Land Trusts in Florida

For Privacy, Liability Protection, Avoiding Probate, Ease of Ownership and 30
More Benefits

Mark Warda and Joseph E Seagle

Land Trust Service Corporation

Contents

Preface

Welcome to the latest edition of Land Trusts in Florida. Mark Warda wrote the first 10 editions of this book, and I'm joining him in this eleventh edition to add my experiences to Mark's voice.

I met Mark through his writings in this book way back in 2001 when I was starting as a real estate title attorney with a small firm and title agency in Orlando. I had been practicing for about five years already but in North and South Carolina. Those states don't have the concept of land trusts, so – when I was faced with a title report showing multiple mortgages in place on a property we were trying to close – the concept hit me in the head like a load of bricks.

The seller held the property in a land trust and had been acting as his own trustee and attorney. There is an adage that "a man who is his own lawyer has a fool for his client." He misunderstood how to secure a beneficial interest in a land trust for a loan and had recorded at least seven mortgages against his own property in favor of his borrowers rather than himself each time he sold the property on seller financing. He convincingly explained that I simply didn't understand land trusts and how they work, so he took his closing elsewhere. I don't know if anyone could ever close it for him.

We attorneys don't like to be ignorant about a legal subject, so I sought out more information about these "land trusts" the man was telling me about. I stumbled across this book and read it from cover to cover. In a professorial and approachable manner, Mark explained the Florida land trust in a way that gave me an idea: I could open a trustee company too! So I did.

My trust company, TRSTE, LLC, was ancillary to my own title agency and law firm I opened in 2004 when I struck out on my own. The trust company was great for my title insurance agency, providing a means for our real estate investor clients to buy and sell properties under one roof without ever having to attend a closing since we handled all the physical signing of closing documents in-house as trustees. Our private lenders loved the ability for us to hold properties in trust in a way that allows them to repossess the property quickly if the borrower defaults.

I met Mark, worked with him, and was a colleague as we collaborated with other attorneys on the Land Trust Subcommittee of the Florida Bar's Real Property, Probate, and Trust Section. The committee met regularly and wrote the latest two Florida land trust statute amendments. Mark and I also became sounding boards for each other whenever we had crazy land trust issues that invariably arose.

Mark had discussed his retirement before the 2020 worldwide COVID-19 pandemic with me. I was focused on growing my title agencies and didn't have the time to devote to taking on another practice, so we shelved the idea. Once the pandemic was over, Mark told me that he planned to retire and wanted to know if I was interested in taking over his practice and trust companies. Serendipitously, I had recently decided to close my residential title agency and was selling my timeshare title agency. The sale of the agency would provide plenty of capital to buy Mark's shares and closing the residential agency would open up my time to devote to integrating and growing the land trustee business. We closed in April 2023, and I consolidated all our companies under one brand, My Land Trustee. Mark regularly corresponds with everyone on our crew and provides insight, history, and advice whenever something we've not seen before comes up. He also publishes books about landlords, personal property trusts, and other trust-related issues.

I hope you enjoy this latest edition of the book that started it all for me.

— Joseph E. Seagle, Esq.

Introduction

The land trust is the most useful and the least known legal device used by real estate investors, developers, attorneys, CPAs, and financial planners. Those discovering the benefits of land trusts start using them for all their properties, but very few investors know how or why they work so well.

Considering that law school property law professors must teach complicated legal concepts from the 1500s, you will understand there is little time left for a simple 1963 statute. Statutes that tell you the procedure are not as exciting as analyzing trust concepts born in 1536. The beginnings of these statutes are discussed in Chapter 1.

This book was first published in 1984, just twenty years after Florida's land trust statute was adopted. Since then, many investors have begun using land trusts, and the Florida Bar has held seminars for attorneys every few years. Because of these changes, the land trust is much better known today than in 1984.

This book explains and simplifies the law and uses of land trusts for Florida attorneys and property owners. It is believed to be the most thorough analysis of the subject available in Florida. Chapter 2 explains the benefits of land trusts, while Chapter 3 explains how they work. Chapters 4 through 6 detail how to set up, finance, and operate a land trust.

Sometimes it becomes necessary to take land trust issues to court. Chapter 7 will touch on the ways this should be done. It will eventually become necessary to sell land trust property, and Chapter 8 will explain how to do this. Many federal and state tax, securities, and racketeering laws govern issues related to land trusts. Chapters 9 through 12 will explain these laws and how they operate in land trusts.

Chapters 13 and 14 raise possible drawbacks to land trusts and issues for trustees. Check the Florida Statutes in Appendix A for some land trust laws. For further analysis of specific problems, reference is made to case law from Florida, Illinois, and other jurisdictions, and these cases are listed in the Index of Cases. For your convenience, some checklists and forms appear in Appendices B and C for your use with land trusts. Throughout the book, we've included stories that illustrate our personal experiences and notes in practice about the topic being discussed. We denote these by setting them out in italics. We have changed the names and other details of the stories and have taken a license to combine multiple experiences into one story to illustrate the points and to protect our client's confidentiality. Since no book can be expected to answer all questions regarding each case and because some of the material is technical, readers who are not attorneys and do not understand the book fully are urged to consult an attorney before setting up a land trust.

Chapter One

How and Why Land Trusts Started

Land Trusts were first invented about 500 years ago for some of the same reasons they are used today, for privacy and to eliminate some of the burdens of land ownership. Before stocks and bonds were invented, land was the primary form of wealth in those days. Like nearly all forms of government, the feudal system wanted to control this wealth. Landowners had to pay taxes and do military service for the overlord. They could only pass it to their oldest sons, they could forfeit it for conduct deemed treason, and they could lose it in payment for their debts.

To avoid some of these burdens, clever lawyers invented the land trust by which land could be transferred to someone else (a trustee) to hold for the real owner (the beneficiary). For example, a young man could put his land in his uncle's name. The uncle would be too old for military service and the nephew wouldn't lose the land if he ran up debts or offended someone higher in the social system.

In 1536, King Henry VIII decided to end the booming trust business and passed the Statute of Uses. This statute said that where land was placed in a trustee's name for the use of another person, "the use was executed," and the title reverted to the beneficiary.

The lawyers took some cases to court, and in 1545, the English courts held that the Statute of Uses only applied to passive trusts (trusts in which the trustee had no legal duties). It did not apply if the trustee had some minor duties to perform, making the trust active.

As each American state joined the Union, it adopted most existing English laws. Therefore, in most states, the Statute of Uses is the law, and a passive trust is void. In some states, the state legislature also passed a version of the Statute of Uses.

But in some states, such as Illinois, the courts decided that passive trusts could be good. Therefore, they ruled that if a trustee had any minor duty, such as signing a deed twenty years in the future, then that little duty was enough to make it an active and, thus, legal trust.

In Florida, the legislature decided that land trusts would be a good thing and passed a law in 1963 that allowed land trusts. In 1984, after a court held a land trust trustee liable for something he shouldn't have been liable for, the legislature amended the law to fix this problem and protect land trust trustees.

In 2002, 2006, 2007, and 2013, the legislature again amended the land trust law to make it better and to clarify the principles of land trust law. The 2006 amendment added a bonus in that beneficiaries were declared to not be liable for the land trust property, and we clarified that passive trusts do not violate the Statute of Uses in 2013.

Land trusts today offer the same benefits that they did over 500 years ago, protecting property owners from some of the burdens of ownership and keeping people's wealth private. As the government gets bigger and its burdens greater, the land trust will become even more valuable to property owners.

We hope this book will be helpful to those who wish to bring the historic benefits of land trusts to places they haven't been before.

Chapter Two

Benefits of Land Trusts

We find another benefit of land trusts just about every year. This chapter explains the most popular uses we have found so far.

Privacy

One of the most important benefits of the land trust is privacy. When you use a land trust to buy property, no one knows—and it is almost impossible to find out—that you are the owner.

There is no public record of the beneficiaries of a land trust. The trustee is listed as the owner, and only the trustee knows the beneficiary's identity. Those checking the courthouse records will find no record of the beneficiaries of a land trust. This privacy insulates owners from annoyances of ownership and keeps their wealth from public view. While some may object to such secrecy of ownership and claim it helps criminals hide their wealth, many feel land ownership should be no more public knowledge than bank balances or stock holdings.

When the first editions of this book were published, the Internet was not yet invented. Looking up a person's properties necessitated a trip to the courthouse and poring over dusty books and microfilms. Today, you can access many property records in your own home with the click of a mouse. In some areas, you can click and see an interior layout or even an aerial photo of the property.

Now, anyone can instantly search the property records of all sixty-seven of Florida's counties. If you buy a gold coin on eBay, the seller can see a bird's eye view of your house and how many other properties you own. The system even shows which property is a person's homestead and gives the street address. But by placing property in a land trust, you can hide the ownership of your properties.

Beneficiaries must be disclosed in Arizona and Hawaii (two other states allowing land trusts), but Florida still allows secrecy. To avoid abuses by organized crime, the Florida Racketeer Influenced Corrupt Organizations (RICO) Act put some limitations on land trusts, as discussed in Chapter 12. However, the land trust offers privacy for those not involved with organized crime.

> *NOTE: A land trust is not absolute protection against disclosure. It is a barrier that will hide your ownership from public view. However, as with other types of wealth, a court can order you to disclose what you own if you have lost a lawsuit. Courts can order an attorney to disclose the identity of a client who owns a land trust. United States v. Aronson, 610 F. Supp. 217 (1985).*

But instances of disclosure are rare. The land trust will protect most people, most of the time. It will also give you the time and freedom to deal with your property if court action is taken against you. Usually, while a lawsuit is pending, you do not have to disclose your wealth. If your property is in land trusts, you would be free to sell it, even while the case is pending, and spend the money—unless there was a court order forbidding you to do so.

Liability Protection

Another significant benefit of the land trust is that the Florida Land Trust Act provides that the beneficiaries are not liable for the property! This means that you are not liable just for being a beneficiary if someone is hurt on the property or if there is money owed for homeowner fees, utilities, taxes, or other matters. It is as if you have a free LLC (limited liability company) with each land trust, and you don't even need to put your name in the public records. (However, you could be liable if you did something on the property that caused an injury.)

This provision of the land trust statute was added in 2006. There have not yet been any court cases over this issue. So there is a possibility that in a horrible case, such as a child killed by a pit bull, a court might find a way to hold a beneficiary liable. However, the statute's plain wording is that a beneficiary is not liable for the property, and changing that would take quite a stretch.

Avoiding Probate

Another significant benefit of a land trust is that the property owned by the trust does not have to go through probate when a beneficiary dies. A land trust can allow property to pass automatically to whomever one chooses without court proceedings. The trust document usually names successor beneficiaries, contingent or remainder beneficiaries. Upon the death of the first beneficiary, the remainder beneficiaries immediately become the trust owners. This avoids both the cost and delay of probate proceedings.

A land trust avoids probate and the complications of a will. Suppose you decide to remove someone from your will. In that case, you must either have the will rewritten or execute a codicil (an amendment to a will) and have it signed before two witnesses, usually in the presence of a notary public. However, to change the beneficiary of your land trust, you sign an amendment and have it accepted by your trustee, and it is done.

Although the property in a land trust avoids going through probate, it does not avoid all the probate claims. In most cases, a person's debts do not have to be paid out of land trust property, but the spouse's forced share and federal estate taxes may need to be paid by the successor beneficiary of a land trust. A forced share is an amount in the statutes that a spouse may choose instead of what a will gives that spouse. In Florida, the forced share is 30% of the estate.

Avoiding Ancillary Administration

Ancillary administration is a court proceeding in a state other than the one in which a person died to determine the ownership of a deceased person's property in that state. It is like a second probate proceeding. For persons who do not live in Florida, a land trust is an excellent way to avoid a Florida ancillary administration, even if they still need a probate in their home state. This can be especially valuable for citizens of other countries whose ancillary administration may be expensive because court documents must be translated from another language. Likewise, Florida residents who own property in other states should investigate the possibility of setting up land trusts in those states to simplify their estates.

Keeping Liens and Judgments Off Property

When a property is held in a trust, judgments and liens against the individual beneficiaries do not attach to the land. *First Federal v. Pogue, 389 N.E.2d 652 (1979).* Therefore, a beneficiary may freely sell their beneficial interest even with numerous certified judgments against their name in the public records, which would typically be liens against all their properties. This also applies to IRS liens and welfare liens. *Chicago Federal Savings & Loan v. Cacciatore, 185 N.E.2d 670, 25 111. 2d 535 (1962) and Nelson v. Fogelstrom, 284 N.E.2d 339, 5 111. App. 3d 804 (1972).*

Liens filed by municipalities, such as code enforcement liens, sometimes apply to "all properties owned" by the person in that county. But if each property is in a separate trust the lien should not affect other properties.

One type of lien that does attach to a land trust and requires payment from the land trust trustee if the property is sold is a RICO lien filed against a beneficiary. A RICO lien is a lien filed by a state attorney against a person believed to be involved in organized crime. Before a trustee transfers a property, the trustee is required to complete a RICO lien search of the beneficiaries. This is explained in more detail in Chapter 12.

Using a land trust allows persons with judgments filed against them to buy and sell property without having the judgments attached to the property. Of course, if asked under oath what assets he or she owns, a person must disclose the ownership of beneficial interests in land trusts under penalty of perjury. That means it is a crime if you do not disclose that you are a land trust beneficiary when asked under oath about your property.

Theoretically, a creditor can still seize a person's beneficial interests in trusts (if they are known), but no Florida cases clearly define how this should be done. If a certificate represents the beneficial interest, then the certificate would probably be subject to a levy (seizure and sale of the property to pay a creditor) by the sheriff in the county or state where the certificate is located. It would be much harder to reach if the certificate were sent out of state.

If there is no certificate, then the creditor could probably obtain a writ of execution against the interest in the trust. A writ of execution is a court document that claims specific property.

The land trust will not wholly shield a debtor from a determined creditor, but it should slow down the process of collecting a debt and might cause an inexperienced attorney to give up in frustration. Any attempt to seize an interest in a land trust could probably be delayed by filing an appeal since there are no Florida cases on how it should be done. Such a scenario would provide a good argument for settlement by the creditor at a reduced amount.

In the event a judgment is filed against the trustee in his or her individual capacity, it would not attach to any properties held by the trustee as trustee. *Yandle Oil Co., Inc., v. Crystal River Seafood, Inc., 563 So. 2d 839 (Fla. 5 DCA 1990).*

> *Example: If a bank owed money to its landlord, the landlord could not seize the property of the bank's customers that the bank was holding as trustee for its customers.*

The property may be reached if the trust is not set up correctly and determined creditors work through an aggressive bankruptcy court. In re Steven S. Saber, 233 B.R. 547 (S.D. Fla. 1999).

> **U.S. Attorney's Office finds trust properties**
>
> *We once held about 10 properties for a family. The husband was charged with breaking federal laws and ordered to pay restitution for the crimes, totaling over $1 million.*
>
> *The US Attorney's Office knew that the defendant, our trust beneficiary, held properties in the land trusts because they had access to his tax returns. However, they allowed the defendant to assign his interests in the trust to his wife, who then refinanced the properties. From the refinance and new mortgage, she was able to "buy out" the USAO's interest in the properties by paying them an agreed-upon settlement sum.*
>
> *It's important to note that the USA's restitution lien did not attach to the lands held in trust. Instead, it attached to the husband's beneficial interest in the trusts. The case did not include any allegations related to RICO violations, so – until the USAO contacted us to inform us of the settlement, and our client directed us to assign the beneficial interests out of his name to his wife – his property was "safe."*

Avoiding Litigation

Property owners are easy targets for lawsuits. Even a frivolous lawsuit may be worth filing if the defendant has numerous properties that can be tied up in litigation or seized. However, if it looks like a person has no assets, it may be difficult for a disgruntled person to find a lawyer to take the case, even one with a lot of merit.

If you plan to own several properties, a part of your asset protection planning should include keeping your name off the property records. That is what a land trust is designed to do.

***

A Tale of Two Physicians

On a Wednesday, Dr. C and his wife arrived at the office for a consultation. He was a little frazzled because his wife had been involved in a car accident that was deemed to be her fault several weeks before. As we discussed their situation, we found they had worked with us years before to protect their assets, including five rental homes they own.

At that time, we advised them to put each home in a separate land trust with our company acting as trustee. We also advised them to hold all of their accounts and other assets as a married couple so they would enjoy Florida's "tenancy by the entireties" protection against judgment creditors. However, we advised them to always own their cars in their separate names and to never drive each other's cars if possible.

In this case, the wife was driving the car titled solely in her name when she t-boned the other car. Fortunately, we could confirm to them that their rental homes would be safe for two reasons. First, if the damages sought by the other driver exceeded their auto and umbrella liability policy limits, an asset hunter would not see that they own the five rental homes free and clear of any other liens. Secondly, they could only name the wife as a defendant in any lawsuit and obtain a judgment solely against her. Thus, their judgment would not attach to the assets they own as tenants by the entirety.

They left our office relieved.

However, on Friday, a different physician sought our advice. His wife as well was in an accident that was her fault and had caused catastrophic, permanently disabling injuries to the other driver. As we proceeded through the same analysis, we discovered that the car she was driving was titled in the doctor's and his wife's names. This meant that both of them would be named in any lawsuit filed by the other driver.

While they had an extensive auto liability policy and a $1 million umbrella policy, it was clear that the other driver's injuries would far exceed these amounts. So we then examined what other assets the family held.

They held quite a few free-and-clear rental properties in land trusts. However, to save money on trustee fees, they named the doctor as the individual trustee of each land trust. Therefore, an asset hunter will see the doctor's name directly related to each of these properties and think they are available to satisfy a judgment, even though that may not be the case.

Unfortunately, we had to inform the doctor that – because he had acted as his land trustee – his name is all over the public records. This would give the other driver's attorneys leverage in future settlement negotiations and entice them to refuse to settle for the policy limits of the doctor's family's insurance policies.

Also, since they would both be named in the lawsuit and thus subject to the judgment, any assets they own separately or together as husband and wife would be at stake of being taken to satisfy the judgment from the traffic accident.

He left the office worrying about what the future holds.

Ease of Control by Multiple Owners

When several parties own interests in a property, it is often difficult to have deeds, mortgages, and other documents executed and notarized by all parties. This is a special problem when some owners are out of state, but the land trust helps here. With a trust, only the trustee needs to sign the documents. The beneficiaries can sign a DIRECTION TO TRUSTEE (see Form 5). This form does not have to be witnessed or notarized and can even be faxed or e-mailed.

The beneficiaries can also empower one person to give directions to the trustee without their signatures. This is usually done by giving that person a power of direction. (See Power of Direction in Chapter 4.)

Ease of Transferring Interests

Another benefit of land trusts is that they make property transfers easy. A transfer only needs a simple signature since interests in a land trust are personal property (not classified as real estate). It does not require witnesses or a notary. The Florida courts have clearly established this position. *Goldman v. Mandell, 403 So. 2d 511 (1981).*

Ease of Changing Contingent Beneficiaries

While a will requires a formal ceremony for execution, a person can change the successor beneficiary of his or her land trust with a simple signature. Percentages given to successor beneficiaries can be changed as properties change, and persons can be cut out of their inheritances without delay or expense.

> *Example: As real estate guru Jack Shea points out, if your teenage daughter runs off with a ne'er-do-well musician, you can take her off the trust as a contingent beneficiary with a simple signature. If he starts producing platinum albums, you can just as easily add her back in.*

Gifting Simplification

To avoid the gift tax, it is expected to use the annual exclusion of $18,000 (as of 2024) per year tax-free. (This amount rises with inflation in $1,000 increments.) An individual can give a tax-free gift of $18,000 to as many people as he or she wants per year. For couples, $36,000 in joint gifts can be given each year to each person without paying a gift tax. Putting a property into a land trust simplifies the process of transferring $18,000 or $36,000 of equity each year. (This is explained in more detail in Chapter 9.)

Ease of Foreclosure or Repossession

While a real estate mortgage foreclosure requires lengthy court proceedings and gives the mortgagor a right of redemption, a beneficial interest given as collateral can be recovered much more quickly. This is because the Uniform Commercial Code (UCC) allows personal property to be repossessed quickly when payments are not made.

When the beneficial interest in a land trust is given as collateral, a chattel mortgage (security agreement) and a UCC-1 Financing Statement are used as security. In such a case, foreclosure is a much simpler procedure governed by Section 679.304 of the Florida Statutes. There is a SECURITY AGREEMENT (CHATTEL MORTGAGE) (Form 17) and a UNIFORM COMMERCIAL CODE FINANCING STATEMENT (UCC-1) (Form 18) in Appendix C.

At present, Florida law is not clear in this area. As explained in Chapter 5, some cases say the UCC procedure can be used and others say it cannot. However, since few transactions go as far as an appeals court, most transactions should be able to take advantage of the quick procedures under the UCC.

The "Belt-and-Suspenders" Option

We have many private lenders who use the land trust (suspenders) and a mortgage (the belt) to ensure they are firmly secured by the real estate that is the collateral for their loan. In this case, the lender is the "primary beneficiary" while the borrower is the "secondary beneficiary" of the land trust. The trustee executes the promissory note and a mortgage in favor of the lender. The borrower executes a personal guarantee of the loan's repayment.

Extensive terms inside the land trust agreement clarify that — so long as the borrower/secondary beneficiary performs under the note and terms of the trust (which mirrors the mortgage), then the secondary beneficiary directs the trustee concerning the property. However, suppose the borrower defaults on the note or terms of the trust agreement. In that case, the lender, as the primary beneficiary, after a short notice and cure period, can take control of the land trust and thus take possession of the property held in trust.

At that point, the lender can do what it takes to protect the property and maximize the value of the lender's repayment. If other liens, such as contractors, have attached to the property, the lender can still foreclose on the recorded mortgage. The lender would direct the trustee to consent to the foreclosure to speed up the process. This would extinguish those contractors' liens and allow the foreclosure sale to occur sooner rather than later. This, too, helps maximize the value of the property to help ensure the lender loses as little money as possible on the defaulted loan. Should the property still not be worth enough to cover everything owed to the lender, then the lender may still sue the borrower under the personal guarantee it signed.

Safer Lease-Option Agreements

Sometimes property is leased with an option to purchase or the right to buy the property. Under such an arrangement, the tenant often acquires vested rights (legal rights that are very difficult to take away) in the property that may prevent the owner from using a simple eviction action when the tenant fails to pay the rent. When a tenant puts a mere $1,000 or so down for this option and defaults (fails to pay), it is unfair to require an owner to pursue a lengthy foreclosure or ejectment proceeding to get the property back.

One recent attempt to avoid this problem has been to divide the transaction into two parts. The tenant can sign a regular lease of the real property (the actual building or land) with the trustee and sign a separate option agreement to buy the beneficial interest of the land trust from the beneficiary. The option agreement can allow credits for each month the lease is in force and provide for nullification of the option upon default of the lease. For more protection, the option agreement can be drafted as a contract for option, which does not become an option unless all terms of the lease and the option have been fulfilled.

Florida courts have not ruled on such an arrangement. It is possible that, in an extreme case, a court would call it a mortgage that must be foreclosed. However, if the lease specifically states that both parties agree it is to be governed by Florida Statutes, Chapter 83, Landlord Tenant Law, the owner should be allowed a quick eviction. An option agreement with another party on the beneficial interest should not prevent the right to use eviction procedures. Dating the option contract later than the lease would make a stronger case to separate the agreements.

In such a case, a separate suit would have to be brought by the tenant regarding the option, and under the reasoning of the case *Ferraro v. Parker* (see Chapter 5), the owner should win. Without possession of the property, the defaulting tenant would not likely be able to pursue lengthy litigation in circuit court over an untested area of law.

Retaining Lower Real Property Tax Assessments

One traditional benefit of the land trust has been keeping tax assessments lower by not letting the tax assessor know that the property was transferred or the purchase price. For example, you can get a long-term property owner to put it into a trust and sell you the beneficial interest of the trust. It looks to the world like he still owns it, and there is no automatic jump in the assessment based on the new purchase price.

A law affecting this benefit was passed in 2008. It requires a notice (Form DR-430) to be given to the property appraiser when 50% or more of the beneficial interest in a land trust or ownership interest in a corporation or LLC changes when they hold non-homestead property.

The law arose because large companies used transfers of LLC membership interests to avoid paying documentary tax on sales. The form lets the property appraiser know that a transfer occurred, so if another occurs within three years, the documentary tax will be assessed on the prior transfer. The form does not require disclosure of the price paid for the interest, and it's important to note that documentary taxes are still paid directly to the Department of Revenue on the price paid for the beneficial interest in the land trust.

With that said, it should be kept in mind that any change in the real estate title can trigger a reassessment of the property for real estate taxes. An assignment of a beneficial interest in the trust does not change the title of the real estate, so it should not trigger a reassessment, even though the DR-430 is filed.

Finally, one attorney suggests that if there are two or more layers of ownership, the law might not apply to the second layer. For example, if an LLC owns a land trust and you sold the LLC membership interests, that might be exempt from filing the DR-430. Also, the transfer disclosure doesn't need to be filed if a deed is also being recorded. So getting an assignment from a seller who puts their homestead property into trust would be exempt.

Keeping the Purchase or Sale Price Secret

When a deed is recorded in the courthouse, the documentary stamp tax (tax on real estate transfer) must be noted. The tax is based on the amount of the sales price. Anyone can use this to find out the sales price. Although the documentary stamp tax must be paid on the sale of the beneficial interest in a land trust, there is no public record of the tax paid, unlike recorded deeds. The tax is paid to the Department of Revenue in Tallahassee with no disclosure required as to which property it was for! As we will explain in Chapter 4, when you purchase a property into a land trust, you can set it up so that the taxes are not noted on the deed, and no one can know what you paid for the property.

Limiting Mortgage Liability

When a person signs a note and mortgage or assumes an existing mortgage, that person can be liable for a deficiency judgment in the event of foreclosure. A deficiency judgment is any amount still owed when the money from the sale of the property does not cover the amount owed on the mortgage. If a trust purchases a property, the transaction can be structured so that only the trustee executes the documents (as trustee without personal liability). Even though it is not explicitly stated in the documents, a mortgage from a trustee allows the lender to look only to the property in the trust as security for the loan. No deficiency judgment can be entered against the beneficiary (unless he also personally guarantees the loan).

Of course, institutional lenders require personal guarantees from the beneficiaries, and sophisticated sellers may also require them. However, many sellers take back mortgages from trusts without question. Since many real estate sellers in Florida do not use attorneys, they often accept offers from trustees without realizing they have no recourse against the buyer.

Improved Financial Statement

If a person owns property worth $300,000 with a $240,000 mortgage against it, the value ($300,000) is put on the asset side of his or her financial statement, and the debt ($240,000) is put on the liability side. The property adds $60,000 to his or her net worth, but the $240,000 debt is weighed heavily by lenders. Owners of numerous properties often cannot get loans because their debt ratio (the size of their debt compared to the amount of their assets) is too high.

If a property is in a land trust and only the trustee signed the loan documents, the beneficiary is not liable for the loan. Therefore, in the above case, the owner could list the beneficial interest in the trust as a $60,000 asset with no debt. The debt is a liability of the trust, payable out of the income of the trust property, and the beneficiary owns only an asset worth $60,000 (the value minus the debt, or $300,000-$240,000 here).

This works only in cases where the trustee signed the mortgage and note or when the property was taken subject to an existing mortgage. If you own a property in your name and signed a mortgage on it, then putting it into a trust will not take the mortgage off your credit report unless the lender releases you from the loan, which is unlikely.

Ease of Negotiation

Negotiation can be a stressful and confrontational process. When a trust buys, sells, or rents a property, the beneficiary or other negotiator can act as the "good guy" and portray the trust as the "bad guy." The other party can be told that the terms of the trust arrangement do not permit certain types of deals. The negotiator can work closely with a buyer or seller to put a deal together, but he or she can explain that the trust has certain rules, such as the trust must receive 20% down or the trust cannot have a negative cash flow on a property. This way, the negotiator can get the terms desired without personally upsetting the other side. Sometimes, it is helpful to write out some trust rules ahead of time so that one can be honest in one's presentation. They can be amended later if desired.

Avoiding Partition

When a property is owned jointly by two or more persons, any of them may go to court and require partition and sale of the property. This way, a disgruntled partner can ruin the progress of an ongoing project, or feuding siblings can break up a family farm.

In Illinois, land held in a land trust is not subject to partition. *Breen v. Breen, 103 N.E.2d 625 (1952).* Because of the legislative intent in the land trust statute, Florida courts should follow this holding. Still, a Florida Statute (Sec. 64.091) allows the partition of personal property in some instances, which is the legal ownership in a land trust. For extra protection in Florida, the LAND TRUST AGREEMENT (Form 4) and beneficiary agreement should specifically say that partition of the property is not allowed.

Avoiding Personal Problems of Beneficiaries

When several partners own property jointly, the death, incompetency, divorce, bankruptcy, or other problems of one of them can ruin a project. When a property is in a land trust, these problems do not affect the property; they only affect the one beneficiary's interest. Of course, the beneficiary agreement should spell out what is to happen in the event of each of these occurrences. There is a CO-VENTURE AGREEMENT (Form 11) in Appendix C to help you shape such an agreement and a PARTNERSHIP AGREEMENT (Form 12).

Holding a Judge's Property

The Committee on Standards of Conduct Governing Judges has issued an opinion that a circuit judge could continue to own an interest in a land trust with former law partners and other businesspeople in the community. This way, a judge would not have to give up his or her real property holding upon becoming a judge. Of course, the judge would have to disqualify him or herself in proceedings regarding the trust since there would be a conflict of interest. Also, like any other property the judge or any elected official may hold, they still must disclose it on their financial disclosures.

Ease of Property Management

When a tenant cannot pay rent and explains personal problems to a landlord, it is often difficult for the sympathetic landlord to insist on strict compliance with the lease. However, a land trust can allow the landlord to sympathize with the tenant and blame the trustee for the fact that an eviction must be filed. Rather than confront the tenant personally, the landlord can explain that the eviction is beyond his or her control. Rules can be created for the land trust to allow the landlord to be honest with the tenant, limiting tenant flexibility.

Saving Title Insurance Premiums

When a property is sold, it is usually necessary to have a new title insurance policy insuring the new deed. However, when an interest in a land trust is sold, the title can remain in the same trustee, and the interest can be transferred by ASSIGNMENT OF BENEFICIAL INTEREST (see Form 6). This would avoid needing a new title insurance premium, which can be expensive on large developments.

When such an event is contemplated, it is best to use a neutral party, such as a bank or corporation, as a trustee so that the buyer will be comfortable with the arrangement and not need to replace the trustee.

Avoiding Violating Real Estate Licensing Laws

Florida's real estate brokerage law (Florida Statutes, Chapter 475) requires that brokers be licensed before performing any brokerage services for a fee. Such services include helping to buy, sell, lease, auction, or option the property. The land trust statute or the land trust itself states that the interest of the beneficiary of a land trust is personal property for all purposes, and the statute says that it will be liberally construed. Therefore, an unlicensed person should be able to conduct transactions on an interest in a land trust.

An interest in a land trust that does not come under real estate brokerage laws might be considered a security if the interest was like a passive investment. Therefore, a broker of land trust interests might need to be licensed as a securities dealer. (See Chapter 11 for more information on when securities laws affect land trust transactions.)

Buying Properties at the Foreclosure Auction

When mortgage lenders sell a property they took back in a foreclosure, they often have a rule that their contract is not assignable or that the property may not be sold for a certain time after purchase. However, if you use a land trust as the contract purchaser, the beneficial interest of the trust can be sold several times before or after closing without assigning the underlying real estate contract or changing the deed.

Also, if an auctioned property is purchased in the name of a land trust, there may be disgruntled tenants, squatters, or any other problems with the property that was just purchased as-is. In that case, having your individual or even company name associated with the property is unfavorable. Purchasing inside a land trust at the auction keeps your or your company's name out of the chain of title regarding that problematic property.

Improved Situation in Foreclosure

Between 2008 and 2012, the U.S. real estate market experienced its greatest crisis in several generations, and many property owners were "upside down" on their mortgages (owing more on their properties than they were worth). Many investors and homeowners gave up their properties. A land trust can help someone in a foreclosure situation in two ways.

First, if a property is put into a trust before foreclosure, the lender may take the property back without hunting down the borrower for a deficiency judgment. Most foreclosures are handled by "foreclosure mills," that is, law firms that only do foreclosures and do them quickly and cheaply. If it is easy to serve legal papers on the trustee and quickly take the property back but hard to find and serve the borrower, then the lender might just go for the property and not even try for a deficiency judgment. In some cases seen by the authors, the bank did not even sue the borrower, only the trustee! In 2013 the Florida foreclosure law was changed to allow a lender only one year, not five, to seek a deficiency judgment.

Second, if a defendant in foreclosure has other properties and puts them in land trusts before a foreclosure judgment is entered, then the foreclosure judgment, even if it includes a deficiency against the borrower, will not be a lien against the other properties. Eventually, the lender might be able to get at them. But in the meantime, you have the flexibility to sell them, borrow against them, or otherwise deal with them.

Anyone facing foreclosure should consider putting their other properties into land trusts.

Buying Distressed Properties

Many real estate investors use land trusts when buying properties close to foreclosure. By putting the property in a land trust, the investor can gain enough control to negotiate a short sale or refinance the property. Some investors prefer to become or have their company become the trustee. Others use a neutral trustee and become the director of the trust. When becoming the director, be sure to spell out your rights and duties to avoid the fiduciary responsibilities of the 2006 changes in the law. See Chapter 4.

There are cases when a seller simply must transfer title to the property because they need to move, but the property's value is close to the mortgage's outstanding balance. In that case, no real estate broker wants to take the listing to sell the property because there isn't enough value to cover the closing costs and their commission. In that event, some real estate investors will buy the property "subject to" the current mortgage. This means that the investor buyer will step into the current owner's shoes and make the monthly payments to the mortgage holder while renting out the property or otherwise make it profitable for them to continue holding it. The investor is not "assuming" the seller's mortgage. That would mean that the lender has formally approved the property transfer and released the original borrower from the loan while substituting the investor as the new borrower. While such assumptions are permitted sometimes in FHA and VA loans, they are not commonly done with conventional mortgages.

Most real estate investors like to purchase properties subject to the current mortgage because the seller's interest rate under the mortgage is much lower than current market mortgage rates. Therefore, they can make a small profit on rent. However, many sellers will balk at this type of transaction. Their most common objection is that their credit score may be ruined if the investor-buyer defaults on their mortgage. Also, what happens if the new owner takes out a second mortgage against the property and then just walks away (illegal equity stripping)?

To overcome these objections, the seller can be the initial beneficiary of a land trust. The property is then conveyed into that land trust so there are no documentary taxes on the public records about that conveyance. The seller then conditionally assigns their beneficial interest to the investor-buyer. The assignment is conditioned upon the buyer's continued payment of the seller's mortgage and otherwise not defaulting or taking out additional financing without the seller's authorization.

Suppose the buyer defaults on the mortgage or otherwise breaches the conditional assignment. In that case, the seller can go through the steps to terminate the assignment and re-take control of the trust. At that point, the seller can re-sell the property or take other actions to protect their credit scores.

A full discussion of subject-to purchases is beyond the scope of this book, but the authors have extensive experience in this type of transaction and have seen it work out for the best of both parties more often than not.

Avoiding Seasoning Problems

Seasoning is the length of time a property has been owned. Some lenders refuse to make loans on properties that are being sold quickly at a profit or to refinance properties that have not been owned very long. A land trust can allow a property to stay with the same owner (trustee) while the beneficial interest is sold, appearing that the same party has owned the property for an extended time. We see this scenario often when a wholesaler purchases a property and then re-sells the property within a few weeks or a month at most. The second sale starts the clock again. However, if the wholesaler sells the trust's beneficial interest instead of the land, the transaction will not appear in public records. Future lenders can assume that the same owner has held title to the property since the beginning, even though it may have changed hands multiple times over the months leading up to the refinance or sale.

> *Example: A party buys a property that needs much work and puts it in a land trust. The beneficial interest can be sold to someone who remodels the property, who can later sell the beneficial interest to someone who finds a purchaser. Since the title remains with the same trustee the whole time (the original party buying the property), the property transfers would not show up as a seasoning problem.*

Protecting Retirement Accounts

Buying real estate with self-directed IRAs, especially Roth IRAs and other retirement accounts, has become more popular. Still, since real estate is risky, the entire account is at risk. Retirement account funds should only be used to buy real estate in ways that protect the account from risk such as using a land trust or LLC.

Suppose the IRA is wrapped inside a limited liability company. In that case, the operating agreement and articles of organization must be specially drafted to comply with IRS and ERISA requirements for checkbook-control IRAs. However, it is much faster and cost-effective to simply have the self-directed IRA custodian be the beneficiary of a land trust that holds title to the property instead, and the IRA's owner can hold the power of direction over the trustee for ease of daily management. This segregates the liability of the property held in the land trust away from the IRA's other assets (cash, investment accounts, etc.) without having to open a separate IRA account for each asset the IRA holds. It also maintains the anonymity of the IRA account from the public records.

Avoiding Condominium and Homeowner Association Judgments

Some homeowner and condominium association documents provide that the owner of a unit is personally liable for any dues and assessments. This means that even if you move away from the property and lose it in foreclosure, you could be liable for several years' assessments. Some condo associations don't allow companies or trusts to buy units, or they require personal guarantees by the beneficiary, so this might not work in every case.

Another caveat regarding such associations is that we have encountered situations where associations refuse to allow beneficiaries to speak or ask questions at meetings since their names do not appear on public records. This has occurred even when the trustee has provided a notarized written statement to the association to appoint the beneficiary as the trust's representative and proxy for the meetings.

Avoiding Mortgage Rules

Since the 2008-2012 Great Recession, more rules and laws have been passed to protect borrowers from themselves. Some of these have monstrous penalties for inadvertent errors. Most of them apply to the borrower who initially takes the loan. Suppose you sold a property to a land trust that you control and put a mortgage on it. A buyer who purchases the property from the land trust, who buys the property subject to the existing mortgage, would probably not be in the same position as someone who signed the loan agreement.

Protecting Mortgages You Hold

When you take back a mortgage in your name on a property you sell, you tell the world that you have a very liquid and valuable asset. Someone suing you would love to get it. But if you take back a mortgage in a mortgage land trust, no one knows it is your asset and passes it to your heirs without probate.

If you structure it so that the buyer of your property doesn't know you are financing it (because you refer him to a mortgage trust lender that he doesn't know you own), then if he has complaints against you for the property, he will not be able to withhold payments as easily as he would if you, as the seller, held the mortgage.

Buying a Neighbor's Property

Land trusts have been used in situations where neighbors were bitter enemies, and one wanted to buy the other out. The selling neighbor would never have sold to his neighbor, but when an offer came from a land trust, he accepted it, not knowing the neighbor was the real purchaser.

***

Horse (Farm) Trading

We once had a client who owned a horse farm. He wanted to purchase more land and heard that his neighbor was considering selling his farm. However, the two neighbors had been on the outs for over a decade, so there was no way the neighbor would sell his farm to him.

So he came to us. We prepared the purchase contract in the name of a land trust as the buyer and signed everything. He even deposited the earnest money deposit in our law firm trust account so it would be sent from there to the closing agent rather than from him. We negotiated the final terms at his direction. Eventually, we closed on the purchase of the property, again running the balance of the purchase funds through our trust account to the closing agent so no one would know the source of the purchase funds. A few years later, after the seller died, the client directed us to deed the property to his company that owned his other farm. The neighbor never discovered who bought his farm.

Timesharing Property

A condominium unit or even a single-family home can be put into a land trust and owned by several families, with an agreement as to when each one can use the property. Using the land trust can avoid restrictions on multiple owners and simplify changes of ownership.

How the Big Boys Do It

Most of the largest developers in timeshare (vacation ownership) now use some form of the Florida land trust to hold and sell all of their inventory throughout the country. They form Florida land trusts and convey properties from various states into the trust. Then they sell percentage interests of the trusts to purchasers. Sometimes those trust interests are converted to points, much like hotel or airline points, that the owners can use to book cruises, hotels, and condo units anywhere in the world.

Equity Stripping

Owning free-and-clear properties makes you a good target for lawsuits. But if you own mortgaged properties with little equity, they are valueless to a creditor. A land trust can be set up to put a mortgage on your properties and make them look like there is no equity. You can own or control the mortgage trust.

***

A Note About Spouse's Forced Share

In earlier editions of this book, a benefit of the land trust was to avoid a spouse's forced share of an estate. However, the law was changed to entitle a Florida spouse to 30 percent of a person's estate, including trust property.

Since land trusts are very private, it is possible that an interest could pass without the knowledge of the spouse. However, any intentional attempt to avoid the law could subject the parties to penalties if discovered. If you wish to avoid a spouse's share, you must sign either a premarital or postmarital agreement or use an offshore asset protection trust. Enhanced life estate (Lady Bird) deeds may also work to avoid this forced share. Check with a lawyer to be sure your agreement or deed complies with the latest laws.

FinCEN BOI Reporting

Under the Corporate Transparency Act of 2021, most entities are required to file a Beneficial Ownership Information Report online with the Financial Crimes Enforcement Network (FinCEN), which is part of the U.S. Department of Treasury. 31 U.S.C. Sec. 5336. FinCEN's mission is to safeguard the financial system by combating money laundering, among other types of financial crimes. Unfortunately, many foreign and domestic criminals — including terrorists, oligarchs, corrupt politicians, and drug traffickers — often buy real estate and other assets inside limited liability companies, shell corporations, and other entities to launder their ill-gotten gains. For several years, FinCEN targeted using LLCs buying real estate for cash in particular geographic locations for threshold amounts of money. These were called "Geographic Targeting Orders." However, this was like playing a game of "whack-a-mole" for law enforcement since criminals would simply move around the country to different non-targeted geographic areas to purchase properties, or they would purchase properties that fell under the price threshold.

Congress passed the Corporate Transparency Act to close the loopholes that criminals exploited. As part of this Act, FinCEN was authorized to create a database of most limited liability companies, corporations, limited partnerships, and other entities that only exist once they file documents to be created with their Secretary of State or another officer in charge of creating and maintaining such entities in a jurisdiction (i.e. the Division of Corporations of the Florida Department of State). Under the Act, any entity created before January 1, 2024, has until December 31, 2025, to register its Beneficial Ownership Information Report in the FinCEN BOI database. Any company created between January 1 and December 31, 2024, has up to 90 days after creation to file its BOI report. Any company created after January 1, 2025, has 30 days to file its BOI report. Failure or refusal to file the report carries stiff fines and potential jail time.

The reports are pretty detailed, requiring disclosure of the attorney, paralegal, or other person who filed the articles of organization or other formation documents with the state. Further, all officers and any owner of an interest that exceeds 25 percent must also be identified in the report. If there are any changes to the ownership or controlling officers of the entity, those amendments must be reported within 30 days of the change.

Land trusts in Florida are not required to file anything with the Florida Department of State to exist. Therefore, they are not subject to BOI reporting requirements like LLCs and other such entities.

Chapter Three

How a Land Trust Works

What a Land Trust Is

A trust is an arrangement whereby one person (the trustee) holds the title to the property for the benefit of another party (the beneficiary). For example, you bring a million dollars to a bank trust department, tell them to invest it for you, and send you the income every month. The money is still yours, but they hold and invest it for you in trust. They have a fiduciary duty to be prudent in investing your money and protecting it.

A land trust, also called an "Illinois type" land trust, is an arrangement in which a piece of real estate is deeded to a trustee merely to hold for the beneficiary, but with no duties except to hold it and sign a deed, mortgage, or other legal instruments when requested.

One unique feature of the land trust is that the trustee is considered to hold both legal and equitable title to the real estate. Under the terms of the trust agreement, the beneficiary's interest in the real estate is transformed into personal property. This is a very unusual legal arrangement and is different from most types of trusts because usually, a trustee holds legal title to the property, and the beneficiaries hold equitable title to the property. In all other kinds of trusts, if the same person holds the legal and equitable title, there is a legal "merger" of the two interests, and the trust dissolves. But the land trust statute prevents this.

Converting the beneficiary's interest to personal property protects it from real estate liens and other problems that may arise from owning real estate (like allowing partition). With that said, there's no requirement that the deed into the trustee state that the beneficiary's interest in the trust is considered personal property. This statement may be isolated to appear only inside the land trust itself. This is important because some county property appraisers argue that if the beneficiary's interest is personal property only, it creates a change of title that allows a re-valuation of the property and removal of all valuation caps. Furthermore, it can prevent a beneficiary who continues to reside in the property from obtaining the homestead tax exemptions and caps. Therefore, the statement that the beneficiary's interest in the trust is only as personal property should only appear inside the land trust agreement and not on the deed to the trustee.

Another unusual aspect of the land trust is that even though the beneficiary has no legal interest in the real estate since the trustee is only holding title, the beneficiary has all of the duties and responsibilities to manage it. The beneficiary usually collects the rent, pays the taxes, and does all the other things an owner of the property would do.

Allowing a trust to exist where the beneficiary has no legal interest in the property but all the duties to manage it is a legal fiction that the law allows, which doesn't make logical sense. Some legal commentators have compared it to Alice in Wonderland. ("The real estate is no longer real estate because we say it isn't.")

Unique features of a land trust

1. Legal and equitable title are vested in the trustee

2. Beneficiary's interest is converted to personal property

3. Trustee has no duties except to sign deeds and mortgages

4. Beneficiaries have all rights to possession and management

What a Land Trust is Not

A land trust is not a typical living trust or inter vivos trust. It is like these trusts in that it is made during one's lifetime, but it is different in that it does not hold title to securities, bank accounts, or automobiles, as most living trusts do. It is possible to create a hybrid trust combining a land trust with a living one. But because of the risks involved with real estate, it is not a good idea. It is better to keep each piece of real estate in a separate land trust.

A land trust is not a business trust or a Real Estate Investment Trust (REIT). These types of trusts carry on businesses and manage real property. The land trust only holds the title. It does not have a taxpayer identification number or a bank account. Some investors set up a separate living trust with the same name as the land trust and get a tax number and a bank account for that trust to collect rent from the tenants living in the land trust property.

A land trust is not the type of real estate trust used in some states where the trustee operates the property, as described in *State ex rel Stanley v. Cook, 146 Ohio St. 348, 66 NE2d 207 (1946)* and *In re St. Charles Land Trust, 206 So2d 128 (La.App 1967)*.

As used in this book, a land trust is not a typical land conservation trust as described on numerous sites on the Internet. However, a land trust can be used for such a purpose if a nonprofit corporation is made the beneficiary.

Florida Requirements for a Land Trust

A valid Florida land trust must fulfill three conditions found in Sections 689.071 of the Florida Statutes:

1. The recorded instrument (usually a deed) must confer on the trustee the powers contained in Florida Statutes §689.073,

2. The trustee must have no greater duties than listed in 689.071(2)(c), and

3. There must be a written trust agreement.

Once these requirements have been fulfilled, the trust is entitled to the benefits of the land trust statute. These characteristics differ from those of other states, which may have different statutes or may not have a statute but may operate under a series of court decisions.

The statute also states that if the recorded instrument or the trust agreement says the beneficiaries' interests are personal property, they will be treated as such. This is not mandatory but advisable because personal property is legally more straightforward.

Deed Powers Statute

From 1963, when the first land trust law was passed, until 2013, the trustee's powers were listed in the land trust statute itself. But after a long, drawn-out court battle over a multimillion-dollar estate that went through several appeals, a court held that using the land trust deed powers for a living trust deed could change the law and the rights that apply to a living trust.

This made every living trust lawyer in Florida wonder if he committed malpractice using that language in his deeds. So, in 2013, the Florida Legislature created Florida Statute Section 689.073, which included deed powers that could be used for both land trusts and living trusts.

Different Florida Statutes

A previously enacted statute, Section 689.07, has nothing to do with land trusts and should not be confused with the land trust statute. This statute states that where a person's name appears on a deed, merely designated "as trustee" with no indication of who the beneficiaries are or of the nature of the trust, then the person named as trustee is deemed to have title to the property in his or her name and not as trustee. This statute aimed to eliminate title problems in cases where people added "as trustee" to their names on deeds. Using a deed with merely the words "as trustee" can have unfortunate consequences.

> *Example: If you put your property in a friend's name as trustee and a large judgment is filed against him, you can lose your property because the statute says the property will be considered his, even though the deed said as trustee.*

Other problems arise when an instrument not complying with either statute is recorded. If a deed that named both a trustee and beneficiaries was recorded, it would not fit the requirements of either statute. If the only problem is clearing the title, the simple solution would be to obtain the signatures of all interested parties. However, if the property were involved in litigation with complex issues of liability or ownership, the court would probably look to other areas of law, such as general trust law or contract law.

> *NOTE: Be sure that any deed you use for a trust complies with Florida Statutes, Section 689.071; not Section 689.07.*

The Florida Trust Code (Chapter 736) has numerous rules and requirements that apply to trusts in Florida, but these do not apply to land trusts. Section 736.0102(3) of the law states, "This code does not apply to any land trust under s. 689.071 except to the extent provided in s. 689.071(7), s.721.08(2)(c) 4. or s. 721.53(1)(e);" and section 689.071(12) of the Land Trust Act says "Except as otherwise provided in this section, chapter 736 does not apply to a land trust governed by this section." Also, a recent opinion confirmed this to be the case. *Freeman as Trustee of Fiddlesticks Land Trust U/A/D September 25, 1984 v. Berrin, 352 So. 3d 452 (Fla. 2d DCA 2022).*

Validity of Land Trusts in Florida

While land trust use may be legally questionable in some states, the Land Trust Act clearly establishes its validity in Florida. The statute even states that it will be liberally interpreted. Florida courts have upheld the validity of both land trusts and the statute since its passage. *Grammer v. Roman, 174 So. 2d 443 (1965).*

In 2002, 2006, 2007, and 2013, the Florida legislature clarified, revised, expanded, and unanimously passed the Florida Land Trust Act, which is well-established as the law of Florida. (Well, in 2013, it was unanimous except for one legislator who voted no. However, he told the author it was "by mistake"!)

Title to the Property

In a land trust, both legal and equitable title are vested in the trustee. (Fla. Stat., Sec. 689.071.) The beneficiary has no interest in the real estate as such. What the beneficiary owns is an interest in the trust. The statute provides that language in the deed can deem this interest to be considered personal property. In most land trust deeds, it is so designated. This setup is like owning stock in a corporation that owns land. You do not own land; you own stock (the beneficial interest). However, in no other way is the land trust like a corporation or any other legal entity.

Why Does it Matter?

Understanding the difference between "equitable" and "legal" titles is essential. Legal title is the owner's name that appears on the recorded deed. However, equitable title is the bundle of rights that goes with property ownership. For instance, someone other than the legal title holder may have the separate equitable right to lease, sell, encumber, convey, subdivide, mine, drill, and otherwise do things with the property. In many estate planning trusts, under Chapter 736 of the Florida Statutes, the trustee holds the legal title to the property. At the same time, the beneficiary retains the equitable title to live in the property. In most cases, all equitable title rights belong to the trustee under a land trust. However, in some cases, the beneficiary may need to retain the equitable right to possess or reside in the property as their homestead so they can enjoy homestead real property tax exemptions, savings, and other benefits.

It is imperative to review the deed into the trustee to ensure this is clarified to the county property appraiser and tax collector so the homestead savings are preserved.

Owner of the Property

Where a statute or regulation refers to an owner of property, there is no set rule as to whether this would be the trustee or the beneficiary. Most Illinois cases indicate that the beneficiary is the owner. *Robinson v. Walker, 211 N.E.2d 488 (1965)*. However, the Illinois courts also recognize that the term "owner" does not have a fixed meaning; in some cases, the trustee has also been held to be an owner. *Coombs v. People, 64 N.E. 1056 (1902), In re Argonne Construction Co., 10 B.R. 570 (1981)*. In Florida, it would depend upon the context in which the term "owner" is used, and we hope a court would use common sense in applying the law to the party to which it was meant to apply.

Third Parties

Third parties dealing with the trustee of a land trust can rely upon the deed, giving the trustee full powers, and need not review the trust agreement itself. In fact, they have no right to look at the trust. Florida Statutes, Section 689.073(2) says that a person dealing with the trustee does not have to look to the trust to see if the trustee has the right to sell, lease, or mortgage the property and does not have to see if the beneficiaries are paid. If the trust powers discussed above are not in the deed into the trustee, then a title agent handling a refinance or sale of the trust property must review the trust agreement, determine if the beneficiaries retained any equitable title to the property, and — if so — require the beneficiaries to sign the mortgage or deed along with the trustee. In that event, any anonymity of the beneficiary's identity is gone once the deed or mortgage is recorded in the public records.

Occasionally, an unenlightened title company or attorney dealing with a land trust will ask to see the trust. So long as the trust powers were included in the deed conveying the property to the trustee, then such request can be declined, and Section 689.073(2) pointed out to them. To protect the title company or attorney, the statute's next subsection says that the trust's beneficiaries cannot sue a person dealing with a trustee. If the title company or attorney still demands to see the trust, you should choose another title company or attorney to handle the transaction.

Attorneys' Title Insurance Fund (The Fund) is a title insurance agency organized by a group of Florida attorneys, now part of Old Republic. In their underwriting book, Fund Title Notes, Title Note 31.02.03A is titled "No Examination of Trust Required." It explains that agents do not need to see the trust. Most Florida real estate attorneys should have a copy of this book, and many other title insurance underwriters also have it. It is considered the authority on title insurance issues faced daily by Florida's title insurance agents.

***

Merger

In historical trust law, a merger occurs when the legal interest of the trustee and the beneficiary's equitable interest are held by the same person. For example, if a beneficiary becomes a trustee, merging the two interests dissolves the trust. This was early Florida law and has been applied to land trusts. *Axtell v. Coons, 89 So. 419 (1921)*; and *In re Steven S. Saber, 233 B.R. 547 (1999)*. However, it does not make any sense to apply it to land trusts because the trustee in a land trust already holds both legal and equitable title. As an Illinois court said, "The Illinois land trust is a species of trust that, unlike other trusts, is immune to the doctrine of merger under most circumstances." *Chrysler Credit Corporation v. Louis Joliet Bank and Trust Co., 863 F.2d 534 (1988)*.

To counter this issue, the Land Trust Act was amended in 2013 to clearly state that the merger doctrine does not apply to land trusts. F.S. §689.071(5)).

Trustee Duties

Although the land trust statute has always said that such a trust was valid if the powers of the trustee were in the deed, some title companies were afraid that if the trust agreement was passive, they would need a deed from the beneficiary based on Florida's Statute of Uses (F.S. 689.09).

The 2013 amendment to the law clearly states that the Statute of Uses does not apply to a land trust (F.S. 689.071(4)). The law limits the duties that a land trust trustee can have to the following:

- The duty to convey or deal with the trust property as directed by the beneficiaries
- The duty to sell or dispose of the trust property at the end of the trust
- The duty to perform ministerial and administrative functions
- Any duties under F.S. Chapter 721, if the property is a timeshare

If a trustee has more duties than this, there is a danger the trust would not come under the land trust statute and might include all of the duties and burdens under Chapter 736.

***

Necessary Documentation

The two documents necessary for a land trust to be legal in Florida are:

1. a deed containing the proper language, such as a WARRANTY DEED TO TRUSTEE (Form 2) or QUIT CLAIM DEED TO TRUSTEE (Form 3), and

2. a LAND TRUST AGREEMENT (Form 4).

Even though a land trust trustee does not have fiduciary duties, federal tax regulations (301.6903-1) require that the IRS be given notice of the trust. Usually, this is done using IRS Form 56, Notice of Fiduciary Relationship. (See Chapter 9 for more information on this requirement.)

Optional Documentation

If there are two or more beneficiaries (other than husband and wife), then there should also be an agreement between the beneficiaries spelling out their legal relationship. That relationship can be a partnership or a joint venture or set up as a legal entity, such as a corporation or a limited liability company (LLC). A CO-VENTURE AGREEMENT (Form 11) and a PARTNERSHIP AGREEMENT (Form 12) are provided in Appendix C.

The trust agreement itself is the only evidence that a beneficiary needs of his interest in the trust. However, some people use trust certificates to show fancier proof of ownership. These might come in handy if the property must be taken out of state to avoid creditors or taxes. The drawback is that if they are lost, preparing an affidavit before the property can be sold may cause delays.

Full details for setting up a land trust are explained in detail in Chapter 4.

Necessary Parties

The necessary parties to a land trust agreement are a beneficiary and a trustee.

Beneficiary.

The beneficiary of a land trust is the person who presently owns the trust. This is unlike the beneficiary of life insurance, who owns it when they die. As explained later, the person who owns it when you die is the successor beneficiary. The beneficiary of a land trust can be a person, corporation, partnership, limited partnership, limited liability company, other legal entity, or a combination of these.

One Illinois case has held that the beneficiaries need not be explicitly specified in the trust if the trustee receives instructions on distributing the interests. *Teeple v. Hunziker, 454 N.E.2d 1174 (1983).*

Trustee.

Until 1992, the trustee could only be a human being, a bank, or a specially licensed trust company. A corporation could not be a trustee unless it had $1 million in assets and complied with Florida Statutes, Sections 658.21 and 660.41. However, a change in the law permitted any corporation or LLC to serve as a land trust trustee. This change was an excellent boost for land trusts. Many people were afraid to serve as trustees individually because of the possibility of environmental and other liabilities.

Now anyone can set up a corporation to serve as trustee. In 2002, the Florida legislature amended the land trust statute to clarify that entities other than persons and corporations could be trustees. This would include limited liability companies. In 2006, the Florida legislature again amended the statute to clarify that any legal entity could be a trustee, including an out-of-state corporation. Some attorneys feel that professional associations (P.A.s) and nonprofit corporations cannot be trustees of land trusts, but there is no court case or law on this issue. However, while there is no case law, The Fund has stated in underwriting seminars that a law firm or other professional association acting as a trustee is an ultra vires activity because it is not the practice of the profession for which the P.A. is licensed. As such, at least some title insurers may refuse to insure a transaction where a professional association or professional limited liability company acts as the land trust's trustee mortgaging or selling the property.

Family and Friends Make Bad Trustees

We are trustees of thousands of land trusts in almost every Florida county. As such, we are named as parties in lawsuits and served by sheriffs and process servers several times a month. In our law practice, we are sometimes asked to prepare trust agreements for clients who want to save some money, so they name their mothers or personal assistants as their trustees. We warn them that — based on experience — being a trustee could be traumatic for laymen.

In one case, a client insisted on naming his mother as his land trustee even after we told him some horror stories. However, he persisted so we complied with his request. Within a month, he called us to ask us to take over the trust from his mother as her successor trustee. He explained that she had started receiving junk mail and several text messages daily from people wanting to buy the property. Further, a tenant had decided to bring a housing discrimination case in federal court, and a U.S. Marshal had come to his mother's home to serve her with the lawsuit, causing her to worry now that her personal name is listed as a defendant (albeit as trustee of the land trust) in a case alleging that she is racist.

In another case, a client named his longtime assistant and friend as his trustee. However, when finances got tight, his assistant (unbeknownst to him as the trust's beneficiary) took out a large mortgage against the property to get a large amount of cash. He eventually learned of what she had done when the lender served a foreclosure complaint on him at the property held in trust.

Optional Parties

Besides the beneficiary and trustee, a land trust can have remainder beneficiaries, successor trustees, and directors.

Successor Beneficiary

When the beneficiary dies, a successor beneficiary becomes the trust's owner. This beneficiary can be a person or any type of legal entity, including a charity.

Under traditional land trust law, naming a successor beneficiary does not require that the trust be formalized like a will, with witnesses. *Conley v. Petersen, 25 111. 2d 271, 184 N.E.2d 888 (1962); First National Bank of Joliet v. Hampson, 88 111. App. 3d 1057, 410 N.E.2d 1109 (1980).* Since the trust interests are personal property, it is like putting "pay on death" (POD) or "transfer on death" on a bank account. However, having witnesses could make it less likely that relatives could challenge the trust.

Successor Trustee

Suppose the trustee is a person (as opposed to a corporation or other legal entity). In that case, you can name a successor trustee in the trust agreement or deed if the trustee dies or is incapacitated. You can also name an alternate successor if the first successor is unavailable or unwilling to serve.

You would not name a successor when the trustee is a corporation or other entity since the entity can not die. If it dissolved, it could still convey the property through its officers, managers, partners, or directors as provided by Florida law.

Director

A land trust director is a person (or persons) with the power of direction, meaning they can instruct the trustee on what actions to take regarding the property. Normally the trust's beneficiaries hold the power of direction according to their interests in the trust. The 2013 amendment to the statute allows a person to hold the power of direction to limited parcels of the trust property.

Having someone other than the beneficiaries act as the director can be useful in many situations, such as:

• if you want to give interest in the trust to other members of your family but want to retain control;

• if you have several investors and want one of them to be able to direct the trustee;

• if you want to loan money to a property owner but want to be in control without having a mortgage;

> *Example: An investor wants to help a homeowner get out of a property that is being foreclosed. Instead of getting a deed from the homeowner into the investor's own name (and paying documentary taxes), they obtain a deed to a trustee who holds the property for the homeowner (no documentary tax). However, the investor is the trust director and can negotiate a short sale, find an end buyer, and profit from the work.*

The land trust statute sets out the director's rights and duties:

The trust agreement for a land trust may provide that one or more persons have the power to direct the trustee to convey property or interests, execute a mortgage, distribute proceeds of a sale or financing, and execute documents incidental to administration of the land trust. The power of direction, unless provided otherwise in the trust agreement of the land trust, is conferred upon the holders of the power for the use and benefit of all holders of any beneficial interest in the trust agreement of the land trust. In the absence of a provision in the land trust agreement to the contrary, the power of direction shall be in accordance with the percentage of individual ownership. In exercising the power of direction, the holders of the power of direction are presumed to act in a fiduciary capacity for the benefit of all holders of any beneficial interest in the land trust, unless otherwise provided in the trust agreement. A beneficial interest in a land trust is indefeasible, and the power of direction may not be exercised so as to alter, amend, revoke, terminate, defeat, or otherwise affect or change the enjoyment of any beneficial interest in a land trust. Florida Land Trust Act, Section 689.071(8)(f).

Including fiduciary duties for the director can limit the availability of remedies for someone wanting to protect his or her financial interest, as in the example above. So, if the Director needed to protect his own interest in the property, it would be very important to spell out in the trust agreement any rights of the Director that overrule this fiduciary duty.

Types of Property

Land, mortgages, leases, and other interests in real estate can be held in a land trust. However, a land trust is neither a classic living nor an inter vivos trust. These are usually trusts established by individuals wanting to hold all their assets in trust to avoid probate. For example, a land trust cannot hold stocks, bonds, or other property not related to real estate. A living trust can be created using the trustee powers in the new statute 689.073, but if a living trust directly owns real estate, other assets in the trust could be at risk for real estate liability.

A better setup would be to have a living trust own the beneficial interest in a land trust. A separate land trust should own each property so a liability at one would not cause the loss of the others.

***

Daycare Babies and Dog Fight Training Arenas

A frantic client called Joe one afternoon. We held four homes in trust for her, all owned free and clear. She had saved money for years and slowly built a small rental empire for her retirement. A tragic accident had happened at one of her homes earlier that day. The tenant ran an unlicensed daycare inside the home while the tenant's boyfriend operated a dog fighting training operation in the backyard. The client had no idea any of this was happening. Unfortunately, one of the daycare toddlers got out of the daycare and wandered into the dog training area. A dog mauled the child, causing permanently disfiguring and disabling injuries. A life-flight helicopter was needed to transport the child to the hospital.

While worried about the child, the client was also concerned about what would happen to her as the landlord. I reminded her that she held this house in a land trust where we were the trustee. Then I pointed out that her other homes were likewise held in separate land trusts, insulated from this property. As such, while it was possible that she could lose this home in a lawsuit for the child's catastrophic injuries sustained there, it was unlikely they would be able to name her directly in the lawsuit or go after any of her other homes to satisfy a judgment. Instead, they would sue us as trustee of the trust that held the property and as the landlord listed on the lease with the tenant. While rents were payable to her separate LLC that operated all of her rentals, that LLC never retained any cash in its accounts. Therefore — while it too could possibly be named in the forthcoming lawsuit — it would be an "empty vessel" for anyone attempting to satisfy the judgment.

In short, she protected her real estate assets in land trusts by separating them from each other and herself.

Documentary Taxes

Documentary taxes are not due when a property is deeded to a trust in which the grantor is the beneficiary, nor when deeded out to a beneficiary or deeded to a successor trustee. This is spelled out in the Florida Administrative Code, section 12B-4.013(28). A cover letter citing this rule should be included to avoid delay when recording a deed, or — better yet — the Administrative Code citation should be included on the deed to show the recording clerk and future title examiners why no documentary tax was paid when the deed was recorded.

When a beneficial interest is assigned in a land trust, documentary taxes are due. Chapter 8 discusses this in more detail.

Agency Law

Agency law concerns the issue of who can legally do something that will bind another person. Court cases involving land trusts have held that the trustee is not the beneficiary's agent. Therefore, a trustee's acts do not create liability for the beneficiary. *Lawyer's Title Guaranty Fund v. Koch, 397 So. 2d 455 (1981)*. The 2006 amendment to the land trust statute added language that explicitly protects a beneficiary from liability. However, the trustee's acts would be binding upon the property in the trust.

Likewise, the beneficiary is not the trustee's agent and cannot create liability against the trustee. *Gallagher & Speck v. Chicago Title & Trust Co., 238 111. App. 39 (1925).* However, to avoid any doubts (and litigation) in these areas, the land trust agreement should specifically say that neither party is an agent of the other.

As a practical matter, the beneficiary sometimes signs documents as an agent of the trust. For example, a beneficiary might sign as the agent to list the property for sale with a real estate agent or to sign a contract to sell the property. It is possible to add those rights to the trust agreement to make it clear that the beneficiary can do such things. However, this is not recommended. Instead, it is always the best practice to have the trustee sign any contract, permit application, lease agreement, or other legal documents related to the trust property to maintain anonymity and to ensure the "agent" is never dragged into litigation related to the instrument that they would have signed instead.

Beneficiary Liability

Before the 2006 amendment to the land trust statute, beneficiaries had no protection from liability for the property unless they set up an LLC to hold the beneficial interest.

That amendment added the words, "Except as provided in this section, the beneficiaries of a land trust are not liable, solely by being beneficiaries, under a judgment, decree, or order of court or in any other manner for a debt, obligation, or liability of the land trust."

Even with the statutory protection, the beneficiary will be liable for their own acts. Because the beneficiary must manage the property, the beneficiary can be liable for mismanagement. Thus, a trust is not insulation from lawsuits for a beneficiary's own wrongful acts.

Setting up the beneficiary as a corporation or limited liability company (LLC) might add protection. However, there would still be the problem of the company's owner doing the wrongful acts and being liable.

A slightly better plan would be to set up a company to operate the property. The beneficiary could be an individual and possibly get lower insurance rates, and an operating company with no assets could do the actual management and signing of leases. This would be better than using the beneficiary, who owns the equity in the property.

An LLC is usually better than a corporation, as it offers more asset protection with less formality. It is also allowed more passive income than an S corporation, and — if the property or beneficial interest must be conveyed to the LLC members, it is not a taxable event as it would be in the case of a distribution to a corporation's shareholders.

***

A 5-gallon Bucket is Not a Septic Tank.

An investor who often bought dilapidated homes, renovated and sold them would always use our trust company to hold title to the properties he was renovating and flipping. He or his general contracting company signed all of the permit applications for work on the homes and personally oversaw all the work. He was furious with us when he was named in a lawsuit related to a home we had held in trust and recently sold.

The new owners started smelling a foul odor from their new home's crawlspace. When they investigated, they realized that their toilets were flushing into a five-gallon bucket under the house instead of through pipes to the septic tank in the backyard. He was unhappy with us, saying that we had promised that—so long as he held the property inside a land trust—he personally would not be named in a lawsuit related to the property.

This is when we pointed out to him that — since he personally did the renovations on the home (and apparently not very well) — then he was in the "line of fire" of the lawsuit for being negligent in doing the work. He wasn't being sued for failure to disclose the defects or misrepresentation. We had signed the contract to sell the home, so as trustees, we would have been named in the lawsuit for that cause of action. But he is the one who did the work that caused the damages to the buyers. That's why he was being sued.

For this reason, we recommend hiring licensed contractors to do any renovations on properties held in trust. Under Florida's building codes, this is required in most cases (i.e., new windows, doors, roofs, plumbing, electrical, and HVAC, just to name a few). Even if it's just to repair a rotten board on a porch step, it's best to hire a licensed and insured contractor to do the work rather than doing it on your own. Whoever replaces the rotten board will be liable if that board gives way and injures a tenant or their guest.

Trustee Liability

The trustee is not personally liable for the trust's debts, obligations, or liabilities unless provided for in the land trust agreement or if the trustee is negligent. (Fla. Stat., Sec. 689.071(7).) This section was added to the land trust statute to overrule a court decision that held a trustee personally liable. *Taylor v. Richmond's New Approach Association, Inc., 351 So. 2d 1094 (1977).* A trustee is personally liable only for torts (wrongful acts) that the trustee personally commits or for obligations where it is personally at fault.

In a 1990 case, a judgment was entered against a trustee (an attorney) personally on a loan of $25,000 to the trust from one of the trust's beneficiaries. The trial judge's rationale was that since the beneficiary who lent the money to the trust never signed the trust and since the trustee never kept an accounting or performed any other fiduciary duties, the trust never existed. This was a wrong decision, and the appeals court reversed the judgment.

The court of appeals held that under an Illinois-type land trust, the trustee has no duty to keep records or perform any other fiduciary functions that usually apply to trusts. The court also held that the trust was not invalidated because one beneficiary who owned 5% of the beneficial interest did not execute it. *Schwartz v. Hill, 562 So. 2d 779 (1990).*

Personal Property

Occasionally, a purchase of real property will include considerable personal property such as furniture or equipment. Although there are no cases regarding this issue, Kenoe says there is no inhibition to provide in the trust agreement for the trustee to own this personal property. It can be transferred to the trustee by a bill of sale. See Kenoe on Land Trusts, § 2.66.

Due-On-Sale Clauses in Mortgages

As a general rule, a land trust cannot be used to avoid a valid, existing due-on-sale clause contained in a mortgage. In an Illinois case, the court held that a conveyance to a trustee for the original owner did violate a due-on-sale clause that forbade the transfer of "any interest" in the property. *Damen Savings v. Heritage Standard Bank, 431 N.E. 2d 34 (1982).*

However, the federal Garn-St. Germain Act provides that a lender cannot call a loan due to "a transfer into an inter vivos trust in which the borrower is and remains a beneficiary and which does not relate to a transfer of rights of occupancy in the property." (12 USC 1701j-3(d)(8)). This law applies only to primary residences where the trust beneficiary also continues to reside in the property. Therefore, lenders routinely allow properties to be put into trusts. As long as there is no indication to the lender that the beneficiary has changed, there is usually no problem.

Since putting a property into trust may also involve a subsequent change of occupancy, it would be prudent to request a letter from the lender stating that putting the property into trust will not cause an acceleration of the loan. If the lender declines to send such a letter, one can send a letter to the lender stating that "unless we hear from you to the contrary, we will assume that putting our property into trust will not violate the due-on-sale clause." This may not be legally binding, but it may help provide a later defense of waiver or laches, especially if the beneficial interest has not been sold.

The prudent lender will require notification from the trustee of a change of beneficiary. Under the federal regulations for the Garn-St. Germain Act, the lender can require this, and if the borrower refuses, the transfer is a breach of the mortgage. Suppose the lender does not require notification, as a practical matter, once a property has been conveyed to a land trust. In that case, the beneficial interest can be transferred without the lender finding out.

If a trustee purchases a property and the mortgage signed by the trustee contains a due-on-sale clause that only covers conveyances of the title, then a transfer of the beneficial interest would not violate the due-on-sale clause. *Wachta v. First Federal, 430 N.E. 2d 708 (1981).* However, most mortgages provide that the loan can be accelerated upon transferring "any interest, " including a beneficial interest.

The change of a trustee under an installment contract with a due-on-sale clause did not trigger acceleration. *Conner v. First National Bank, 439 N.E. 2d 122 (1982).*

A question arises occasionally whether violating a due-on-sale clause is illegal or unethical. This issue came before the U. S. Supreme Court. *Field v. Mans, 516 US 59 (1995).* This was a bankruptcy case in which a creditor said it was fraudulent for the debtor to ask permission to transfer the property after it was already transferred. The court said that even though the creditor could have easily checked the records, this could be considered misleading and fraudulent. In a concurring opinion, Justice Ginsburg quoted a conversation the Court had with the creditor's lawyer in which he admitted that if the debtor never said anything when he violated the due-on-sale clause, there would have been no problem. While this concurring opinion is not binding law, it indicates that at least one United States Supreme Court justice feels that violating a due-on-sale clause without saying anything to the lender is not fraudulent.

***

Subject-To Transactions and the Due-On-Sale Clause

When an investor takes a property subject to the current mortgage(s), one question always arises: "What happens if the lender calls the loan because the due-on-sale clause is being breached?"

It's fortunately rare that this occurs. In our experience, the lender will accelerate the note and mortgage when there is an unapproved transfer of title if the lender finds out that the transfer has occurred and there is some other technical breach of the loan agreements. For instance, conventional loan lenders typically track payment of real property taxes and maintenance of insurance on the mortgaged property. Whenever the property is transferred, the tax bill will change since there is a new owner, and the insurance will likewise change to reflect the new insured owner. When the lender receives notice of these changes, they may send a notice to their borrower to ask them to prove that they are the beneficiary of the trust and that they still reside in the property as their primary residence.

If the property is in a land trust and is no longer the borrower's primary residence, they cannot make such a representation to the lender. At that point, the investor who purchased the property inside the land trust subject to the borrower's mortgage would need to find some way to pay off the mortgage within 30 days or face foreclosure.

We have developed a subject-to conditional assignment of beneficial interest (not included in this book). In this assignment, the borrower is the initial beneficiary of the land trust at closing. They assign their beneficial interest in the trust at closing to the investor buying the property subject to the borrower's mortgage. The assignment, however, is conditioned upon the investor's continued compliance with the borrower's mortgage. So long as the investor continues to pay the mortgage payments on time, keep the property properly insured, and pay the taxes, the investor holds the beneficial interest and the power of direction over the trustee. However, suppose the investor fails to hold up this end of the bargain after some notice and due process. In that case, the conditional assignment of beneficial interest will terminate, reverting it to the borrower, who will then control the trust and can direct the trustee to convey the property back to the borrower if they want it.

This consumer protection mechanism for the borrower helps the investor overcome the inevitable objections when they approach such borrowers to buy their properties without paying off their mortgage debts. Also, if the borrower's lender demands to see the land trust agreement, they will see an agreement where the borrower is the beneficiary. Even if they demand to see the conditional assignment of beneficial interest, they will see that it is subject to reversion to their borrower at any time. This can all help to argue against allegations of a breach of the due-on-sale clause in the mortgage.

Chapter Four

Setting Up a Land Trust

There are two ways to set up a land trust, buying a piece of property directly into a trust or putting property you already own into a trust.

Buying Property into Trust

The best way to set up a land trust is to do so when you purchase a property and have the seller deed the property directly to the trust. This way, your name never appears in the public records. The other way to structure it is to buy it in your name and deed it into trust.

You would only use the latter method if your lender required the property to be in your name to do the financing. Whenever possible you should avoid lenders with this requirement. As long as the lender receives a title policy covering the mortgage and a personal guarantee of the note (or you signing the note as the maker), using a land trust should make no difference to the lender. (More information on this is in Chapter 5.)

If you wish to keep your purchase price of the property secret, then you should set up the land trust with the seller as the initial beneficiary. At the closing, the seller will sign the trust and then deed the property into the trust. Since it is their trust, only a minimum (70¢) documentary tax is paid on that deed. Then, the seller immediately signs an assignment of beneficial interest to you, and the correct amount of documentary tax is paid on the assignment using form DR-228, which is sent to the Florida Department of Revenue in Tallahassee and is not in the public records.

In most counties in Florida, the seller customarily pays the documentary tax on the transaction, so he or she should pay them on the assignment rather than the deed. The buyer can pay the 70-cent minimum stamp tax on the deed to the trustee.

To be sure the transaction is handled this way, you should spell it out in the contract. A clause like this should work:

> It is agreed between the parties that at or before closing the property will be conveyed to a trust of which Seller is the initial beneficiary (said conveyance to be exempt from transfer tax). At Closing Seller will convey the property to an entity or persons designated by Buyer or Buyer's assignee by

signing an Assignment of Beneficial Interest to said Buyer's designee. ___ Buyer/ ____ Seller shall pay the Documentary Tax on the Purchase Price whether a land trust is involved in the Closing or not.

Suppose you fail to require it in the contract. In that case, a suspicious or skittish seller might not want anything to do with your trust if you spring it at closing, but if you explain why you are doing it and the fact that they are immediately assigned out of the trust, the seller should consent. If not, you might offer the seller some incentive for doing it, such as an extra $100. The author once gave a seller a copy of this land trust book and a will book for agreeing to work with a trust to retain the confidentiality of the sales price at closing.

Suppose you are buying property at some type of foreclosure sale, such as a sheriff's execution, tax deed auction, or foreclosure sale. In that case, it is advisable to first deed the property to a strawman and then to the trustee. (A strawman is a person who holds title for an instant just to ensure property passes legally.) This is because there is a legal question of whether a sheriff or court clerk can sign a deed to a trustee and convey the statutory trust powers. So you have the sheriff's or clerk's title certificate go to a strawman, and then the strawman immediately deeds the property into the land trust with a proper land trust deed containing all the needed clauses.

The strawman can be any person or entity. Often, it is an attorney or their assistant. It can be a corporation, but then some secrecy will be lost because anyone can check the officers and directors on the Secretary of State's website.

A straightforward solution is to have the land trust trustee take title merely "as trustee" with no powers and immediately deed it to the trust with a corrective deed containing the correct powers, full name and date of the trust, and other clauses. As explained in Chapter 3, "as trustee" has no legal effect in a deed, vesting title solely in the grantee, so while the deed would fail to create a true "trustee's deed," as between yourself and the person or entity acting as your trustee, it is a strong indication that the grantee is only your trustee and does not hold the property solely for itself.

The most important thing to consider when using a strawman is to be sure that he or she has no judgments or liens of record. If so, those will immediately become liens on the property. Even if you put "as trustee" after the strawman's name, the lien could be attached to the property because of Florida Statutes section 689.07, which was discussed in Chapter 3.

Contract For Purchase

When contracting to buy a property into a land trust, there are two ways to write the contract: 1) you can write the contract in your name and assign it to the trustee, or 2) you can write it in the name of the trust.

Signing the Contract in Your Name

The easiest way to buy the property is to sign the contract in your name and make sure it is assignable, then assign it to your land trust trustee since the contract is not recorded in the public records. You would also want to ensure that the assignment completely releases you from personal liability to perform the contract after the assignment is complete. To make sure the seller does not object to the trust at closing, you can put a clause in the contract similar to the following:

> Buyer may assign its rights and obligations under this Contract, and be released from any further liability.

Making the Trust the Buyer

The other way to write a contract is to designate the trust as the buyer. The buyer or purchaser on the contract would be written as follows:

> [name of trust], with [name of trustee], as trustee, with full power and authority, to protect, conserve, sell, lease, encumber, or otherwise manage and dispose of the property under Florida Statutes §689.071 and §689.073.

Since you are buying the property for yourself through a trust, you could sign as an agent of the trust you will be setting up, but this is a gray area of the law; and there is a chance that you might not be able to sue the seller if he or she refuses to sell. Further, if you sign the contract — even as an agent of the trust — you have destroyed your anonymity and potentially placed yourself in the cross-hairs of litigation if you or the other party breaches the contract. If you do not plan to sue the seller or be sued for not buying the property, this should not be an issue. You can avoid these issues if you sign the contract yourself, as described earlier, and assign the contract to the trust. But remember, the best practice is to have the trustee of the trust sign the contract in the first place as trustee of the trust. Now that contracts are customarily signed electronically, you can negotiate the contract and then have the trustee sign the final contract within seconds. Further, this lets the trustee know that a forthcoming contract will need trust documentation created.

If you prefer to have the trustee sign the contract, know that an issue has been raised as to whether a trustee might be personally liable for signing a contract if no deed is recorded since the statute seems to require some recording. The trustee should not be liable since the statute applies to all interests in land and is to be liberally construed. Still, adding language to the contract for extra protection would be best, insulating the trustee from personal liability. You can do this by adding this special provision to the contract:

> The parties agree that this instrument is executed by the trustee, not personally, but as trustee in the exercise of the authority conferred upon such trustee. No personal liability or responsibility is assumed by nor shall be enforceable against the trustee, either express or implied.

Amending the Contract.

If you forgot to make the contract assignable, you can sign an Amendment of Contract with the seller. Just use a blank Amendment to Contract form and state that the contract is being amended as follows:

> The Buyer under this contract shall be [name of trust], [name of trustee], trustee, with full power and authority, to protect, conserve, sell, lease, encumber, or otherwise manage and dispose of the property under Florida Statutes §689.071 and §689.073.

Putting Property into Trust

If you already own a property you wish to put in trust, you can usually deed it to the trustee. You will lose some secrecy because it has been in your name, and past deed records are open to the public forever. People will always be able to find out that you once owned that property and you deeded it to the trustee. Since you will probably not pay taxes on the transfer, they will also know that you put it into your own trust. (You could unnecessarily pay the transfer taxes, but that is expensive; in some cases, this could be unethical or illegal.)

Putting your existing property into trust does give you most of the benefits of having a land trust; you just don't have complete secrecy. You have some secrecy, however, because your name will come off the tax rolls shortly after recording, and you will no longer be listed as owner. While a sharp asset investigator can find out you once owned the property, a cursory asset search will show that you currently do not own any property.

Putting a Mortgage Into Trust

Unlike Illinois, Florida allows land trusts to hold mortgages, which can offer the same privacy and probate avoidance as real estate.

When selling a property out of a land trust and taking back a mortgage, the mortgage can be granted to the selling land trust trustee using similar trustee powers as a deed into trust. Under a liberal reading of the statute, the exact wording would work. Still, some title companies might want to see specific language giving the trustee the power to assign or satisfy the mortgage. So the mortgagee clause could read, for example, as follows:

> ...to ABC Trust Company, Trustee of Trust No. 123 dated February 17, 2014, with full power and authority to protect, conserve, sell, lease, encumber, or otherwise manage and dispose of, as well as to foreclose, satisfy, or assign mortgages on said property pursuant to Florida Statutes §689.071 and §689.073, Mortgagee, whose post office address is...

The trust agreement should also be revised slightly to cover the powers to satisfy or assign the mortgage and the contingency that the trustee might take the property in a foreclosure action. The following are some revised clauses to the ones included in the land trust agreement.

1. **TRUST**. The Trustee is about to hold title to a mortgage on real estate under the provisions of Sections 689.071 and 689.073, Florida Statutes, with full power and authority to protect, conserve, assign, satisfy, sell, lease, encumber, or otherwise manage and dispose of said mortgage and the property, in the event it comes into trustee's possession through foreclosure or otherwise, and agrees to hold the mortgage and the title, proceeds, profits, and avails thereof, if any, which may come into its possession, in Trust for the uses and purposes and under the terms herein set forth.

2. **PROPERTY**. The Trustee will take title to a mortgage encumbering various properties, the legal descriptions of which shall be attached on Schedule A.

3. **INTEREST OF BENEFICIARIES**. The interests of the beneficiaries hereunder and of any person who becomes entitled to any interest under this Trust shall consist solely of a power of direction to deal with the mortgage on and title to said property and to manage and control said property as hereinafter provided, and the right to receive the proceeds from rentals, mortgages, sales, payments, or other dispositions shall be deemed to be personal property and may be treated, assigned, and transferred as such. No beneficiary now has, or shall hereafter at any time have, any right, title, or interest in or to the mortgage or any portion of said real estate as such, either legal or equitable, but only an interest in the earnings, avails, and proceeds as aforesaid; it being the intention of this instrument to vest the full legal and equitable title in and to the mortgage and said premises in the Trustee under Florida Statutes Section 689.071 and 689.073.

If a separate trust is set up to hold a mortgage, which is either given by property owners or assigned by holders, the trust agreement should also have the above clauses, and the mortgages or assignments should also have the powers previously mentioned. An ASSIGNMENT OF MORTGAGE is included in Appendix C. (See Form 25)

Choosing the Trustee

The basic concept behind a trust is that you are giving your property to someone you can trust. Because a trustee would have the ability to freely sell or mortgage your property, you should use someone whom you know will not steal it or otherwise harm your interest in it.

A bank is probably the most trustworthy entity available, but the fees at many banks are unreasonable. Because banks are used to dealing with active trusts that require much time to manage, their charges for serving as trustees can reach thousands of dollars a year. Unless a bank agrees to set a fee designed for land trusts that do not require the same work or risk as other trusts, you will probably not want to use one for your trusts.

Most attorneys, if they are the kind that charge reasonable fees and deal fairly with their clients, can be trusted to be land trust trustees. Since a land trust is a written document spelling out all terms, and transfers by deed and mortgage are public records, the only time you would have trouble with an attorney as a land trust trustee would be if the attorney was a complete fraud and was ready to lose his license and go to jail. Even then, it would be more likely that an attorney would take cash out of someone's probate or trust account than do something dishonest with trust property in public records.

Relatives can often be used as trustees if there is a close family relationship and you know they will not sell or mortgage your property without your permission. The same last name can be a giveaway to an asset investigator, so a relative with a different last name is better.

Friends as trustees

A client once designated a close family friend as his land trustee to hold title to his home. When the sheriff showed up to serve notice that the home was being foreclosed, he learned that his friend of over 25 years had hit hard times financially. She, therefore, deeded the property out of trust to herself and her husband. They then signed a mortgage secured by the property, taking out a loan of over $500,000.00 and taking the money into their personal bank account. Afterward, she returned the property to herself as trustee of the land trust. It cost the client tens of thousands of dollars and years of time to clean up the title and quiet the title for his home.

Fake trustees

Some investors once thought they had the perfect plan to keep ownership secret and avoid trustee fees. They made up a fake name and deeded the property to that imaginary person as trustee. Unfortunately, it was impossible to have the trustee's deed notarized when it came time to sell the property!

Now that corporations that are not banks can legally serve as trustees of land trusts, there are many new possibilities. Attorneys who were afraid to serve as trustees personally have used their professional association, but some feel this is not allowed under its corporate purpose. Further, we have been in Continuing Legal education courses for lawyers where title insurance underwriters have said that a law firm is not allowed to act as trustee because that is not the practice of law. The law firm acting as trustee would thus create a title defect that title insurance may not cover. So it would be better for a lawyer or other professional to form a separate company to serve as a trust company rather than using their professional practice firm to do so. After many client inquiries, the authors have formed a trust company. See www.mylandtrustee.com for details.

You can also form your own corporation or LLC to serve as a trustee. However, the big problem with doing so is that the names of the officers, directors, managers, and registered agents are permanent public records available on the Division of Corporation's website. Anyone can type in your name and find every corporation you were ever involved with.

If you wanted to keep your name out of the public records, you would need at least one other person to be the sole officer and director (of a corporation) or manager (of an LLC). You could then be the sole shareholder (of a corporation) or member (of an LLC), since shareholders and members are not public record. Another way to keep your name off of the public records of a corporation or LLC would be to use a trust to be the officer or manager. This is the topic of a whole other book, Personal Property Trusts by Mark Warda.

When deciding whether to form an LLC or a corporation to be your own trustee, you should consider whether you will ever want to obtain conventional (Fannie Mae or Freddie Mac) financing secured by the trust property. If so, then you should form a corporation since the guidelines of those entities specifically state that a "corporation" regularly engaged in the business of acting as a trustee can be the mortgagor in such a conventional loan.

Choosing the Beneficiary

The beneficiary of a land trust can be an individual, a corporation, an LLC, a partnership, a trust, or any entity. Individual ownership might make it easier to get insurance, and since the land trust protects assets, using a company would not be necessary. For the land trust to obtain the homestead tax exemptions and Save-our-Homes valuation caps, the beneficiary must be the individual who occupies or resides in the property owned in the trust.

However, an LLC offers double asset protection. A corporation offers single-asset protection in that if it does something wrong, its shareholders are not personally liable (unless they did something themselves to contribute to the liability).

The LLC offers this same protection, but it provides double-asset protection because if the owner of an LLC does something wrong unrelated to the LLC, his creditors cannot take his LLC interests away from him (so long as the LLC has more than one member). Instead, they can only get a "charging order" against the LLC. A person who owns a corporation can lose his corporate stock to his creditors regardless of how many shareholders there are.

The only drawback to having two-member LLCs is that they must file a separate tax return (form 1065), while a single-member LLC does not because a disregarded entity passes income to its members' tax returns. This can be expensive for persons who own several properties. With that said, in the latest revision to Florida's LLC Act, it was clarified that there may be "non-economic" members of an LLC who are not entitled to receive distributions from the LLC, nor are they required to make any monetary contributions to the LLC. As such, the LLC should not need to file a partnership tax return in that event, but a CPA should be consulted to ensure it would apply to your situation if you have a multi-member LLC — even with non-monetary members.

Another solution is to set up a single-member LLC for each land trust property and have them all owned by one multi-member LLC. The income from the single-member LLC passes through to the multi-member LLC, which files one tax return for all properties. The owners of the multi-member LLC receive a Schedule K-1 from the multi-member LLC, which they file with their tax return.

The following is an illustration of how the ownership of several properties would be set up using single-member LLCs owned by a multi-member LLC

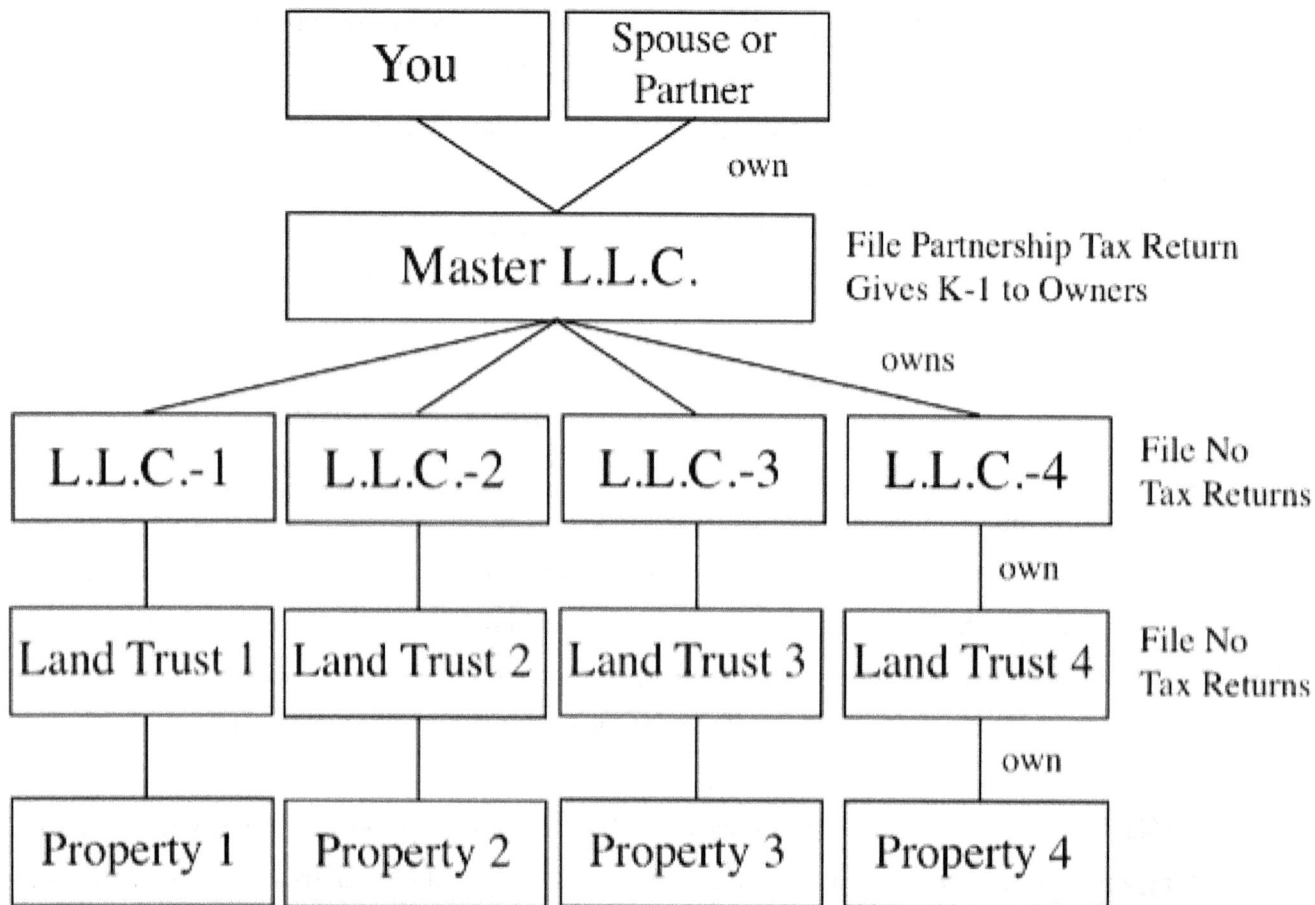

Land trusts with separate single-member LLC's as beneficiaries to collect rents (no outside operating or property management entity).

However, as a better practice and for extra protection, a separate management or operating company can be set up to sign leases and deal with the tenants. That way, the tenants have no contact with the LLCs that own the trusts. The operating company would have no assets and would only collect rent and pay bills.

When liability protection was added to the land trusts via the latest statutory amendments, some people did away with the individual LLCs that owned each land trust and had the multi-member LLC own them all. Still, you should have a separate operating LLC as shown below:

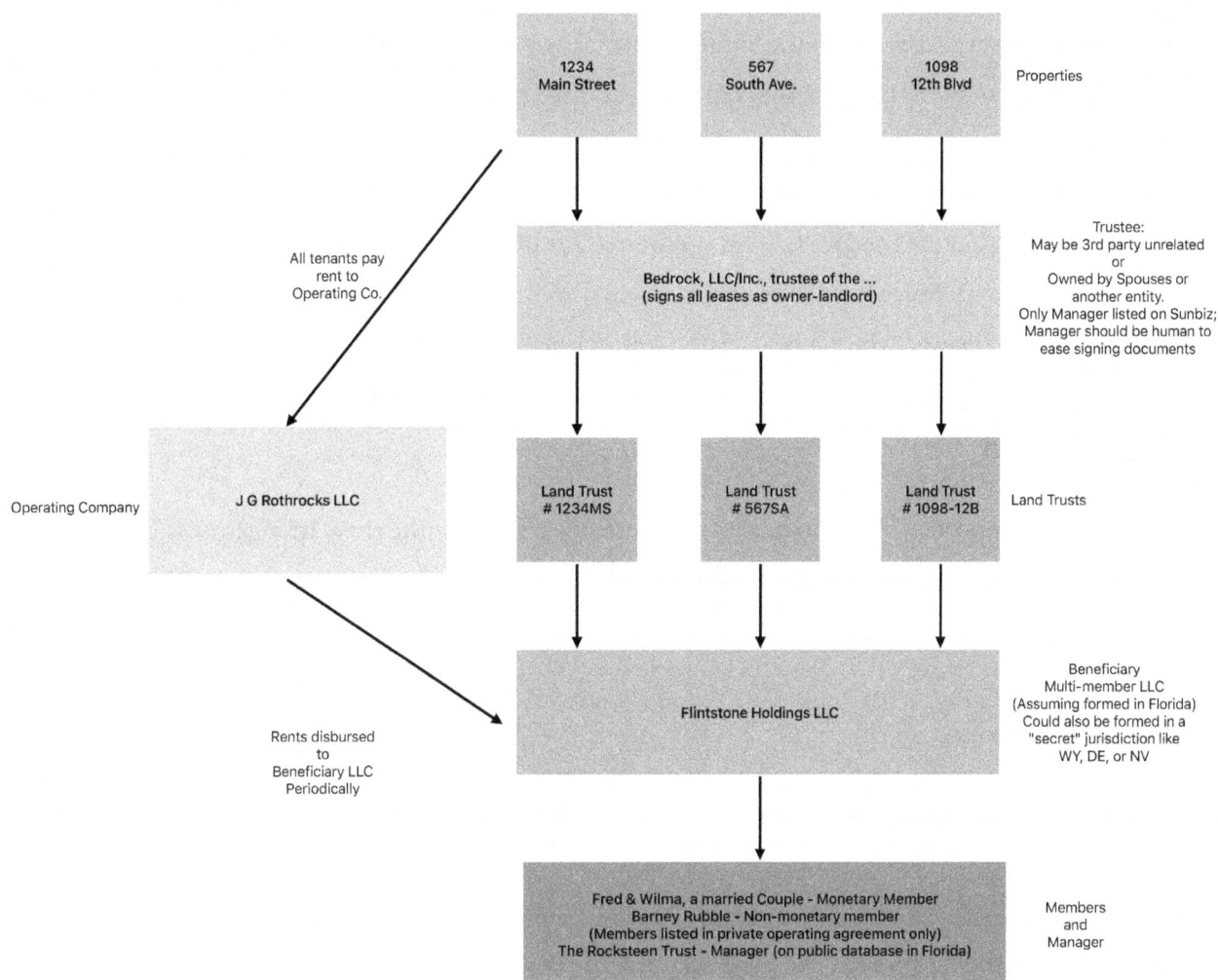

Land Trust structure with one multi-member LLC as beneficiary plus outside operating company.

If you are having trouble getting insurance for an LLC, you can eliminate the multi-member and just have one LLC management company. If the land trusts are owned by a husband and wife in an estate by the entireties, then they would have similar protection to an LLC. However, while tenancy by the entireties can provide a lot of asset protection in Florida, we recommend that you consult with an asset protection attorney to ensure you have taken steps to mitigate liability exposure against marital assets.

Naming the Trust

A trust can be given any number or name. A professional trustee may require or prefer numbers related to its record-keeping system. Very often, the property's street number is used as the trust number, and since two properties can have the same number, the date of the trust is usually given as part of the name. For example, "Trust No. 5678, dated March 13, 2024."

When an investor wants the public or mortgage company to think a previous owner still owns a property, she may name the trust the "Smith Family Trust" and then take an assignment of the beneficial interest from the seller/owner-beneficiary. Some title companies may think that this name means the Smiths still have an interest in the property and may want someone in the Smith family to sign a deed. However, the land trust statute says the trustee has full powers, so the trust name should not affect those powers.

If a trust name is used and if business is transacted in the name of the trust (such as on a bank account), then the name should be registered with the Florida Department of State's Division of Corporations (Sunbiz) as a fictitious name (Florida Statutes §865.09). This is required for using a name that is not your legal name or your registered company's name. Since it is the beneficiary who is doing business in the name of the trust, registering the beneficiaries as the owners of the fictitious name will sacrifice secrecy.

Preparing the Deed

The deed is the most important document in a land trust since it creates the trust arrangement. Even if a trust is never executed, the trustee has all the powers conferred in the deed. When you draft the deed, consider the following points important.

Full Powers to Trustee.

The deed must grant full powers to the trustee. At least those listed in the statute should be mentioned as follows.

> ...to [name of trust], dated [date trust was created], [name of trustee], as Trustee with full power and authority either to protect, conserve, sell, to lease, encumber, or otherwise manage and dispose of as provided in Florida Statutes, Sections 689.071 and 689.073.

In the past, it was normal to put the trustee's name first, but since county databases often do not have enough room to fit the entire name, sometimes the trust number or even the word trustee would be left off. The result of this was that a city code enforcement department filing a legal action or a lien would erroneously file it against, for example, "John Doe" or "John Doe, Trustee" without the trust name. This would cause a problem for all other properties held by that trustee in that county. Putting the trust name first makes it more likely to appear on the ownership rolls.

Some attorneys and title companies have argued that because a trust cannot hold title—only the trustee can—the trustee's name must appear first. This is not true. As long as the trustee's name is clearly in the deed, the order of the words does not matter legally.

Some people have named the grantee something like "Trust No. 123, the trustee hereinafter mentioned" and then named the trustee in a paragraph on the second or third page of the deed. The hope is that the indexer will not even list the trustee's name. This is not illegal as long as the deed names a legal person or entity as a trustee.

It is advisable to refer specifically to the statute to show the intent to create a land trust and to utilize the liberal interpretation allowed by the statute.

Some feel that when the trustee executes other documents, such as a condominium declaration, all other powers should be given. Under the statute, full rights of ownership vest with merely the above words, so this would seem unnecessary. Still, since a title insurer may raise the issue, adding other powers to a deed is advisable when their use can be expected. If the trustee may at some point take back mortgages and need to sign satisfactions, assignments, or foreclosure complaints, it would similarly be advisable to add those powers.

Person or Legal Entity as Trustee.

The deed must have a person or legal entity as a trustee. There is a lot of confusion on this issue. Some people want to make the trust the grantee on the deed. A trust is not a legal person (unless it is a registered business trust), so title cannot be given to the trust itself. It must be given to a person (natural or artificial) as trustee for the trust.

To make it more likely that the deed will be indexed in the records under the trust name, some people put, for example, "...to Trust No. 1234, dated February 17, 2014, Acme Trust Corp., Trustee "

Some people write "...to the Smith Trust whose trustee is hereinafter mentioned..." at the top of the deed and then put the trustee's name in the fine print on page two. The hope is that the clerk recording the deed will index only the trust's name and not the trustee's.

Personal Property.

The deed may contain a provision stating that the beneficiary's interest is personal property, as provided in §689.071(6). However, if the trust property is to be the beneficiary's homestead, this paragraph should be left out of the deed since some county property appraisers will deny the homestead exemptions if they see this in the recorded deed. In any event, the provision should be listed at least in the trust agreement itself.

Personal Liability.

The deed should provide that the trustee has no personal liability. Although the statutes relieve the trustee of liability, such language in the deed should take care of possible exceptions that might be found in the law.

Successor Trustee.

If the trustee is a natural person (and not a corporation or LLC), the deed should provide for a successor trustee in the event of the original trustee's death. If the trustee is a corporation or LLC, which would not die as a person would, no successor trustee is needed. However, it is still prudent to list a successor trustee for an entity because the entity may be dissolved on purpose or by neglect, meaning a new trustee should be able to step into the role in that event.

Free and Clear.

The deed should state that persons dealing with the trustee take title to the property free and clear of the beneficiaries' claims.

Straw Man.

Where a sheriff gives a deed in an execution sale, a clerk of court in a tax deed sale, or as a mortgage or lien foreclosure certificate of title, it is best to convey it to a straw man and then to a trustee with a deed that gives the trustee powers. Otherwise, a question may arise as to the capacity of the sheriff or clerk to grant trust powers.

Third Party.

The deed can come from the beneficiary who is setting up the trust or from a third party selling to the trust. However, there is some question about a third party's capacity to grant trust powers to another's trust. Therefore, the best method is for a third party to deed the property to a trust of which he or she is the beneficiary and then assign the beneficial interest to the intended beneficiary.

State Law.

The deed must comply with state law regarding form and formalities. For example, two witnesses and a notary are required, and there must be a blank 3" square in the upper right corner. The deed can be on letter- or legal-size paper, and the notary can be one of the witnesses. The witnesses must print their names and addresses legibly beneath their signatures.

Preparing the Trust Agreement

Since 2006 a land trust has been required to be in writing. It should be executed prior to the deed, but there have been no cases indicating that there is any penalty if it is executed later.

1. It should provide that it is being established under Florida Statutes, Sections 689.071 and 689.073.

2. It should provide for the trustee's duty to deal with the property at the beneficiaries' direction and to convey the property to the beneficiaries at the end of twenty years. This term is chosen because of the Rule Against Perpetuities, but it can be extended whenever necessary. (The Rule Against Perpetuities states that future owners of property must be able to be determined within twenty-one years of the participants' lives.)

3. It should state that neither party is the agent of the other.

4. It should allow compliance with Florida's RICO law. (See Chapter 12 for more information.)

5. It should provide for the trustee's resignation and a successor trustee.

6. It should clearly eliminate personal liability on the part of the trustee.

7. It should provide that the beneficiaries' interests are personal property.

8. It should clearly spell out the beneficiaries' interests, which are usually designated as percentages. To avoid probate, ownership can be in joint tenancy and provide for remainder beneficiaries who acquire their interests upon the deaths of the existing beneficiaries. To designate joint tenancy, the wording should include "as joint tenants with full rights of survivorship and not as tenants in common."

Many other clauses aid in the trust's operation and eliminate potential problems. A basic land trust agreement form is included in Appendix C.

When designating a person who will be beneficiary after the death of the original beneficiary, it is important that the successor not be given a present vested interest. It must be clear that the successor beneficiary has no interest until the death of the original beneficiary, that the successor beneficiary does not have to consent to any actions regarding the trust, and that the successor beneficiary can be changed at any time. The following wording is suggested:

[current beneficiary], with X% of the beneficial interest hereunder, has full power to assign or deal with all of the rights and interests of the beneficial interest. Upon the death of the said beneficiary during the existence of this trust, and provided that the beneficial interest shall not have been previously assigned or otherwise disposed of, then the interest hereunder shall vest in and be owned by [successor beneficiary].

Beneficiaries often complete a form similar to the LAND TRUST DATA SHEET (Appendix C – Form 1), which the trustee uses to prepare the trust and other forms.

At the Closing

Since many closing agents are unfamiliar with land trusts, misunderstandings can cause issues at or prior to closing. The following are the most common issues. Answers to other issues are found throughout the book.

Assignment.

If you sign a contract to buy a property in your own name and later decide to buy it into a trust, the closing agent will probably want an assignment from you to the trustee. (Appendix C – Form 26).

Taking title.

It is important that the deed to the trustee is prepared correctly, so you need to provide specific instructions to the title company and be sure they follow them exactly. Form 31 in the index can be used as a letter to a title company.

Showing the trust.

The title company will often ask to see a copy of the trust. If you are selling a property out of trust, it is clear that the title company has no right to see it, but if they are preparing a deed to a trustee, there is a plausible argument that they need to be sure the trustee really has the powers before they can put them in the deed. Since trust will not be recorded, just looked at, there is normally no harm in showing it when buying a property.

Who can sign.

Normally the trustee signs all the closing documents. Any document that will be recorded should have the trustee's original signature and be notarized and — sometimes — witnessed. The trustee can email or sign unrecorded closing documents, such as the settlement statement or disclosures. All of the closing documents subject the signer to legal liability to the title insurer, the buyer or seller, the buyer's lender, or all of them, so it is important to segregate that liability away from the beneficiary and solely into the trustee of the trust. For other documents that won't subject the beneficiary to legal liabilities (i.e., applications for utility services at the trust's property), Form 30 is a letter authorizing someone to sign on behalf of the trust.

Property Management Agreement

Using an LLC you set up with no assets as a property manager or operating company can add protection to your property. Instead of dealing with either the beneficiary that owns the trust or the trustee, the tenants can have their only contact be the property management or operating company that signs the leases and collects the rents. This way, neither the beneficiary nor the trustee would be necessary parties to litigation between the tenant and the landlord/manager.

Form 33 included in this book is a basic form and may need to be amended to meet your circumstances. You might be able to obtain a form from a local Realtor or property management company. Alternatively, you could write a simple property operating agreement with artificial intelligence.

Trust Certificates

Trust certificates are not really necessary since the trust agreement itself is proof of the beneficiary's interest in the trust. However, they could be useful if the interest needs to be moved out of state to avoid creditors or to do a transfer out of the state of Florida to possibly avoid transfer taxes. Also, some beneficiaries might prefer some more "official looking" evidence of their interest that they can put with their deeds and other valuables. It can be shown to loan officers and is more easily understood by a personal representative if the beneficiary dies. A trust certificate can be a plain piece of paper with the beneficiary's interest spelled out or in a fancier form. A TRUST PARTICIPATION CERTIFICATE is included in Appendix C. (See Form 22)

For those who are buying and selling properties in their trusts, certificates may be more trouble than they are worth since they must be located and forwarded to the trustee for each transaction. Legally, the trust agreement itself is adequate evidence of the trust.

Beneficiaries' Agreement

A beneficiaries' agreement is useful when two or more unmarried individuals own interests in a trust. If a married couple owns the entire beneficial interest in an estate by the entireties, then it would not be necessary. To eliminate any possible conflicts, it is preferable to have a detailed agreement between the parties. At a minimum, it should contain provisions to avoid double taxation and securities law violations. This can be done by providing for equal control of management and restricting the sale of a beneficiary's interest. Other useful provisions would provide solutions for:

- deadlocks between beneficiaries;

- contributions of capital;

- default by a beneficiary;

- death of a beneficiary; and,

- withdrawal by a beneficiary.

The agreement can often be either a co-venture or partnership agreement. An explanation of the rights and liabilities of partnerships is beyond the scope of this book. Still, the main difference is that partners are agents for each other and liable for each other's actions in the scope of the partnership business. Also, they must file a partnership tax return.

Form 11 in this book is an example of a simple CO-VENTURE AGREEMENT. Form 12 is a more lengthy PARTNERSHIP AGREEMENT. Creating a lengthy co-venture agreement or a simple partnership agreement is also possible. In a case in Miami, a court held that a partnership agreement among several beneficiaries imposed personal liability on them for a lease entered into by the trustee. In a footnote, the court seems to describe the trust as one under Florida Statutes, Section 689.07, but then it cited Florida Statutes, Section 689.071. Therefore, it is not clear why such liability should apply in a land trust. In order to guard against this happening again, a beneficiary agreement should mention that the beneficiaries are not agreeing to be personally liable for the trustee's debts. *First D.M.V., Inc. v. Amster, 545So.2d936 (1989).*

Occasionally, beneficiaries will want to give each other rights of first refusal to buy each other's interests. These are valid and are very useful in many situations. A Florida case on the subject has held that when there is such an agreement, the beneficiary wishing to exercise the right must strictly comply with the terms. *Green v. First American Bank and Trust, Trustee, et al., 511 So. 2d 569 (1987).* In this case the beneficiary made an offer matching a third party's offer except for the broker's commission. The court held that this did not comply with the agreement and held that the offer must match with no exceptions.

Often, beneficiaries provide each other with options to purchase each other's interests in the event of death or withdrawal. Such agreements must be carefully drafted. In one case, the option failed to provide for credit for the mortgage balance or for apportionment of the fractional interest in the property, and the court held that the remaining partner had to pay the full value stated. *Santo v. Santo, 497 N.E.2d 492,146 Ill. App. 3d 774 (1986).*

Obtaining Insurance

Insurance is one of the biggest issues facing land trusts or any other non-human Florida property owners. Most insurance agents and their underwriters seem to misunderstand land trusts. With the number of large hurricanes that have hit Florida in recent years, many insurance companies have left the state or raised their rates to the point that the premiums are cost-prohibitive.

Since the trustee holds the legal and equitable title for the beneficiary, who is the real owner, the trustee should be the "insured" party on the policy. The beneficiary should be listed as an "additional insured," like a mortgage holder.

With the Internet at their fingertips, agents routinely look up properties to be insured and require that the "owner on the public records" must be the insured party. Most underwriters say they cannot offer liability insurance to corporations or LLCs, so using a corporate trustee can be an issue. In that case, the insurance company will exclude any liability coverage from the policy and only insure against hazards like storms, fire, vandalism, and theft. Separate business owner liability policies are available, so it is possible to get hazard insurance from one company and a separate liability policy from the same or different company. The authors' clients have reported that the combined premiums for the separate hazard and liability policies are comparable to a single policy that includes hazard and liability coverage.

Some clients do not carry liability insurance since the land trust statute protects a beneficiary from liability. But if the beneficiary is directly responsible for doing something wrong that causes someone injury, or if the property has equity, it would be best to have a policy in place. Because of the kinds of judgments we've seen in recent years, a business and personal umbrella policy of one to two million dollars is prudent protection to have.

For this reason, it's imperative to find an insurance agent who is knowledgeable about personal and business policy coverages.

Multiple Properties

Any number of properties can be put into one trust, but then all the properties are at risk of loss if something happens at one property. The land trust offers liability protection to the beneficiary and their other properties but not to other properties in the same trust. The same trustee can be used for any number of trusts if each has a different name or number, but each property should be in a separate trust.

Sale and Mortgage Back

When a property is sold out of a trust, it is possible for the trust to take back a mortgage on the property (also known as "seller financing"), even if the mortgage is the only interest remaining in the trust. There is not as much reason to have separate trusts for mortgages since there is no risk of liability from them, so many investors have one trust to hold all their mortgages.

An even better arrangement is to assign the seller-financed mortgage to a separate trust (or LLC) since, as a bona fide purchaser for value of the seller-financing promissory note, the assignee would have more protections than a seller lender if the borrower defaults and foreclosure is needed.

Other Interests in Land

The statute allowing the creation of land trusts applies to any interest in real property in this state, including but not limited to a leasehold or mortgagee interest. Therefore, a land trust could be used for other interests, such as agreements for deed, options, and timeshares.

Out-of-State Property

Clients often ask if they can put their out-of-state property in a Florida land trust. The general rule is that because the law allowing the Florida land trust is a Florida statute, it traditionally only applies to interests in land in Florida. Unfortunately, not many states have laws allowing land trusts. However, an organization that is in charge of creating uniform state laws has created a uniform land trust law that can be adopted in all states. Hopefully, someday, more states will allow land trusts.

Florida-based timeshare developers use Florida land trusts to hold title to thousands of timeshare interests across the country, and they use nationwide title insurers to act as the land trustee because they are permitted to be trustees under local laws in the states where the timeshare resorts are located. The developers convey the property in states like Arizona, South Carolina, North Carolina, California, and other timeshare-resort-focused states to the Florida land trusts based in Orange County, Florida. To comply with the Florida statutes, they record a deed or notice of timeshare interest in Orange County, Florida, to create the interest in Florida land. From that point forward, all the sales and purchases of the timeshare are via buying and selling interests inside the land trusts they've established to hold the various resorts from around the country. This is a unique case study in how a Florida land trust can hold real estate outside of Florida, but it is not practical for most smaller real estate investors to use.

Some states have land trust statutes, and a few have court opinions that allow land trusts. The following are those that appear to allow typical land trusts as of the time of publication, along with the statutes authorizing them. To determine whether the law allows a trust to suit your needs, you should check with an attorney with experience in the jurisdiction you are considering.

- Hawaii — Haw. Rev. Stat. Ch 558

- Illinois — 765 ILCS 430/1 and 765 ILCS 405/1

- Indiana — Ind. Code. Sec. 30-4-2-13

- North Dakota — N.D. Cent. Code. Sec. 59-03-02

- Virginia — Va. Code. Ann. Sec. 55-17.1

The following states have court opinions that have recognized land trusts.
- Arizona — *Land Title & Trust v. Brannon, 103 Ariz. 272, 440 P.2d 105 (1965)*

- Arkansas — *Randolph v. Reed, 129 Ark. 485, 196 S.W. 133 (1917)*

- California — *In re Tutules Estate, 204 Ca. 2d 481, 22 Cal. Rptr. 427 (1962)*

Trusts similar to land trusts may be used in many other states, but they have additional requirements that make them somewhat different from pure land trusts. For example, in some states, the trustee must manage the property, collect the rent, or take an active role in operating the trust property for the trust to be valid. For additional information on land trusts in other states, see Mark Warda's book Land Trusts for Privacy & Profit.

Mexico.

The land trust has found new uses in Mexico, where non-citizens are prohibited from owning oceanfront property. An American can effectively buy such property by using a long-term land trust with a Mexican citizen as a trustee. For more information, see "Purchasing Beachfront Property in Mexico: How Americans Circumvent Mexico's Constitutional Prohibition," published by the Illinois Business Law Journal located at www.law.illinois.edu. In

Revenue Ruling 2013-14, the IRS acknowledged that Mexican land trusts should be regarded as disregarded entities, allaying fears that they might be treated as foreign trusts.

Power of Direction

The use of a director for a trust has provided an effective way to operate a trust when some of the beneficiaries cannot easily sign a direction to the trustee or when one person needs to control the project. For example, having a director is useful when a project has several partners, and some are out of town, or when one person puts up most of the money and desires control over the decisions.

The 2006 revised land trust law made statutory provisions for using a director for the first time, but it states that the director has fiduciary duties to the other beneficiaries unless otherwise spelled out in the trust. "Fiduciary duties" mean that the director must look out for the best interests of the others. It also says that a director cannot "alter, amend, revoke, terminate, defeat, or otherwise affect or change the enjoyment of any beneficial interest" in the trust.

A transaction in which the director has put up most of the money could cause a conflict. This director will want his or her first duty to be to protect his or her investment, which might go against the interests of the other beneficiaries. To avoid problems in such a situation, the rights and duties of the parties should be clearly spelled out in the trust agreement or in an amendment to the trust agreement. If the trust agreement spells out that certain beneficiaries' interests will be terminated, revoked, amended, etc., in the event of certain circumstances, then it would not be the director who did so but the operation of the trust.

When using a director in a simple non-conflict situation, the following clause can be added to the trust agreement.

> POWER OF DIRECTION. [name of director] shall have the sole power of direction for this trust and the Trustee shall follow any instructions from said Director without consent of other beneficiaries.

Whenever you have an arrangement in which one person makes financial decisions for others, a court could rule that a security is involved, and thus, there could be civil or criminal penalties for violations of securities laws. If you are using a director, be sure to read Chapter 11 on securities laws.

Under an Illinois case, the land trust director does not need to be a beneficiary. *In re Estate of Schaaf, 312 N.E.2d 348, 19 111. App. 3d 662 (1974)*. Florida law does not contradict this, so Florida courts would probably follow it.

Foreign Beneficiaries

In recent years, the concern over increased foreign ownership of U.S. real property has resulted in disclosure requirements for properties held in land trusts. The laws that apply in this area are the International Investment

Survey Act of 1976, the Agricultural Foreign Investment Disclosure Act of 1978, and Florida's Business Corporation Act.

International Investment Survey Act.

The International Investment Survey Act of 1976 requires various types of persons involved with real estate transactions to file reports with the federal government. It requires initial and annual reports and penalties for violations can include imprisonment and fines of up to $10,000. The reports are confidential and not available to the public. The complex rules are explained in the Code of Federal Regulations, Title 15, Sections 806.1 through 806.18.

Agricultural Foreign Investment Disclosure Act.

The Agricultural Foreign Investment Disclosure Act of 1978 (AFIDA) applies only to agricultural land. The reports are public information, so foreign persons who wish confidentiality should not invest in U.S. agricultural land. The rules for AFIDA are located in the Code of Federal Regulations, Title 7, beginning with Section 781.

Florida Business Corporation Act.

The Florida Business Corporation Act (Fla. Stat., Ch. 607) requires foreign corporations that are transacting business in the state to register and have a local resident agent (Fla. Stat., Sec. 607.1501(1)). Foreign corporations are all corporations that are not incorporated in Florida. However, a corporation that merely owns property in the state is not considered to be carrying on a business (Fla. Stat., Sec. 607.1501(2)(m)). (Trusts with foreign beneficiaries must also comply with the Florida RICO Act as explained in Chapter 12.)

Florida Conveyances to Foreign Entities Act.

As of July 1, 2023, Florida prohibits certain types of property from being owned by persons or entities from the following foreign countries of concern: China, Russia, Iran, North Korea, Cuba, Venezuela, and Syria. A government official, entity, political party, business, or person who is from or lives in one of the listed countries is not allowed to own:

- agricultural land;

- property within 10 miles of a military installation that is at least 10 acres in size; nor

- property within 10 miles of critical infrastructure facilities such as airports, spaceports, seaports, chemical plants, power plants, water or sewer plants, etc.

If the property was acquired before July 1, 2023, the owner must register with the State. If they purchase it after July 1, 2023, they must divest their ownership or face criminal charges and civil fines.

The law does not apply to people from prohibited countries who are resident aliens (Green Card holders) or naturalized citizens of the U.S.

A foreign person from one of these countries may purchase up to one residential property up to two acres so long as it is over five miles from a military installation, the buyers have a U.S. non-tourist visa or asylum, and they register with the State within 30 days of acquisition.

Title insurers will require an affidavit from anyone purchasing property within 10 miles of a military installation or critical infrastructure facility, stating under penalties of perjury that they are not subject to this law and they are in compliance with the statute. Since it is difficult to know whether a property is located in one of these "red zones," we expect that this will be a form signed in every closing after July 1, 2023.

Violations of the law are a second-degree misdemeanor up to a third-degree felony for the buyer and a first-degree misdemeanor for the seller.

In light of this law, trustees should require the beneficiaries to execute affidavits, signed under penalties of perjury, stating that they are not prohibited from owning the trust property. The trustee will usually be required to sign such an affidavit at closing, certifying that no beneficiary is prohibited from purchasing the property directly or indirectly through a trust or other entity.

As this book is going to press, the law is being challenged as unconstitutional in several court cases, along with similar laws passed in other states. For this reason, readers are encouraged to follow the news related to this law and its constitutionality.

Because foreign investors may be concerned about political persecution at home, they often wish to avoid disclosing their identity in any way. Anyone with such concerns should work with an attorney specializing in foreign investment in real estate.

Notary and Witnesses

There is no law requiring the notarization of a land trust agreement, but because it involves an interest in real estate and may someday need to be recorded for some unforeseen reason, it is sometimes notarized. The authors do not include notary acknowledgments on their trust agreements for fear that someone may inadvertently record the agreement itself, destroying the anonymity provided by the document. However, unless they have obtained other assurances, a trustee may insist on it being notarized if you are a new client so that they can verify the identity of who they are dealing with to avoid violating the PATRIOT Act.

There is no legal requirement that a land trust be witnessed, but because it may pass property at death, having two witnesses would provide one less reason for a disgruntled heir to try to contest it.

Documentary Taxes

Florida law is clear that documentary taxes are not owed on a deed from a property owner to his own trust (except the minimum 70¢ for any nominal consideration recited in the deed). This is explained in the Florida Administrative Code (F.A.C.), section 12B-4.013(28)(a). Some county recording clerks and Department of Revenue employees are not aware of this, so you may need to teach them. However, if you include — on the deed itself — the proper reference to the applicable exemption under the Administrative Code, the clerks and the Department of Revenue will most likely not audit the deed. They audit (review) every deed that is recorded with only nominal or no consideration and may assess a tax lien for unpaid documentary taxes at any time within three years after the deed was recorded. There is also no tax on deeds to successor trustees (where the beneficiary is the same). The F.A.C. sections are included in Appendix A.

Recording

The deed to the trustee needs to be recorded in the Official Public Records of the county where the trust property is located. The trust agreement should not be recorded or the trust's anonymity protections would be destroyed by showing the beneficiaries. As explained earlier, the recording fee should only include 70¢ documentary stamp tax if a person puts his own property in his own trust. The recording fee is $10 for the first page and $8.50 for each additional page.

Notice to the IRS

As explained in Chapter 9, notice should be sent to the Internal Revenue Service when a trust is formed and a fiduciary relationship begins (Rev. Rul. 63-16).

Forms

Appendix C contains 39 forms for land trust transactions. Before using a form, be sure you understand its legal ramifications. Some mistakes can only be fixed by going to court!

The forms may need to be adapted to your situation. For example, the Warranty Deed to Trustee (Form 2) is for one grantor and for a trustee who is a person who may die and needs a successor trustee, while the Quit Claim Deed to Trustee (Form 3) is for two grantors and is for a company trustee that does not need a successor since it doesn't die. You may need to make a warranty deed for two grantors to a corporate trustee, in which case you would adjust the deed accordingly.

The forms in Appendix C and many other forms relevant to real estate investors are available as part of the Investor DocKit, which can be purchased at InvestorDocKit.com.

Chapter Five

Financing a Property in a Land Trust

The financing of a land trust can be structured in two ways: 1) with a mortgage of the real estate signed by the trustee or 2) with a pledge of the beneficial interest signed by the beneficiaries. Some lenders require both for their extra protection.

Mortgage of the Real Estate

When property in a land trust is to be mortgaged, the trustee signs the mortgage document, and most commonly, the beneficiary signs the PROMISSORY NOTE (Form 14). However, since a copy of the note may be recorded along with the mortgage, which may cause a loss of secrecy, the trustee may sign the note. Because the copy of the note that is attached to the mortgage is not indexed by the recording clerks, including such a note with the mortgage is not a big risk unless a very thorough asset investigation is expected.

A wise lender will require a personal GUARANTY OF PROMISSORY NOTE BY BENEFICIARY (Form 15). However, a wise purchaser/borrower will draft his or her purchase contract so that only the trustee signs the note with no liability on behalf of the beneficiary. This is called a "non-recourse" loan.

Although the land trust statute prevents the trustee's personal liability unless specifically provided in the documents, it is always wise to add a clause to the note and mortgage, freeing the trustee from liability. A court might interpret standard mortgage language as creating personal liability in a tough case. A trustee who executes documents regularly should have a rubber stamp, as described in Chapter 14. At a minimum, the typed name of the trustee under his or her signature should include the words "as trustee of trust [name of trust], and not individually."

Even if a beneficiary does not personally sign the note, they may be held liable if fraud or deceit can be proven. *Lake Shore Savings & Loan Assn. v. American National Bank & Trust Co., 234 N.E.2d 418, 91 111. App. 2d 143 (1968)*. However, a beneficiary will not be held liable merely because they directed the trustee to sign the note. *Conkling v. Mcintosh, 58 N.E.2d 304, 324 111. App. 292 (1944)*.

A mortgage signed by a trustee of a land trust can be on any standard form. Still, the name of the trustee should be followed by the exact designation of the trust and powers as cited on the deed, such as "Trustee under Trustee No. 6 dated 1/29/07 with full power and authority either to protect, conserve, sell, or to lease, or to encumber, or otherwise manage and dispose of as provided in Florida Statutes, Sections 689.071 and 689.073."

Conventional Lenders

It is not easy to get a conventional mortgage loan on a 1-4 family residential land trust property because most lenders don't understand land trusts and because most of them sell the loans to Fannie Mae or Freddie Mac, which allow land trust loans in Illinois. We have seen cases where the mortgage loan originators and underwriters are experienced; they can find the applicable guidelines in the Fannie Mae and Freddie Mac underwriting guidelines. Fannie Mae Selling Guide, Sec. B2-2-01, General Borrower Eligibility Requirements (12/14/2022); or Freddie Mac Underwriting Guide, Section 5103.7.

Once these guidelines are reviewed and followed, it is possible to obtain a conventional Fannie or Freddie loan secured by a 1-4 family residence that is held in a Florida land trust.

The case is typically easier to make for commercial and industrial properties, and the loan can be made directly to the land trust. In those cases, it is common that the bank is a local or regional bank making a portfolio loan that will be held by the bank rather than sold on the secondary mortgage-backed securities market. As such, the lender and borrower will usually have local legal counsel representing them and drafting the loan documents. Local counsel should understand how land trusts work, and they will be able to coordinate with each other to ensure the documents are drafted in a way that obligates the trust on the mortgage while ensuring that the beneficiary — and others — personally guarantee payment of the loan.

Private and hard money lenders often prefer or even require that borrowers hold title to the mortgaged property in a land trust. Some private lenders even require that they be listed as either a contingent beneficiary inside the land trust agreement or that the beneficial interest is also conditionally assigned to the lender so they can take control of the trust quickly if the beneficiary-borrower defaults on the note or mortgage. Once the lender takes control of the trust, they may take possession of the property, collect the rent directly, and even complete renovations and sell the property to recoup their loan. If they must foreclose, they can direct the trustee to consent to the foreclosure so that it occurs faster and easier than if they were foreclosing the borrower directly through their LLC or other entity that holds title to the property.

There is no reason not to make a loan on land trust property. The lender is in exactly the same position as with a property that is not in a trust. All title insurance companies will issue title insurance policies on mortgages on land trusts.

Pledge of the Beneficial Interest

An alternative to mortgaging the real estate is to pledge the land trust beneficial interest. The use of a PROMISSO-RY NOTE accomplishes this, a COLLATERAL ASSIGNMENT OF BENEFICIAL INTEREST, a SECURITY AGREEMENT, and a UCC-1 FINANCING STATEMENT under the Uniform Commercial Code (UCC) (Florida Statutes, Chapter 679). The PROMISSORY NOTE (Form 14) documents the indebtedness. The COL-LATERAL ASSIGNMENT OF BENEFICIAL INTEREST (Form 16) gives the lender a claim on the beneficial interest. The SECURITY AGREEMENT (Form 17) and STATE OF FLORIDA UCC-1 FINANCING STATE-MENT (Form 18) protect that interest if the lender must repossess the beneficial interest because of failure to pay. An advantage to the lender in this situation is that they should not have to go through a costly and time-consuming foreclosure action to get the property. They should be able to quickly seize the property as provided in Florida Statutes, Section 679.304, and the borrower should have no right of redemption. A procedure like this was used successfully in one case. *Ferraro v. Parker, 229 So. 2d 621 (1969).*

Under Illinois and Florida law, a transaction that pledges real estate as collateral for a loan must be treated like a mortgage and foreclosed like a mortgage. (F.S. §697.01.) A 1922 Illinois case held that a land development arrangement executed simultaneously with a trust was to be treated like a mortgage. *Devoigne v. Chicago Title & Trust Co., 136 N.E. 498.* However, in 1957, the court held in another case that where the trust was created earlier and not as part of the financing arrangement, there was no mortgage and no right of redemption. *Horney v. Hayes, 142 N.E.2d 94 (1957).* In more recent cases, Illinois courts have held that factors indicating that an equitable mortgage exists include:

1. creation of the trust simultaneous with the loan;

2. creation of the trust for the purpose of the financing arrangement;

3. a requirement in the loan documents that the property be sold upon default; and,

4. inclusion of more than just the beneficial interest in the pledge.

Two other Illinois cases on the issue are *Melrose Park National Bank v. Melrose Park National Bank, Trustee, 462 N.E.2d 741 (1984)* and *Commercial National Bank of Chicago v. Hazel Manor Condominiums, Inc., 487 N.E.2d 1145 (1985).*

In 1986, a different appeals court ruled that where a valid land trust has been created, the interest is personal property and, as such, may be foreclosed under the Uniform Commercial Code (Florida Statutes Chapter 679). In this case, the court noted that the borrower neither alleged nor proved that the transaction was, in essence, a mortgage. *Magnuson v. Jones, 491 So. 2d 1315 (1986).*

Unfortunately, a case has confused the law regarding the foreclosure of beneficial interests under the UCC. *Kirkland v. Miller, 702 So. 2d 620 (1997).* A beneficial interest was pledged, and the trial court allowed a

UCC foreclosure. The defendant appealed, and the appeals court said the plaintiff had to foreclose the right of redemption as if it were a mortgage.

The fact that the court did not even understand the case is clear since it ruled that this was not a valid land trust. Actually, the validity of the land trust (which was created four months earlier) was not the issue in the case. The issue was whether the sale of the beneficial interest secured by a collateral security agreement should be treated like a mortgage or foreclosed under the UCC.

A court might rule the same way in a similar case. However, if the parties were more equal, the UCC foreclosure would be more likely to be successful. (See Chapter 7 for more information on foreclosing a beneficial interest.)

The 2006 amendment to the land trust statute specifically says that "Chapter 679 applies to the perfection of any security interest in a land trust." (Fla. Stat., Sec. 689.071(8)9c), so creditors should be able to foreclose using the UCC rather than the mortgage foreclosure process. However, the law is unclear when a court can use Section 689.01 to require a foreclosure.

Procedures.

In Florida, it is important that a STATE OF FLORIDA UCC-1 FINANCING STATEMENT (Form 18) is filed with the secretary of state in Tallahassee to perfect the security interest. Fla. Stat., Sec. 679.3101; and *In re Povia, 224 B.R. 209 (1998)*. A UCC-1 is most easily and quickly filed electronically online at www.floridaucc.com.

> NOTE: This differs from Illinois, where the Uniform Commercial Code is worded differently, and filing is unnecessary.

To secure a loan in this manner, the beneficiary-borrower should execute the PROMISSORY NOTE, CONDITIONAL ASSIGNMENT OF BENEFICIAL INTEREST, SECURITY AGREEMENT (chattel mortgage), and a UCC-1 should be filed. There is no requirement that the lender sign the UCC-1 nor the borrower, but the Security Agreement that the borrower signs should make it clear that the lender may file and renew the UCC-1 without any further authorization from the borrower.

It is important to be sure that all beneficial interests are included and that no previous pledges or assignments have been made. This can be done with an affidavit or estoppel certificate from the beneficiaries and the trustee stating that there are no other interests.

When the beneficiary is an artificial entity, such as a corporation or limited partnership, the lender should be sure that the entity's registration is current and that the proper officers have authorized the transaction. An LLC's members or a corporation's directors may execute a resolution of incumbency that certifies that the loan has been authorized by the members and the names and titles of the person or persons who are authorized to execute the loan documents.

Foreclosing a beneficial interest under Florida Statutes, Chapter 679, would not require going to court since the statute allows a private, non-judicial sale of the collateral. However, if the subject property is a residence and the former beneficiary lives there, court action may be necessary to get the former beneficiary out by obtaining a writ of possession from the Clerk of Court as ordered by a judge. This would be an eviction if a landlord/tenant relationship could be established or an ejectment if it could not.

To release a UCC-1 FINANCING STATEMENT, use STATE OF FLORIDA UCC-3 UNIFORM COMMERCIAL FINANCING STATEMENT AMENDMENT, (Form 19). This, too, can be filed online at www.floridaucc.com.

Chapter Six

Operating a Land Trust

Questions arise during the life of a land trust about who the proper party is to execute documents and how to deal with changed situations.

Leasing the Premises

A premises lease can, in most cases, be executed by either the trustee or the beneficiary. This is because the trustee is the actual titleholder, and the trust grants the beneficiary the power to manage the property. *Southeast Village Associates v. Health Management Association, 416 N.E.2d 325 (1980).* The doctrine of estoppel would bar a tenant from contesting the beneficiary's right to sign a lease of the property. *Avila South Condo Assoc, Inc. v. Kappa Corp., 347 So. 2d 599 (1977).* However, the lease must be drafted in the name of the party signing. It was unenforceable when a lease was drawn up in a trustee's name and signed by the beneficiary as its agent. *Feinberg v. The Great Atlantic and Pacific Tea Co., 266 N.E.2d 401 (1970).*

One way around this would be for the trustee to sign a power of attorney that specifically gives the beneficiary the power to sign a lease. However, there is a question as to whether a trustee can delegate its powers to someone via a power of attorney, and it is much easier for the beneficiary to sign leases in their own name as a property manager. There would not be a problem with real estate brokerage laws since the beneficiary is the actual owner. Using a corporation or LLC as the operator of the property as its property manager would provide some insulation to the beneficiary, individually. However, with electronic signing being so ubiquitous and easy, there is no reason why the trustee cannot quickly and easily sign the lease as the landlord/property owner and keep the beneficiary's name out of the contract completely. There is a danger that — if the beneficiary is signing the lease or any legally binding contractual agreement — the beneficiary could be named along with the trustee and the property management company in any lawsuit related to someone being injured, discriminated against, or otherwise hurt at the trust property. Except in extreme emergencies when the trustee cannot be reached, the trustee should sign the lease and all other contractual documents related to the property in their capacity as its trustee to keep the beneficiary's name and signature off of those documents.

If exculpatory language is used in a lease to protect the trustee from liability, it should also include the beneficiaries. In an Illinois case, exculpatory language protecting a trustee was held not to apply to the beneficiaries who were later brought into the case. *Levi v. Adkay Heating & Cooling Corp., 274 N.E.2d 650,1 111. App. 3d 509 (1971).*

Day-to-Day Activities

There should not be many activities in the day-to-day ownership of the property that require action by the trustee. Some instances when the trustee might be needed include the following.

If a quasi-judicial hearing on a building code violation was held, the hearing master might want some written proof that the person appearing at the hearing (usually the beneficiary) is authorized to do so. An AUTHORIZA-TION TO REPRESENT PROPERTY OWNER can be used for this purpose, but check to be sure that the hearing you are going to does not have its own unique form that must be used (see Form 30).

If construction work requiring a building permit is to be done on the property, a notice of commencement must be filed in the county records. Contractors usually ask for the owner/trustee to sign this. Florida Statutes, Section 713.13(l)(a) says that this can be done by the "owner's agent," so the beneficiary (or anyone authorized by the trustee) could do so. However, again, it is the best practice to have the trustee sign the permit application, construction contracts, and notices of commencement to keep the beneficiary's name off of these legally binding documents to avoid claims of personal liability in the event of a lawsuit to enforce them.

For public housing programs in which part of the rent is paid by a government agency, written authorization from the record owner is usually necessary to pay the rent to someone else. The programs usually have a form for this, and the trustee might need to sign it to avoid having the checks made out to the trust.

***

Amending the Trust

Because the beneficiaries can terminate the trust at any time and start a new one, courts have allowed beneficiaries to freely amend the trust at any time. This is true even when no power is given in the trust document as long as there is no specific prohibition. The amendment would usually only be effective when signed by all beneficiaries and accepted by the trustee. As with the trust itself, no witnesses or notary are required for an amendment.

If a party takes over another person's beneficial interest in a trust or a new trustee takes over a trust, either of them may wish to make major changes to the trust instrument. This can be done by a simple AMENDMENT TO TRUST (see Form 34). If the changes are substantial, the easiest way to do this is to execute an amended and restated trust agreement that essentially replaces the previous trust agreement completely.

Changing Successor Beneficiaries

A beneficiary can change the successor beneficiary at any time. An AMENDMENT TO TRUST should be executed stating the change (see Form 34). As long as the previous successor beneficiary was not given a vested interest, no approval is needed from such a previous successor beneficiary.

Death of a Beneficiary

If a land trust is drafted with a properly designated remainder beneficiary, the successor would own the beneficial interest immediately upon the beneficiary's death. The trustee would normally require a certified death certificate before complying with instructions of a successor beneficiary and may require that an acceptance of the trust terms be signed.

The interest would pass to the beneficiary's estate if no successor is named in the trust. The LAND TRUST AGREEMENT (Form 4) form in this book specifies that it passes under the beneficiary's will and not under the statutes that name heirs. If you use a corporation, LLC, or living trust as a beneficiary, you do not need a successor since these entities do not die. Instead, your shares in the corporation or membership interests in the LLC would pass to your heirs according to your will or — if you have no will — according to the intestacy statutes (the "will" that the state has written for you).

There are two ways that claims may exist against a successor beneficiary's interest in a land trust. If the beneficiary's estate was subject to federal estate taxes, the beneficiary might be called upon to contribute to paying those taxes. Also, if the beneficiary did not leave enough property to a surviving spouse, the spouse could claim property in the trust.

Successor Trustees

Changing trustees may become advisable or necessary at some point in a trust's life. The usual way to change trustees is to have the current trustee deed the property to the successor trustee. This would be a Trustee's Deed to the Successor Trustee. (See Form 36), and no documentary tax is due on such deeds so long as the correct Administrative Code section is recited on the face of the deed.

If there is a concern about preserving the title insurance, a Warranty Deed to Successor Trustee can be used. The protection of the original title insurance should transfer through the warranty to the successor trustee.

Problems can arise when a trustee dies or cannot sign a deed to a successor. The 2006 amendments to the land trust law solved this problem by providing specific methods for appointing a successor trustee.

One interesting aspect of the amended law is that if the trust names a successor, then both the existing trustee and the successor trustee must sign the declaration (unless the trustee has died or been incapacitated), but if no successor has been named in the trust, then the successor and beneficiaries can sign the declaration. This means that it is better not to name a successor in the trust since you would then be able to replace the trustee without getting his or her signature.

One problem with this statutory solution is that a title company cannot determine whether the successor is legitimate. What if some people come to a title company saying they are the beneficiaries and successor trustees and produce a bogus trust? Most likely, title companies will want something more than the statutory requirement before insuring title in such a situation. If the original trustee is a well-known professional third-party trustee, they can contact them to confirm that the succession has occurred. Otherwise, it may be more difficult for the title agent to find the former trustee to obtain such verification.

The underwriting guidelines used by Attorneys Title Insurance Fund are explained in Fund Title Notes section TN 31.02.01.

The following are the provisions of the statute:

Deed names successor.

If the deed names a successor trustee, then a death certificate of the trustee should be recorded, and the statute says that no other declaration needs to be filed. (Fla. Stat., §689.071(9)(d).)

Trust Names Successor.

If the deed does not name a successor but the trust does, then a declaration needs to be filed stating:

    1. the legal description of the property;

    2. the name and address of the former trustee;

    3. the name and address of the successor trustee;

    4. a statement of resignation by the former trustee (or statement that he or she is incapacitated or has died) and acceptance by the successor trustee; and,

    5. a statement that the successor was duly appointed by the unrecorded trust agreement. (Fla. Stat., §689.0 71(9)(c).)

If the trustee has died, a death certificate must be filed. If the trustee has resigned (and not died or been incapacitated), a deed to successor trustee would be just as effective as this declaration.

Trust and deed silent.

If both the trust and the deed are silent as to successor trustees, then a declaration needs to be filed stating:

    1. the legal description of the property;

2. the name and address of the former trustee;

3. the name and address of the successor trustee; and,

4. a statement that the successor trustee has been appointed by one or more persons or entities having the power of direction and acceptance by the successor trustee. (Fla. Stat., §689.071(9)(b).)

One final note about recording declarations of successor trustees versus using a deed to note a successor trustee: it may be advisable to use a declaration rather than a deed to avoid the potential that the county property assessor may treat the deed from one trustee to the next as a change of title that permits a revaluation of the real property. Generally, when a new deed is recorded, the appraiser may remove all exemptions and valuation caps to increase the taxes on the property. While this is incorrect, the argument with the appraiser's office can take some time. But if a declaration is used instead of deed, the chances of such a revaluation are minimal.

***

Governmental Liens

Because land trusts are relatively new to Florida, they often confuse government officials. Liens filed against a trustee rarely contain the proper identification of the trust involved. Trustees must be vigilant to avoid blanket liens that may cause title problems for several properties. It is also possible for such liens to be filed against a trustee personally by someone who does not understand the term "trustee." Such liens can be municipal code violation liens, Department of Revenue liens, fire district liens, tangible property tax warrants, or any similar liens.

If any preliminary notice to file a lien is received by a trustee, it should, of course, be sent to the beneficiaries. If the notice does not contain the proper designation of the exact trust to which it applies, such as "trustee under Trust No. 123, dated January 1, 2026," then a letter should be sent to the issuing authority stating that "there is no such entity as 'John Smith, Tr;' my correct position is John Smith, Trustee under Trust No. 123, dated January 1, 2026."

An erroneous lien damaging the trustee's credit may be slanderous. If it affects property owned by other parties, it may be slander of title. If a lien has been filed erroneously without notice, then the trustee should request or demand that it be corrected. This is also another reason why it is dangerous for an individual to act as a land trustee since the sheer number of lawsuits filed each year against the land trusts would destroy anyone's personal credit.

Florida's tort claims statute (Fla. Stat., §768.28) requires that a person planning to sue the state or a division of the state, such as a municipality, must first give notice. If the trustee sends proper notice that he or she intends to sue a subdivision of the state, that is often enough to get some action.

Terminating the Trust

The trust's termination usually occurs when the last piece of property has been conveyed out of the trust. No specific action or documentation is necessary, as the trust ceases to exist when there is no property in it. However, the IRS requires that it be given notice by a trustee when a fiduciary capacity ends (see Chapter 9).

When a property owned by a land trust sells it and takes back financing, sometimes the trust holds the mortgage. This preserves secrecy, avoids probate, and retains many of the original benefits of the land trust. While each piece of real property should be in its own land trust, many mortgages can be in one land trust since holding a mortgage usually does not involve risk. However, if there is some risk, such as problems on a property over which a buyer may sue the seller, then separate trusts could protect other mortgages from claims involving that property.

Chapter Seven

Litigation Involving Land Trusts

Because litigation has strict rules of procedure and land trusts are different from many other forms of ownership, simple errors in litigating land trust issues can cause loss of the case.

Parties to the Lawsuit

The evolution of the land trust has required an evolution of legal theories regarding who is the proper party in litigation involving land trust property. The general rule in Illinois is that both parties are usually necessary since the trustee has legal and equitable title and the beneficiaries have the ultimate interest. However, in Florida, the trustee has the "power to prosecute or defend actions, claims, or proceedings for the protection of trust assets and of the trustee in the performance of his [or her] duties," so the beneficiaries' presence as a party may not always be necessary. *Fla. Stat., §737.402(2)(z)*.

In a mortgage foreclosure suit, it was confirmed that the beneficiaries were not necessary parties. *Cowen v. Knott, 252 So. 2d 400 (1971)*. (This ruling was made under Florida Rule of Civil Procedure 1.210(c), which was replaced by Florida Statutes Section, which was in turn replaced by 736.0802.) However, because the trustee failed to file a defense, the beneficiaries were allowed to defend it.

In a malpractice suit by a trustee against an attorney for failing to see that the land trust received the proper amount of land contracted for, the court held that the beneficiaries were the proper parties and that the complaint could be amended to add the beneficiaries. *Datwani v. Netsch, 562 So. 2d 721 (Fla. 3DCA 1990)*.

Therefore, it appears that the beneficiaries need not be joined when dealing solely with the trust property. However, when dealing with their interests as such or when seeking to bind them personally, they must be joined in any litigation.

For actions in federal court, it appears that Rule 19(b) of the Federal Rules of Civil Procedure may require adding beneficiaries as parties to a suit where their interests are at stake. *Tick v. Cohen, 787 F.2d 1490 (1986)*.

It was fine until the final judgment.

Once, a disgruntled tenant sued our company as trustee of a particular trust. All of the pleadings throughout the case noted that we were the trustee of the trust, and the beneficiary felt no need to hire an attorney to defend the case. The tenant's attorney filed a motion for a summary judgment and had a hearing. The judge granted the motion and entered the judgment. However, the final paragraph said the judgment was against our company directly. No mention of the trustee status or trust name was included in the final paragraph of the judgment. When handling closings in that county for any other properties we held in trust, title companies called us several times a week to tell us we had to pay off the judgment before any closings to sell or refinance trust properties could occur. We contacted the tenant's attorney to request, then demand, that they go back to the judge to correct the error in the final judgment. He refused to do so. Therefore, we filed our own motion to correct the error in the judgment. At the hearing on our motion, the judge chastised the tenant's attorney for poorly drafting the order for the judge's signature and then for refusing to fix it without requiring us to file a motion and attend a hearing. We still had title companies calling us for the next ten years until the judgment expired, asking us to pay off the judgment. But we could point them to the amended corrected judgment easily each time so they would drop their objections. Of course, the title companies were also still wrong because — even had the judgment been against us correctly — it still wouldn't attach to the trust property unless we were also the trust's beneficiary, which we never are. Fortunately, as lawyers and professional land trustees, we handled the issues in-house. But an amateur trustee wouldn't be so lucky.

Guardians ad Litem

A guardian ad litem is a person (usually an attorney) appointed by a court to represent a party to a lawsuit who cannot represent himself. They're appointed when the person cannot be found or may be incompetent. In foreclosure cases, sometimes attorneys ask for guardians ad litem to be appointed to be sure all parties are foreclosed. For a land trust, a guardian ad litem is not needed for the beneficiaries because the trustee holds both legal and equitable title, so when one is appointed in a foreclosure of a land trust, it just adds extra expenses to the owner, who might be trying to save the property.

The 2013 statute makes it clear in section 689.071(8)(i) that a guardian ad litem is not necessary to represent the interests of a land trust beneficiary. If an attorney in a foreclosure requests payment for one, it should be noted that the statute makes one unnecessary.

Identification of the Trustee

In suits involving a land trust, the trustee should be the party (plaintiff or defendant) and should be identified by name, trust number (or name), and trust date in both the caption and the body of the pleadings. A correct identification would read, "John Smith, Trustee under Trust No. 1234, dated January 29, 2014."

A common mistake is merely naming "John Smith, Trustee" as the party. This can cause serious problems with the title to other properties held in trust, even if unrelated to the litigation. If a trustee is served with papers not naming him or her properly, he or she should explain this to opposing counsel and, if necessary, file a motion with the court to correct the error.

A judgment filed against a trustee can be amended later to correctly designate the trust against which it applies. *Johnson v. First National Bank of Park Ridge, 463 N.E.2d 859, 123 111. App. 3d 823 (1984).* This would be accomplished by a Motion to Amend Judgment filed in the original case.

Another mistake is to name the trust as the party. A land trust is not a legal entity, so the trustee's name must be included with the trust's.

Legal Notices to the Trustee

The 2013 revision to the Land Trust Act contains a provision (§689.071(11)) that any legal notices to a trustee of a land trust must either identify the trust property that the notice pertains to or the name and date of the trust if it appears on the deed. This was added to the law because some entities had been sending notices such as "there may be buried munitions on your property" to a trustee of hundreds of properties (one of the authors) without saying which trust properties they pertained to.

If a lawsuit is based on a notice that didn't identify the property or trust, it might be subject to dismissal for not giving proper legal notice.

***

Joining the Trustee Individually

In suits against the trust, plaintiffs (such as mortgagees) occasionally join the trustee individually to attempt to wipe out any possible interest they might hold. While this would be necessary for a trust under Florida Statutes, Section 689.07, it is not necessary for a land trust since the trustee has no personal interest in the property. The land trust statute clearly states that all ownership rights are vested in the trustee as a trustee.

Deficiency judgment against the wrong person

In a mortgage foreclosure suit involving a trust of which one of the authors was trustee, the author was joined individually and as trustee. The plaintiff's attorney made the additional error of demanding a deficiency judgment against all defendants. One rationale used by the attorney was that if the trustee lived in the property (which he did not), some individual interest might need to be foreclosed.

However, this did not provide any reason for demanding a deficiency judgment personally against the trustee. The Circuit Court assessed attorney's fees against the plaintiff under Florida Statutes, Section 57.105 for lack of a justiciable issue. Ridgewood Savings Bank v. Warda, Pinellas County Circuit Court Case No. 84-15780-7 (1985).

Evictions

Some authorities suggest that both the trustee and beneficiary be named plaintiffs in an eviction action; however, the proper party to the lawsuit would be the party named as the landlord on the lease. As stated earlier, the land trust's trustee should be listed as the landlord and sign the lease to maintain the beneficiary's anonymity and ensure that the beneficiary is not named individually in any suit by a tenant. Thus, the trustee, as trustee of the trust, would be the plaintiff to sue a tenant for an eviction. A trustee must have an attorney represent them as trustee in court. The trustee cannot represent themselves even if the trustee is an individual unless the trustee is also an attorney licensed to practice law in Florida. In most counties, anyone — trustees, LLCs, corporations — can file an eviction action for possession of the property from the tenant. So long as the trustee signs an authorization that is filed in the case to give that person authority to file the action on their behalf. However, if a tenant objects or makes any defense, a non-attorney trustee must hire an attorney to represent the trustee from that point forward.

This is very serious.

One author's client was almost put in jail for contempt of court when he asked the judge to "just this one time" go ahead and enter the judgment for the client's LLC as the landlord. When the judge realized that the client was not licensed to practice law, he had the client cuffed and held in the courtroom until all the hearings were completed. Then he ordered the client to come back to court the next day with a lawyer, his spouse, and his priest to throw himself on the court's mercy and promise never to prosecute another eviction for his LLC on his own, without an attorney. Fortunately, the next day, the judge was in a better mood, and the client took an attorney to court with him, who often practiced before that judge. The judge relented and didn't put the client in jail, but the client learned quickly that he couldn't just prosecute evictions on his own when his LLC or a land trust owned the property.

In Florida, the tenant should not be able to contest the right of a beneficiary who signed this lease to bring an eviction action, even though he or she does not have title to the property, but — by the same token — a tenant can sue not only the land trustee that owns the property and the beneficiary who signs the lease under the principals of privity of contract. *Avila South Condo Asso,c, Inc. v. Kappa Corp., 347 So. 2d 599 (1977)*. So why put yourself in that predicament? Let the land trust protect you as it's supposed to do, and have the trustee to sign the leases and prosecute the evictions.

Bankruptcy

The courts have ruled both ways in deciding whether a land trust can file bankruptcy. Early cases said it could file. *Mayo v. Barnett Bank of Pensacola, 448 F. Supp. 250 (1978)*; *In re Matter of Maidman, 2 B.R. 569 (1980)*. Then, after amendments to the bankruptcy law indicated that the beneficiary — not the trust — should file, bankruptcy courts rejected the cases. *In re Dolton Lodge Trust No. 35188, 22 B.R. 918 (1982)*. This was thought to be the correct rule because the land trust is not an active business but a conduit for holding property. Two characteristics of a business trust that is allowed to file bankruptcy are that it is registered with the secretary of state and that it files a tax return. Land trusts do neither of these.

However, three Middle District of Florida bankruptcy cases considered a land trust a business trust. *In re Star Trust, 237 B.R. 827 (1999)*; *In re Metro Palms I Trust, 153 B.R. 922 (1993)*; and *In re Arehart, 52 B.R. 308 (1985)*. These may be erroneous decisions, but a party who needs protection and is in the Middle District of Florida might want to rely on these cases.

The Eleventh Circuit Court of Appeals (which covers Florida) ruled in 2004 that it was proper to dismiss a bankruptcy by a land trust for bad faith filing. *State Street Houses, Inc. v. New York State Urban Development Corp., 356 F.3d 1345 (2004)*. It ruled that the Bankruptcy Reform Act did not change the rules that a bad faith filing can be determined from the following six factors:

1. the debtor has only one asset;

2. the debtor has few unsecured creditors whose claims are small compared to the secured creditors;

3. the debtor has few employees;

4. the property is subject to a foreclosure action;

5. the debtor's financial problems are mainly the foreclosure action; or,

6. the bankruptcy filing appears timed to delay the foreclosure.

One trustee filed for bankruptcy for a land trust, which immediately stopped a pending foreclosure action, giving him time to rescue the property. The bankruptcy was later dismissed. However, an attorney who knowingly does this could be subject to sanctions (penalties).

If a beneficiary files for personal bankruptcy, their interest in a land trust is a property the bankruptcy trustee may liquidate.

Tort Actions

Tort actions against the trust are based upon breach of a duty to maintain the property. In an Illinois land trust, that duty is held by the beneficiaries. Therefore, actions there are proper against only the beneficiaries. A long line of Illinois cases has held a trustee immune from personal liability in such actions. *Fields v. Indiana Ave. Apts, Inc., 196 N.E.2d 485, 47 111. App. 2d 55 (1964).*

In Florida, a trustee is personally liable only if he or she is personally at fault. F.S. §736.1013. Further, under tort law, if the beneficiaries did not personally take or neglect to take actions that caused the plaintiff's injuries, then the beneficiaries are not liable either. However, the trustee, as trustee of the land trust, owes a duty to tenants, invitees, and even trespassers to ensure they are not injured on the trust property. This is so simply because the trustee, as trustee of the land trust, is the owner of the legal and equitable title of the property. Property owners are liable for injuries others sustain on their property simply because they own the property and nothing more.

Therefore, a tort action where someone is injured on the trust property is properly filed to name the trustee of the land trust, in its capacity as trustee, as the defendant. Of course, any other persons who contributed to the plaintiff's injuries would also be named and served.

Guns are not toys

A neighbor and their child sued one author's trust company. The trust property was a condominium unit. The condo's tenants had a party, and a guest decided they would show their gun to others at the party. They started playing around with the gun, and — of course — it went off. The bullet traveled through the condo's wall into the bedroom of the next-door neighbor's son, where it struck the sleeping child in the arm, shattering his humerus.

The 4-year-old, through his mother, sued our company as trustee of the land trust that owned the property. They also named the tenant, who had since vacated the condo and could not be located. And they named the unknown person who shot the gun. Fortunately, the trust beneficiary had obtained a liability insurance policy on the condominium unit. The policy named us, as trustee of the trust, as the "insured." Hence, the insurance company provided legal representation and eventually paid something for the child's permanent injuries to his arm. Had there been no insurance, the child would have gotten a judgment against the trustee as trustee of the land trust. At that point, the only asset in the trust was the condo unit where the party had occurred, so that is the asset the child would have been able to seize and sell to raise money to pay for his injuries.

Creditor Actions

As explained in Chapter 2, Florida law is unclear as to how a creditor should proceed to make a claim against a beneficiary's interest in a land trust.

In Illinois, a creditor can bring an equitable action called a creditor's bill. In Florida, this is covered by Florida Statutes, Section 68.05. A supplementary proceeding may also be possible under Florida Statutes, Section 56.29.

If a limited liability company owned the beneficial interest, it would be especially hard for a creditor to reach because, if set up properly, it would only be subject to a charging order, which gives the creditor no useful rights in the interest.

When a beneficial interest is owned by a husband and wife as tenants by the entirety, it would probably only be reachable by a creditor of both parties. If a creditor had a judgment only against one of the spouses, the creditor could probably not touch the beneficial interest.

Chapter Eight

Selling Trust Property

A property in a land trust can be sold in two ways. Either the trustee can deed the property to the purchaser or the beneficiary can assign their beneficial interest in the trust to the purchaser. If the beneficial interest is assigned, then the property buyer becomes the new owner of the trust. Sometimes, the buyer can keep the same trustee; other times, they may want a new trustee.

Deeding the Property

If the property is to be deeded out of trust to the buyer, the main documents needed are the contract for sale, the deed from the trustee, and the direction to the trustee to sign the contract and deed. As explained in Chapter 12, the trustee must comply with Florida RICO law by having a RICO lien search done on the beneficiaries' names.

Trustee's Deed

The trustee can convey the property by either a trustee's deed or warranty deed, depending on what is called for in the contract. A TRUSTEE'S DEED appears in Appendix C. (See Form 8.)

If the contract requires the trustee to sign a warranty deed, it should be made clear that this is being done in the capacity of trustee for one specific trust. This can be done by clearly naming the trust as part of the grantor trustee's name and signature.

Before signing either the contract or deed, the trustee must obtain a DIRECTION TO TRUSTEE (Form 5) signed by the required beneficiaries. (If the purchase is being financed, see Chapter 5 for an explanation of how to finance a land trust sale.) As explained in Chapter 9, notice should be sent to the Internal Revenue Service when the trust ends and the fiduciary status no longer exists.

Assigning the Beneficial Interest

Rather than receiving a real estate deed from the trustee, a property buyer can receive an ASSIGNMENT OF BENEFICIAL INTEREST (Form 6) from the beneficiaries. In such a case, the trustee would remain the same, and the buyer would step into the shoes of the previous beneficiary.

If the buyer does not wish to use the same trustee, he or she can replace the trustee simultaneously or later. The advantage to buying the beneficial interest and then replacing the trustee over having a deed from the seller's trustee to the buyer's trustee is that the documentary tax can be paid on the assignment rather than the deed, concealing the purchase price from the tax appraiser records and the Official Records. Following is the preferred sequence to maintain secrecy:

1. The beneficial interest is assigned to the buyer (documentary taxes are paid on the assignment directly to the Department of Revenue and not recorded in the Public Records).

2. The trustee deeds the property to the successor trustee or to the beneficiary (no documentary taxes).

The documents needed to sell beneficial interest are a contract and the assignment. Appendix C (Form 39) includes a contract to sell beneficial interest. Usually, a closing statement should be prepared for tax purposes, and — when using a closing agent such as a law firm — other closing documents may be used. A Florida title insurance agency cannot close the sale of a land trust beneficial interest because they may only close transactions where they will issue a title insurance policy. No such policy can be issued on an unrecorded assignment of beneficial interest. Therefore, they usually cannot close such a transaction.

The Assignment of Beneficial Interest does not require witnesses or a notary since it is not recorded on the Public Records. *Goldman v. Mandell, 403 So. 2d 511 (1981)*. However, witnesses would be a good idea if the form provides for successor beneficiaries and if you think someone might contest the successor. The trust agreement should provide for the procedures for lodging the assignment with the trustee; otherwise, the trustee would not know from whom to take direction.

Since the beneficial interest is personal property, even if the trust owns the homestead (primary residence), a spouse should not be required to join in the assignment to convey good title. While no Florida case has ruled specifically on this, Illinois courts have long taken this position. *Duncanson v. Lill, 153 N.E. 618 (1926)*.

If the seller is holding financing on the property, this can be done either with a pledged collateral assignment of the beneficial interest or with a mortgage on the property.

If the trustee does not change when a beneficial interest is sold, the title insurance will remain in effect, covering any title defects before acquisition. Still, the policy would not cover the time since the trustee acquired the property. Further, the coverage amount of the title insurance is limited to what was paid to purchase the property into the trust initially. If the purchase price of the beneficial interest is higher than that amount, the additional amount is not covered by title insurance.

A copy of form DR-228 should be completed and sent to Florida's Department of Revenue. Note that this form does not request the identification of the property, so there is no record of what was sold. The person to sign this form would be whomever the sales contract says should pay the tax on the transfer. The tax is 70¢ per $100 or a fraction thereof of the sales price (except in Miami-Dade County, which has an additional surtax) and applies to the amount of any mortgages on the property.

In 2008, a law was passed requiring that assignments of beneficial interest be disclosed to the property appraiser in the county where the property is located. This is done with form DR-430, NOTICE OF CHANGE OF OWNERSHIP OR CONTROL NON-HOMESTEAD PROPERTY (Form 21). One purpose of this form is to ensure that property buyers do not keep the assessment cap that was instituted in 2008, and there are harsh penalties for paying lower taxes by keeping the tax cap.

If the property assessment has not been kept artificially low by the cap, then failure to file the form would result in no monetary penalty, but filing the form might raise issues regarding documentary taxes (see Chapter 10). If an assignment is used when a deed is filed, then the form does not need to be filed. Seek legal advice as to the pros and cons of filing this form.

Contract for Sale

The rule in Illinois has been that a contract for property sale in a trust is invalid if signed only by the beneficiary. *Schneider v. Pioneer Trust and Savings Bank, 168 N.E.2d 808 (1960).* This is based upon the rationale that to use the benefits of a land trust, a beneficiary must not ignore the formalities of a land trust. However, in 1981, an Illinois contract executed by a sole beneficiary was held enforceable. *First National Bank of Barrington v. Oldenberg, 427 N.E.2d 1312 (1981).* Florida courts could go either way.

The best practice is to have the trustee execute a contract to sell the trust's real property. This preserves the beneficiary's anonymity and helps to further ensure that the beneficiary will not be named personally in a lawsuit by a buyer or seller to enforce the terms of the contract in the event the trustee breaches it. Further, in the case where the contract is to sell the property, having the trustee to sign the contract ensures that the beneficiary will not be personally liable for any representations made to the buyer in the contract.

Lease Option Agreements

One of the most creative ways to use a land trust is to structure a transaction in which the trust leases the real estate to a person, and the beneficiary sells the new tenant an option to purchase the trust's beneficial interest. This way, the new tenant can buy the property from you but still be evicted like a tenant.

The problem with a normal lease option agreement is that even if purchasers have little or no equity in a property, courts grant them much greater rights than mere tenants. Also, it may take months or even years to get them out when they default because the court might order a foreclosure or an ejectment.

With a land trust, the purchaser can be given a lease of the real property that clearly allows for a tenant's eviction and then be given a separate option or even a "contract for an option" (in which they do not get an option until the contract is fulfilled) to purchase the beneficial interest of the trust (which is personal property technically unrelated to the trust's real estate).

Of course, a judge could look at the big picture in equity and require a foreclosure or ejectment rather than a tenant eviction, but this would take sophisticated legal work, and most cases would never get to court or would be settled much sooner.

Oral Agreements

An Illinois case raised the question of whether a contract for the sale of a beneficial interest in a land trust had to be in writing. One party argued that since the interest was personal property, the requirement that contracts for the sale of real estate be in writing did not apply. However, the court ruled that since the beneficiary retains every attribute of real property ownership except the title, such interest would fall within the wording of the Illinois Statute of Frauds, which requires the contract to be in writing. *IMM Acceptance v. First National Bank and Trust, 499 N.E.2d 1012 (1986).*

No Florida case has ruled on this issue, so it could go either way. The Florida Statute of Frauds is even broader than the Illinois statute. See Fla. Stat., Sec. 725.01. However, the Florida land trust statute says that the property should be considered personal property for all purposes.

To be safe, all agreements should be in writing, but considering the lack of clarity in Florida law, an oral agreement might be worth taking to court.

Broker Commissions

Technically, if a broker has an agreement that entitles him or her to a commission on the sale of a piece of real property, and if the beneficial interest is sold without transfer of the real property out of the trust, it could be argued that no commission is due. However, if the transaction were a trick to avoid the commission, a court could rule in the broker's favor under principals of equity, especially if the broker had a well-written exclusive listing agreement. The Florida Association of Realtors Exclusive Brokerage Listing Agreement states that the broker is entitled to a commission for any sale of the property "or any interest in the Property." This additional clause would likely entitle the broker to a commission when a trust sells the property or when a beneficiary sells a beneficial interest in a trust that owns the listed property (or if a member of an LLC sells their LLC membership interest).

In an Illinois case involving a land trust and a real estate broker, the court held that the broker could collect his commission even though just one beneficiary signed the listing agreement and the trustee did not. *Ellis Realty v. Chapelski, 329 N.E.2d 370, 28 111. App. 3d 1008 (1975).*

RICO Lien Search

As explained in Chapter 12, Florida law requires the trustee to conduct a RICO lien search when conveying the property from a land trust. This is a search of the county's official records where the real property is located. Such a search can usually be obtained from a title company for anywhere from $50 to $100 or more. It is not difficult, and an experienced real estate attorney can do it in a few minutes.

Tax Forms

As explained in Chapter 9, the trustee must file documents with the IRS when terminating a trust, and someone involved in the transaction (usually the title company) must issue an IRS Form 1099-S. To avoid withholding part of the proceeds at closing under the Foreign Interest in Real Property Tax Act (FIRPTA), the closing agent usually also requires an AFFIDAVIT REGARDING STATUS UNDER INTERNAL REVENUE CODE SECTION 1445. (See Form 24.)

At the Closing

As with purchasing a property in a land trust, selling one may present problems if the closing agent is unfamiliar with Florida land trust law. The following are the most common issues that come up in a sale. Answers to other issues are found throughout the book.

Assignment. If you sign a contract to sell a property in your own name but it is in a land trust, the closing agent will probably require the trustee to join in signing the contract or to sign a consent to the contract to show that the holder of both the legal and equitable title to the property is selling that property.

Showing the Trust. Florida law clearly says that no one needs to show his or her trust if the trustee's powers are listed in the deed. However, since title agents need to see who has the powers in other types of trusts, they routinely ask to see trusts when a trustee sells property. If a title agent asks to see your land trust, ask if they have seen that the trustee's powers are included in the deed and if they have asked their underwriter if seeing the trust is necessary in this case.

If the closing agent is an attorney writing title insurance on the Attorneys' Title Insurance Fund, then you can point out Fund Title Note 31.02.03A, which says that the closing agent does not need to see the trust.

Who can sign?

Normally, the trustee signs all the closing documents. Any document that will be recorded should have the trustee's original signature and be notarized. In addition to notarization, the deed must be witnessed by two witnesses, but the notary may sign as a witness and sign as a notary public. If the trustee is a corporation or LLC, the closing agent may have additional documents that must be signed to prove the person signing on behalf of the entity has the authority to do so.

Who receives sales proceeds?

Since the beneficiary is the actual financial owner of the property, the sale proceeds should go to the trust's beneficiary. However, the regulations on title and closing agents (and their title insurance underwriters) usually require that they disburse funds only to the title owner of the sold property. In that case, the money will be wired to the trustee or the trust's name. If the trustee is a corporate trustee (or owned by a lawyer), then the funds should be disbursed into a regulated and properly named "trust" or "escrow" bank account of the trustee. If the trustee is not a professional trustee, then there may be a danger when the funds are wired to such a person's regular checking or savings account if they are untrustworthy. This is another reason it is critical to consider carefully whom you choose to serve as your trustee. In this case, you may have to argue and plead with the closing agent to wire funds directly to you as the trust beneficiary. If this should happen, use the AUTHORIZATION TO DISBURSE CLOSING PROCEEDS (Form 29), in which the trustee authorizes the money to be paid to anyone whom the trustee directs.

That said, it is vital to be mindful that title insurers and their agents have been victims of fraud. One of the strongest indicators of fraudulent activity is when a seller demands that proceeds be wired to a person or entity that is listed nowhere (or in an unrecorded document) as having any ownership of the property. This is why they are reluctant and even forbidden to wire funds to an account that is not held in the same name as the owner shown on the public records.

We have heard of beneficiaries demanding to be paid on the settlement statement as an unrecorded lienholder, resulting in zero net proceeds to the trustee. In that case, a title agent would rightfully demand to see a copy of an unrecorded mortgage to the beneficiary signed by the trustee before putting the "payoff" on the settlement statement. The same happens if the beneficiary invoices the trust for "work" completed at the trust property and demands payment on the settlement statement that way.

It is problematic for the closing agent to include payment of large sums to anyone on the settlement statement if the buyer obtains a conventional, FHA, or VA bank loan. The underwriters of such loans are trained to spot fraud like the closing agents are. During the Great Recession of 2007-2012, many fraudulent payments or kickbacks were on the seller's side of the transaction with fake payoffs, invoices, and inflated commissions or fees that were routed — after closing — back to the borrower or a third party fraudster trying to rip off the banks. For this reason, even including a large payment to the beneficiary on the trust's side of the settlement statement will likely hit a roadblock. While an old Illinois court case explains that the beneficiary should receive the proceeds directly, in light of the recent history of rampant mortgage fraud, such payments simply won't be allowed anymore. *Robinson v. Chicago National Bank, 176 N.E2d 659, 321 111. App. 2d 55 (1961).* For this reason, be prepared for the trustee to receive the proceeds at the closing of the sale of the trust property. The trustee should then immediately wire the funds to the beneficiaries in proportion to their interests once the funds clear and settle into the trustee's escrow or trust account.

Which TIN to Use?

A closing agent for a real estate sales transaction is required to report the transaction to the IRS and file a Form 1099-S. For this, the agent must obtain a taxpayer identification number. He or she will often ask for a FIRPTA affidavit (See Form 24).

It is important that the taxpayer identification number or Social Security Number given to the closing agent is that of the beneficiary. If the trustee is a corporation or LLC, the closing agent will sometimes obtain its identification number from the Division of Corporation's website and use that without asking. The trustee's identification number should never be given to the closing agent, and if the closing forms contain it, it should be crossed off, replaced with the beneficiary's, and initialed.

Some closing forms have a box to check if the seller is a disregarded entity (such as a land trust), and in such cases, the beneficiary might be asked to sign that form.

Certificate of Trust.

Some closing agents have a form called Certificate of Trust which needs to be recorded when property is sold by a trust that is not a land trust. It should not be used for a land trust and should not be signed by a trustee or beneficiary.

The form is included in Florida Statutes §736.1017; some of the forms even cite this statute number at the top. But §736.0102(3) states, "This code does not apply to any land trust under s. 689.071, except to the extent provided in s. 689.071(7), s. 721.08(2)(c)4. or 721.53(1)(e)."

At most, a land trustee may execute an affidavit that they are still the trustee and have not received any notice that the beneficiary has revoked the trust or declared bankruptcy.

Closing Affidavit.

Most closing agents ask the seller to sign a closing affidavit, which (among other things) states that the seller knows of no pending liens or claims against the property and that all tenants have been disclosed. When the trustee signs this, he or she should be sure that it is as trustee and not personally. Use the rubber stamps discussed in Chapter 13. Also, the trustee should not sign if it says he or she has personal knowledge because, usually, the trustee has no idea if there are any claims, liens, or tenants. The proper way to word it would be to say the statements in the affidavit are "to the best of the trustee's knowledge."

Chapter Nine

Federal Taxation of Land Trusts

L and trusts allow much flexibility in how real estate transactions will be taxed. This chapter explains what your tax options and requirements are when using a land trust.

Tax Returns

A land trust does not file any federal tax returns. For tax purposes, the trust is disregarded, and all taxable activities of the trust are reported on the beneficiaries' returns. These returns may be individual, partnership, or corporate, depending upon the filing beneficiary's filing status. *Pommier v. Commissioner, 52 CCH TCM 766 (1986); Pieroni Building Trust v. Commissioner, 45 B.T.A. 157 (1941).*

A corporate owner of an interest in a land trust may be a C corporation or an S corporation. A partnership may be either general or limited. Limited liability companies can also be beneficiaries. Limited liability companies may file corporate or partnership returns, or if they have only one member, then they file no return, and the member files either Schedule E or Schedule C with his 1040 return. If you are unsure which is best for you, a tax expert should be consulted before deciding which type of entity to use.

Taxpayer Identification Number

A Florida land trust does not obtain a taxpayer identification number or employer identification number. (A business trust does need a taxpayer identification number, but it is not a land trust.) The beneficiary, whether an individual or company, uses his or their tax number (social security or EIN) on their tax return to report the trust's income and expenses. When asked for the trust's tax identification number, whether on a W-9, FIRPTA form, or closing affidavit, the trustee provides the beneficiary's number and not the trustee's TIN.

Notice of Fiduciary Capacity

Under §6903(b) of the IRS Code and Treas. Regs. §§301.6903- 1(a) and 301.6903-1(b), the trustee must disclose to the IRS that they act as a fiduciary for the beneficiary. Revenue Ruling 63-16 discusses this requirement. This disclosure helps the IRS connect the beneficiary claiming the income and deductions to the trust property. It should be filed within 30 days.

Years ago, Form 56 had a box to check for an Illinois-type land trust. Then it was revised and had no place for this information for land trusts. When it was filed, the IRS would sometimes get confused and send a taxpayer identification number.

In 2001, the IRS published a new proposed Form 56-A in The Federal Register. The proposed form was intended to be used for "Illinois-type land trusts." Since no specific form is required to be used to comply with §6903(b), one of the authors started using this form. But he received a phone call asking where the form came from and requesting that he not use it because it was not yet approved.

In 2003, 2006, 2009, and 2012, notice was published in The Federal Register with requests for comments on the form. When one of the authors contacted the agent in charge to assess the status in late 2003, he was told that it was still on hold because the IRS was being reorganized. They had not yet received comments from all concerned divisions of the IRS as to whether the proposed form was adequate. The person in charge had no idea when it might be approved and seemed to think it might be a long time, perhaps until his retirement. In 2013, a new person was in charge of the form, and he also gave a vague answer about the status.

The best suggestion the first agent could offer was to file Form 56 and attach the proposed Form 56-A to it since it does not have places for the right information. The other possibility would be to send a letter to the IRS stating that it is disclosing a fiduciary relationship pursuant to section §6903(b).

Some people have argued that since the instructions for Form 56 say that the form is optional, they do not have to file it or anything else with the IRS. Well, the form says it is optional because you can opt to file the same information by letter if you do not want to use the form. But Rev. Rul. 63-16 clarifies that they require disclosure for a land trust.

In the authors' experience, the IRS has no idea what to do with this information and likely keeps it somewhere unindexed, never to be seen again. We file them because we like to follow all the rules carefully, but it seems to be a pointless task.

Beneficiary Status

Where there are two or more beneficiaries of a trust (other than a married couple), an agreement should be carefully drafted spelling out their relationship. If this is not done, it is possible that they will be treated as an "association" and subject to double taxation like a corporation.

The six attributes of an association are:

1. associates,

2. objective to carry on a business,

3. continuity of life,

4. centralized management,

5. limited liability, and

6. free transferability of interests.

If beneficiaries can avoid two of these six characteristics, they will not be taxed as a corporation.

Associates.

Whenever there are two or more beneficiaries, they are "associates."

Objective to Carry on a Business.

Unless the trust holds a family residence or raw land, the objective is usually to carry on a business.

Continuity of Life.

Most land trusts do not terminate on death, so there is usually continuity of life.

Centralized Management.

Management can be equally shared by the beneficiaries or controlled by a director. In Revenue Ruling 64.220, a trust had one manager, but a majority vote of the beneficiaries controlled him, and management was held not to be centralized.

Limited Liability.

Beneficiaries are liable for damages caused by their property management so this characteristic is avoided.

Free Transferability of Interests.

Interests can be freely transferable or can be controlled by a buyout agreement.

Therefore, every beneficiary agreement should provide equal control of management or restricted interest transferability. Revenue Rulings 78-371 and 79-77, IRS Reg. §301.7701-2 and *Landsdown Realty Trust v. Commissioner, 50 F2d 56 (1930)* provide further guidance.

This book includes two beneficiary agreements: Form 11, a simple co-venture agreement (in which two or more people own the property but are not partners), and Form 12, an extended partnership agreement.

Tax-Free Sale of Residence

The Taxpayer's Relief Act of 1997 exempts the first $250,000 of gain on the sale of a residence ($500,000 for married couples). This exemption can be used on any residence a person has lived in for at least two out of the last five years. It is unclear whether using a land trust will affect this exemption. Be sure to check with a tax adviser before taking action on this.

Section 1031 Exchanges

Under §1031 of the Internal Revenue Code, certain property may be exchanged tax-free for like-kind property. Although interests in trusts are specifically not allowed to be exchanged tax-free under Treasury Regulation §1.103(a)-1, interests in land trusts are considered real property, which is allowed under §1031. Revenue Ruling 92-105, also *In Re Hubert Rutland, 36 CCH TCM 40 (1977)*.

For more information on this subject, see "Can A Beneficial Interest In An Illinois Land Trust Qualify For Tax-Free Exchange Treatment?" by Jeffrey L. Kwall in the Illinois Bar Journal, November 1982, pages 178-182, and "Illinois Land Trust May Effect s. 1031 Exchange," 33 Tax Management Memorandum 387-388, Dec. 28, 1992.

Since beneficial interests in land trusts can be held by corporations, partnerships, LLCs, and other trusts, they offer many creative possibilities for §1031 exchanging.

Land Trusts may also be used in reverse 1031 exchanges to purchase the replacement property before the relinquished property is sold. Many qualified intermediaries will only use LLCs to hold title to the replacement property before the relinquished property is sold. However, a land trust is faster, cheaper, and easier to set up than an LLC and doesn't require filing formal articles of dissolution once the exchange is completed. An experienced, qualified intermediary who understands this is vital if land trusts are involved in your regular or reverse 1031 exchange transaction.

Estate and Gift Taxes

Putting property into a land trust does not avoid estate taxes. The net value of a trust would be included in a decedent's estate for federal estate tax purposes. However, a land trust can be used to divide up interests in real property to take advantage of the current annual exclusion under IRC §2503(b), as amended occasionally. For the exclusion to apply, the interests given away must be "present interests," meaning that the beneficiaries must receive some control along with the interest. In one case where the grantor conveyed interests but kept all control himself, the exclusion was denied. *McClure v. United States, 608 F.2d 478 (Ct. Cl. 1979)*.

The estate tax has been a political football, and the rules change every few years. Anyone with a large estate should consult a tax professional and an estate planning attorney with experience handling large estates to reduce or avoid estate and gift taxes as much as possible.

FIRPTA

The Foreign Investment in Real Property Tax Act of 1980 imposes a tax on foreign sellers of real estate. It requires the buyer to withhold 10% of the purchase price, or else the buyer is liable for the foreign seller's tax payment. The withholding is required even if the seller is making no profit on the sale, but he can get a refund (eventually) by filing a tax return.

Every buyer of real estate in the U.S. must withhold 10% of the purchase price unless he gets a statement that the seller is not a foreign person or it is a home costing under $300,000 that the buyer plans to occupy as his primary residence for at least the next two years.

This is why, when a property is sold, the closing agent requires a "FIRPTA Affidavit" to be signed by the seller stating whether the seller is a U.S. taxpayer. Since a land trust is a disregarded entity for tax purposes, the FIRPTA Affidavit should be signed by the beneficiary, but most closing agents want the trustee to sign it. The tax ID number on the form should be that of the beneficiary, not the trustee's own number.

When a property seller is a foreign person, he must have a US taxpayer identification number (TIN). This is obtained using IRS Form W-7. Since it can take a long time to obtain such an ITIN, a foreign investor should file the application long before contemplating the sale of a property, or the sale could be delayed. It's recommended that any foreign owner of real property, whether directly or through a disregarded entity like a trust or single-member LLC, obtain an ITIN upon purchase of the property to have it to file annual U.S. tax returns and for the FIRPTA forms when the time comes to sell the property.

IRS Form W-9

Tax law requires that real estate closing agents file 1099-S forms, listing the seller's tax identification numbers and net proceeds of real estate transactions. Financial institutions are also required to make reports of interest paid and received. For this reason, title agents and lenders may request the trustee sign Form W-9, disclosing the trust's taxpayer identification number.

Because the beneficiary is the party responsible for tax on the profits, the trustee can sign the W-9 form with the beneficiary's taxpayer identification number. To avoid confusion, it would be best to use the trust name or number as the taxpayer's name on this form rather than or in addition to the trustee's name. As explained in Chapter 8, since the trust is a disregarded entity for tax purposes, the beneficiary will ultimately receive the proceeds from the sale of the trust property, so the beneficiary's taxpayer identification number should be the one listed on this form.

Chapter Ten

State Taxation of Land Trusts

M any of the same state taxes that apply to ordinary income and transactions apply to land trusts as well. However, some do not apply at all, or apply in a different way from what is usually seen. An accountant or tax lawyer can help you understand and comply with the law if you do not fully understand it.

Real Estate Taxes

Real estate tax bills are sent to the trustee, who is the record owner of the property. It is paid by and deductible by the beneficiaries. The Truth in Millage (TRIM) notices are also sent to the trustee, usually in August, and these should be forwarded by the trustee to the beneficiaries in time to file any appeals that may be desired. Appeals of valuations or exemption denials must be made within 25 days of the property appraiser mailing the TRIM notices. The appraisers sometimes put a mailing date on the TRIM notice that is days before the actual mailing date. This means that when you receive the notice, you may really only have a few days to file an appeal. Therefore, it's imperative that the trustee forward these as soon as possible when received, and for the beneficiary to review them immediately upon receipt. If there is any question about valuation or exemptions, the beneficiary should calendar August 15 of each year to go to the property appraiser's website for the county where the property is located and manually search for and download a copy of the annual TRIM notice to get a headstart on the appeals process.

Homestead Exemption

The issue of whether and how a beneficiary of a land trust can qualify for the homestead exemption has been confused for years but is finally settled. The problem was that while the land trust statute said that a beneficiary could get the homestead exemption, it also said that the trustee had legal and equitable title. Meanwhile, the Florida Constitution says that one must have at least an equitable title interest to qualify for the homestead exemption.

For a while the only solution was to have the beneficiaries get a life estate in the property. This clearly qualifies for the exemption. But once the Attorney General's office issued an opinion in 2008 (AGO 2008-44), property appraisers started applying the exemption where the deed does not say the trustee holds legal and equitable title and where the trust agreement or deed, or both say that the beneficiaries have a "beneficial interest for life" or the right to "occupy" the trust property or similar wording. Further, some counties will still deny the exemption if the deed into the trustee states that the beneficiary's interest is personal property only. Therefore, this provision should be stated in the land trust agreement only, and not on the face of a deed for property that may be entitled to homestead exemptions for the beneficiary.

For example, the following wording could be used on a deed and with similar language in the trust:

> NOTE TO PROPERTY APPRAISER: By accepting this deed, the Trustee confirms that under the terms of the trust agreement, the beneficiaries of the trust have not less than a beneficial interest for life and may occupy the property as their primary residence. Thus, they are entitled to the homestead tax exemption pursuant to the provisions of F.S.§196.041(2) and Section 6, Article VII of the Florida Constitution.

Before setting up a trust for which you want the homestead exemption, you should speak with someone in the appraiser's office and find out exactly what they will require to appear on the deed to be eligible for the homestead exemption.

One problem with getting the homestead exemption for a land trust property is that most property appraisers require that the name of the person getting the exemption be listed along with the trustee on their website. This destroys the anonymity. If the main reason for the trust is to avoid probate, this would not be a problem, but if your main concern is privacy, you might need to forego the tax exemption, which will be costly. Again, speaking with the appraiser's office beforehand can be helpful. We have found that most appraisers now list the beneficiaries' names for homestead trust properties only in their internal databases. In contrast, others make it part of the mailing address lines, which are not publicly searchable.

Documentary Tax

The documentary tax is a tax on the transfer of real estate. It is one of the largest revenue sources for the State of Florida, behind Sales Taxes. It is 70¢ per $100 of the price paid for the property in all of Florida except Miami-Dade County, where the tax is 60¢ per $100, plus a 45¢ per $100 local surtax on transactions that do not involve single-family residences.

This tax is meant to be on real property sales, but the Florida Department of Revenue keeps trying to extend it to transfers of property that are not sales. For example, transferring property to your corporation in exchange for stock is taxable. Transferring property to an LLC of which you are the sole member is also taxable if there is a mortgage on the property. The tax is considerable at 70¢ per $100 in value ($1,400 for a $200,000 property).

Transferring a property to a trust in which the trust beneficiary is the same as the grantor on the deed is exempt from the tax. This is made clear by the Florida Administrative Code (F.A.C.) Sec. 12B- 4.013(28)(a) and *River*

Park Venture 315076 v. Dickenson, 303 So. 2d 654 (1974). However, recording clerks often demand that the tax be paid on such transfers. If you are faced with such a clerk, ask for a supervisor and point out these legal references. With that said the Florida Department of Revenue will audit any deed recorded with no documentary tax paid at all or only a nominal (0.70) documentary tax. If they find that the property was subject to a mortgage or into an LLC or corporation, and the proper exemption language was not included in the deed itself, the Department can — within three years after the recording — issue a tax warrant against the grantor, and that warrant attaches to all real and personal property that the seller owns in the county where the lien is recorded.

Even Department of Revenue employees do not all understand these rules. One wrote to a client of one of the authors demanding tax be paid on such a transfer, stating that it didn't apply if the trustee is a separate entity, which is not what the rule says, and a completely wrong interpretation of it. She did not back down until the author asked to discuss it with the department's attorney.

One author has been involved in numerous documentary tax audits and lien appeals with the Department of Revenue. Many real estate investors and others who don't see the Department's actions daily will disregard the importance of putting the exemption language on the deeds, but they do so at their peril.

A transfer from a trustee to a successor trustee when the beneficiary is the same is not taxable. F.A.C. Sec. 12B-4.013(28)(d).

When a person transfers property to his or her own corporation not in exchange for stock, just as a contribution, no tax is due if there was no mortgage on the property. FS 201.0201(3) and *Crescent Miami Center, LLC v. Florida Department of Revenue, 903 So. 2d 913 (Fla. 2005)*. However, if the property is conveyed into an entity in this manner and then transferred back out to another entity or person within three years, it is presumed that the transfer was for consideration, and documentary tax will be assessed on the prior transfer. This is another reason that form DR-430 must be filed with the local property appraiser any time 50 percent or more of an LLC's membership interest, corporation's stock, or partnership's partnership interest is transferred to another person or entity. It lets the property appraiser know that the interest in the underlying property owner has changed hands so they can be on the lookout for a subsequent transfer to that transferee. This prevents sellers from transferring unencumbered properties to an entity or trust, selling the entity's interest for millions of dollars (no documentary tax due because it's not real estate), and then the entity deeding the still-unencumbered property out to the end buyer (again with no documentary tax). Without this legislative change, the documentary tax would have been nullified by those large companies engaging in such transactions with unencumbered properties.

Most property transfers by owners to their own companies are not sales, and nothing is paid because the owners are taking advantage of the limited liability of a corporation or limited liability company (LLC). Thus, many lawyers argue that there is no sale, no change in underlying ownership, and no reason for a tax to be paid.

In a 2003 ruling, the Department of Revenue said that when two people put their unencumbered property (no mortgage on it) into an LLC, no tax is due. Technical Assistance Advisement No. 03B4-008R, Aug. 29, 2003.

When a property is transferred to another person as a gift, there is no tax on the transfer unless the property has a mortgage, in which case the tax is based on the mortgage amount. F.A.C. Sec. 12B-4.013(18) and (21).

A tax attorney at a Florida Bar land trust seminar said that some people go out on an offshore gambling boat to sell beneficial interests in Florida land trusts to avoid the documentary stamp tax on the basis that the transaction did not take place in Florida. However, since it is Florida real property, the Department of Revenue would probably not hold the same opinion if an audit was done. F.A.C. Sec. 12B-4.013(25).

Assignments of beneficial interest are not recorded anywhere other than in the trustee's and beneficiaries' records; there would normally be nothing to trigger an audit. But if the Department discovers that a trustee is not ensuring that documentary tax is being paid on assignments of beneficial interest, it could demand an audit of all assignments that happened under all trusts held by the trustee. For this additional reason, it's a best practice to pay the documentary tax when it is due on an assignment of beneficial interest.

Sales and Use Tax

Florida sales and use tax must be collected on commercial rentals. The tax would be collected and paid by the beneficiaries who manage the trust's property. The beneficiaries should obtain a sales tax registration number in their own names or in their agent's name who will be collecting and paying the tax.

The same guidance applies to short-term, transient, tourism, or vacation rental licenses (the nomenclature varies by county or city where it is collected), which must be obtained for any property rented for terms of six months or less (e.g. weekly vacation rentals, monthly "snowbird" rentals, and short-term subscription boarding houses). This includes Airbnb, HomeAway, VRBO, and properties advertised regularly on similar home or room-rental sites. For such properties, it is also recommended that an operating company be established to receive the "rents" or subscription fees (i.e., with PadSplit-type scenarios), as illustrated in Chapter 4.

Rental License Tax

More and more cities are developing new landlord license laws to generate income and regulate rental units. Since the beneficiaries have full management control of the property and the trustee merely holds the title, the beneficiaries should be licensed under such laws.

Since land trusts are poorly understood and licensing laws may require owners to be licensed, some cities may have problems convincing government officials that the trustee should not register. It may depend on whether the ordinance wants owners to register or those in the business of renting property. The trustee is the owner but is not in the business of renting property. They only hold the title. There is a practical problem of having the trustee as the licensee since he has no contact with the tenants or access to the property.

In any case, if the license must be in the name of the trustee, it should clearly be in the name of the specific trust. If a federal tax identification number is required, the beneficiary's number should be provided, as this is the tax number associated with the trust.

Tangible Property Tax

There is a tax on the value of tangible personal property (furniture, computers, drapes, etc.) used in businesses and rental properties. The first $25,000 is exempt, so if the value of your property is less, you don't need to file a return.

Your tax adviser can decide whether these returns should be filed in your name, company name, or trust name. Normally, the trustee does not file these.

Chapter Eleven

Securities Laws

M any people, including some attorneys, have shied away from land trusts because of the possibility of violating securities laws. However, a land trust does not involve securities laws. The trust is merely a form of holding title to real estate. Whether securities laws apply depends on the relationship between the parties to the transaction. The general rule is that securities laws do not apply unless one person passively puts up money and expects to make a profit based on the efforts of another party.

If your land trust will have just you as the beneficiary, you and your spouse, or you and your partner who equally participate in the property management, then you don't need to read this chapter. This chapter only applies if one or more beneficiaries are passive with no active management in the daily operations of the land trust property.

What Is a Security?

Under federal and state laws, a security exists when four attributes exist:

- an investment

- in a common enterprise

- with the expectation of a profit

- from the efforts of others

The most famous U. S. Supreme Court case explaining what a security is, is *SEC v. W. J. Howey Co., 328 U.S. 293 (1946)*. In this case, a Florida promoter bought an orange grove and sold individual orange trees to investors who signed management agreements for the promoter to take care of the trees and harvest and sell the oranges. Although the Howey case used the words "solely from the efforts of others," later cases have watered down the word "solely" so that even if the investor puts some effort into the transaction, it may be deemed a security. A good examination of when securities laws apply is contained in the case *Williamson v. Tucker, 645 F2d 404 (1981)*.

What if a Security Exists?

If all of the above attributes exist in a venture, then the interests of those who put up money are securities. In that case, they are subject to several laws. These include the federal Securities Act of 1933, the Securities Exchange Act of 1934, the Investment Advisor Act of 1940, plus state securities laws in all 50 states.

These laws protect investors from losing their money in securities scams and fraudulent deals. The main thrust of the laws is to require complete disclosure of all of the risks involved in an investment. For larger deals, this is accomplished by registration of the offering with the government.

Violations of these laws are serious. There are criminal and civil penalties, and investors who lose money can sue the promoters personally for actual and punitive damages.

Avoiding Securities Law Problems

To avoid the possibility of problems with securities laws, a transaction can be structured so that no security is involved. One way to do this is to give control of the enterprise to all of the participants. This can be done by structuring the venture as a general partnership. You can simplify the management of the project by consolidating day-to-day management in a single manager, but if all of the beneficiaries (partners) retain the power to replace the manager and make ultimate decisions, the transaction should be safe.

However, remember that the courts do not let form rule over substance. If you call all parties "general partners," but some of them are passive investors, you may lose if the matter goes to court.

If the ownership of the beneficial interest is in a corporation or limited partnership, then the issues involving securities law would be the same as with any stock or partnership interest issuance.

Whether certificates are used in the land trust should not affect the determination of whether securities laws apply since the law looks at the substance, not the form of the transaction. There have been cases where even corporate stock has been held not to be a security. *United Housing Foundation, Inc. v. Forman, 421 U.S. 837 (1975).*

***

Exemptions from Securities Laws

Even if structuring the transaction does not allow one to avoid securities laws, it may still be possible to avoid securities problems by fitting into one of the exemptions in the securities laws. Both federal and state laws have "safe harbor" exemptions, which allow limited issuances of securities without compliance with the complex and expensive registration provisions.

In situations where a husband and wife or a few partners are beneficiaries of the trust, and all parties are active in the enterprise, securities laws would normally not apply to their interests in the enterprise. As a practical matter, if your father or aunt wants to put up some money for an interest in a property you are buying, you probably won't get in trouble. They probably won't seek triple damages and criminal penalties if your business fails. (But this can't be said of your father-in-law if he becomes your ex-father-in-law someday!)

Other situations may also be exempt. The following is a brief summary of the possible exemptions:

Florida Private Placement Exemption.

Under Florida Statutes, Section 517.061(10)(a) (West 2024), a Florida private placement exemption can apply if all of the following are true:

1. There are no more than 35 purchasers, or the issuer reasonably believes that there are no more than 35 purchasers, of the securities of the issuer in this state during an offering made in reliance upon this subsection or, if such offering continues for a period in excess of 12 months, in any consecutive 12–month period.

2. Neither the issuer nor any person acting on behalf of the issuer offers or sells securities pursuant to this subsection by means of any form of general solicitation or general advertising in this state.

3. Before the sale, each purchaser or the purchaser's representative, if any, is provided with, or given reasonable access to, full and fair disclosure of all material information, which must include written notification of a purchaser's right to void the sale under number 4 below.

4. Any sale made pursuant to this exemption is voidable by the purchaser within 3 days after the first tender of consideration is made by such purchaser to the issuer by notifying the issuer that the purchaser expressly voids the purchase. The purchaser's notice to the issuer must be sent by e-mail to the issuer's e-mail address outlined in the disclosure document provided to the purchaser or purchaser's representative or by hand delivery, courier service, or other method by which written proof of delivery to the issuer of the purchaser's election to rescind the purchase is evidenced.

These rules may sound simple, but many more rules, regulations, and court cases explain each in more detail. For example, what does "35 purchasers" mean? It sounds simple, but it can mean more than thirty-five people. For example, spouses, persons whose net worth exceeds a million dollars, and corporation founders may not be counted in some circumstances.

Florida Private Offering Exemption.

If you sell your stock to a small group of people without any advertising, you can fall into the federal private offering exemption if all of the following are true.

1. all persons to whom offers are made are financially astute, are participants in the business, or have a substantial net worth;

2. no advertising or general solicitation is used to promote the stock;

3. the number of persons to whom the offers are made is limited;

4. the shares are purchased for investment and not for immediate resale;

5. the persons to whom the stock is offered are given all relevant information (including financial information) regarding the issuance and the corporation; and,

6. a filing claiming the exemption is made upon the United States Securities and Exchange Commission (SEC).

Again, there are numerous court cases explaining each element of these rules, including such topics as what is a financially astute person.

Federal Private Placement Exemption.

If you sell your stock to a small group of people without any advertising, you can fall into the private offering exemption:

1. all persons to whom offers are made are financially astute, are participants in the business, or have a substantial net worth,

2. no advertising or general solicitation is used to promote the stock,

3. the number of persons to whom the offers are made is limited,

4. the shares are purchased for investment and not for immediate resale,

5. the persons to whom the stock is offered are given all relevant information (including financial information) regarding the issuance and the corporation. Again, there are numerous court cases explaining each aspect of these rules, including such questions as what is a "financially astute" person, and

6. a filing claiming the exemption is made upon the United States Securities and Exchange Commission.

Federal Intrastate Offering Exemption.

If you only offer your securities to residents of one state, you may be exempt from federal securities laws. This is because federal laws usually only apply to interstate commerce. Intrastate offerings are covered by SEC Rule 147, and if it is followed carefully, your sale will be exempt from federal registration.

Federal Small Offerings Exemptions.

The SEC has liberalized the rules to facilitate small businesses' growth. Under Regulation D, adopted by the Securities and Exchange Commission, there are three types of exemptions: rules 504, 505, and 506.

Rule 504:

Offering securities of up to $1,000,000 in a twelve-month period can be exempt under SEC Rule 504. Offers can be made to any number of persons, no specific information must be provided, and investors do not have to be sophisticated.

Rule 505:

An offering of up to $5,000,000 can be made in a twelve-month period, but no public advertising may be used, and only 35 non-accredited investors may purchase stock. Any number of accredited investors may purchase stock.

Accredited investors are sophisticated individuals with high net worth or income, large trusts or investment companies, or persons involved in the business.

Rule 506:

Under this rule, the amount of money raised is not limited, but—like Rule 505—it does not allow advertising and limits non-accredited investors to 35. You must register with the state under this rule.

It is important to note that in all cases where an exemption from securities laws is sought, there can be no general advertising or solicitation, and all persons to whom the stock is offered must be given full information about the offering and the condition of the corporation. (To be safe, promoters sometimes list everything they can think negatively about themselves and the stock.)

In all cases, disclosure is important in determining liability, even if an exemption is used. A full and fair disclosure is considered necessary to allow the investor to determine the extent of the risk.

***

Get an Opinion

Because of the complexities of securities regulations, this book can only provide a limited overview of your options. With the criminal penalties possible for violations, anyone putting forward an investment project should consult a specialist in securities law. You should be able to pay for a one-hour consultation to lay out your proposed plan and have the attorney explain the problems and pitfalls and suggest alternatives.

Further Research

For further information on your state's securities laws, you should review the material in CCH's Blue Sky Reporter, which is available in many law libraries. It also has information on federal securities laws. Another great resource for raising private money is attorney Kim Lisa Taylor's books and services on her website (https://syndicationatt orneys.com/).

Each state has an office of securities regulation, and some provide helpful materials. The North American Securities Administrators Association provides contact information for each state.

Chapter Twelve

Florida RICO Act

The Florida Racketeer Influenced and Corrupt Organization (RICO) Act is contained in Florida Statutes, Chapter 895. It aims to ferret out money used in drug deals and organized crime. Because land trusts can be used to hide assets, the Act places certain requirements on trustees of land trusts.

RICO Liens

Under Florida Statutes, Section 895.07, the state can file RICO liens against persons believed to be involved in illegal activities. Whenever a trustee of a land trust is directed to convey property out of trust or to distribute money to a beneficiary, he or she must search the official records of the county in which the property is located to determine if a RICO lien has been filed against the beneficiaries. The trustee must notify the state whenever he or she learns of a lien against a beneficiary. Failure to follow the RICO law is a second-degree misdemeanor. A trustee who distributes property to beneficiaries named in a RICO lien notice is personally liable to the state of Florida for all amounts distributed. RICO liens are effective for six years and may be renewed for an additional six years.

Foreign Beneficiaries

An entity of which 10% or more is owned by a foreign person or entity is designated an alien business organization (ABO). Every ABO or non-Florida foreign entity owning real estate or holding mortgages in Florida is required by the RICO Act to have a Florida registered agent and registered office under Florida Statutes, section 607.0505. This means that any land trust beneficiary, which is an ABO or foreign entity, must designate a Florida registered agent since it is deemed to own Florida real estate. For instance, if a Wyoming LLC is the beneficiary of a land trust, it must appoint a Florida registered agent even though it is not directly "conducting business" in the State of Florida. The Secretary of State has created a REGISTERED AGENT & OFFICE FOR ALIEN BUSINESS ORGANIZATION, FINANCIAL INSTITUTION, OR TELEHEALTH PROVIDER form (Form 13). A form for changing the agent can be obtained on the Florida Division of Corporations website (www.sunbiz.org).

Fortunately, the legislature did not require disclosing the beneficiaries as long as a registered agent is named. The beneficiaries must only be named if the Department of Legal Affairs issues a subpoena. Failure to comply with these requirements could result in a fine of up to $1,000 daily. (A good explanation of the RICO requirements is contained in an article titled "1984 RICO Amendments," found in the October 1984 issue of the Florida Bar Journal, page 501.)

NOTE: All Florida land trusts should contain provisions allowing the trustee to comply with the RICO Act.

Chapter Thirteen

Drawbacks and Pitfalls

After learning all the benefits of a land trust, many people figure there must be drawbacks, or everyone would have their properties in trust. The main reason everyone doesn't have their property in trust is that they don't know enough about them. But you should be aware of a few problems and drawbacks.

Unfamiliarity in Marketplace

Because few knowledgeable people are using land trusts, not all of the people in the real estate industry have experience with them, and some are afraid to deal with them. Some have even told the authors they thought they were "illegal" or "only for tax fraud."

Lenders, insurance agents, title agents, and even some attorneys may be reluctant to get involved with your deal if they know nothing about land trusts. No one wants to admit they are ignorant about something, and it is much easier to say, "We don't deal with trusts," than to learn how.

You may have to check with a few providers before finding one who can do the paperwork correctly for your land trust transaction. But since land trusts are becoming more popular each year, you will find more professionals able and eager to deal with them.

Insurance

As explained in Chapter 4, few insurance agents or their underwriters know how to write insurance for land trusts, and some of them require a separate, more expensive liability policy. However, if you shop around you should be able to find one who can correctly issue the insurance policy. Once a property moves into a land trust, the "insured" is the trustee as trustee of the trust, and the beneficiaries should be listed as "additional insureds" or "loss payees." If the trustee is not a human, then the insurer may exclude liability coverage, and a separate business premises liability policy would be needed. In any event, obtaining insurance on Florida real estate is difficult regardless of who or what holds title to the property, and the land trust (or an LLC or corporation) can add complications to obtaining a policy in an already difficult process.

Tax Reassessment Risks

Some county property appraisers remove any valuation caps and exemptions that are in place on a property when the property is conveyed to a third-party trustee. This is incorrect in most cases, but — if the proper language is not included in the deed, or if the deed is drafted carelessly — there is a risk that the real property taxes on the property will increase significantly in the following calendar year.

Costs

To obtain the benefits of a land trust, one must incur the cost of setting it up and maintaining it. An attorney's fee for setting up a simple land trust would usually be between $600.00 and $1,200, depending on complexities such as financing, subject-to provisions, and closing coordination. Some have been known to charge over $3,500.00 to clients who don't know what a typical charge should be. The yearly trustee's maintenance fees are in the range of $200.00, so it is advantageous to compare prices. A bank in the Miami area has been advertising that it will serve as land trust trustee for a minimum fee of $1,500 per year, and a non-attorney has advertised that she'll be your trustee for over $500.00 a year!

In a traditional land trust, the trustee's only duty is to keep the trust file and occasionally forward mail, so a low annual fee can often be negotiated, especially if the trustee is familiar with land trusts. Any work performed by the trustee is billed separately at an agreed-upon rate.

Trustee

It is important to choose a trustee you can trust. A trustee has full power to sell, mortgage, or lease your property, and in most cases, you cannot simply reverse the trustee's actions. While such an act could be criminal fraud if done without your consent, it's expensive and time-consuming to litigate an action against a trustee for such fraud. Criminal restitution awarded to you will likely never be recovered, and even a civil judgment against a trustee is usually uncollectable. An attorney established in the community or a bank would not present much risk, but if you use a friend or relative, the temptation may prove too great, and you may be cheated.

If you choose not to use a professional trustee, one precaution is to put a small ($1,000) mortgage on the property in trust or record a "Memorandum of Option" to the beneficiary or a relative so the property cannot be sold or mortgaged without some notice to the beneficiary. A MEMORANDUM OF OPTION form is included in this book as Form 23. However, this places your name in the public records or requires involving another relative or friend in your business.

The best practice is to use a professional trustee corporation that is owned by an attorney, CPA, bank, or other professional licensee. Such professionals have too much on the line to risk mishandling your real estate. With electronic signatures so easily and quickly completed now, there should be no concern about the ability to quickly obtain the trustee's signature on documents. Also, larger professional trust companies have multiple officers who can sign documents anytime during business hours (and often during non-business hours). Additionally, they have notaries in the office, so signing, witnessing, and notarizing documents is faster and easier than having your friend or relative forced to take time out of their day to go to a notary, find witnesses, and sign documents on their time for your business.

Finally, if you use a professional corporate trustee (as pointed out in Chapter 5), you may be able to obtain conventional mortgage loans from Fannie Mae or Freddie Mac without having to remove the property from the trust. Also, you won't need to—again—involve your relative or friend in signing stacks of mortgage loan documents at your business closing.

Chapter Fourteen

Concerns for Trustees

Because banks charge quite high fees for trust services, attorneys and others are often asked to serve as trustees by those who wish to take advantage of land trusts at a reasonable cost. Considering the general lack of knowledge about land trusts and the usual fiduciary obligations on trustees, attorneys often hesitate to take on such work.

However, attorneys who agree to serve as land trust trustees and let that willingness be known in the investment community usually attract considerable business. When the authors began offering trustee services to local investors, they soon had hundreds of properties in trust and currently hold over 2,000 properties in Florida in land trusts. This business usually leads to other business, including title insurance and legal work. For a conscientious attorney in a state where land trusts are allowed, there is not much risk now that CERCLA liability has been eliminated.

Fiduciary Obligations

Illinois and Florida courts have clarified that an Illinois-type land trust does not impose the standard fiduciary obligations on the trustee. The first time a court held a trustee liable, the Florida legislature clarified the law to eliminate such liability in the future. The only duty of the trustee is to hold title to the property. There are no accounting, bookkeeping, or other duties. *Schwartz v. Hill, 562 So2d 779 (Fla 2DCA 1990)*.

A few cases have held trustees liable in limited circumstances. In *Flagship Bank of Orlando v. Reinman, Harrell, Silberhorn, Moule & Graham, P.A., 503 So2d 913 (Fla 5DCA 1987)*, a trustee was held liable for not redeeming tax certificates that had been issued on the property. However, this was not the case for a bare title trust like most land trusts. In this case the bank was appointed both trustee and receiver and was specifically authorized by the court to redeem the certificates. The bank's attorney went to the courthouse, but instead of redeeming the certificates, he bid in the sale and allowed himself to be outbid.

Illinois cases that have imposed liability on trustees have usually involved banks that were both trustee and mortgagee. After one particular case, *Home Federal Savings and Loan Assoc. of Chicago v. Zarkin, 89 Ill2d 232, 432 NE2d 841 (Ill. 1982)*, the Illinois legislature amended the law to protect trustees from liability.

Liability

The trustee of a Florida land trust is protected from personal liability except in limited circumstances. Fla. Stat., §736.1013. The land trust statute was amended to include these protections after a court-imposed liability on a trustee in 1977. *Taylor v. Richmond's New Approach Ass'n., Inc., 351 So. 2d 1094 (1977)*. Under Florida statutes §736.1013, a trustee is only liable personally under three circumstances:

1. if the documents the trustee signs provide for personal liability;

2. if the trustee fails to disclose his or her representative capacity and identify the trust; or

3. if the trustee is personally at fault for a tort or obligation;

In *Schwartz v. Hill*, the trustee was held personally liable for a note he had executed as trustee, but this judgment was reversed on appeal. In one suit against a trustee asking for a deficiency judgment on a Department of Veterans Affairs (VA) mortgage foreclosure, the trial court ordered the plaintiff to pay the trustee's attorney's fee to defend when it was pointed out that both the deed and the statute protect the trustee from liability.

In 2002, an appellate court overruled the trial court's holding that a trustee was personally liable. In *Jonathan D. Commander, P.A., et al. v. McCann-Coyner-Clarke Real Estate, Inc., 830 So. 2d 116 (Fla. DCA 2002)*, the trial court held that the attorney's fees clause of a real estate contract with a trustee imposed personal liability on the trustee for attorney's fees under a previous statute making trustees liable for attorney fees in some cases. In rejecting this, the appellate court held that the real estate contract was not a contract for attorney's fees in and of itself ... holding such clauses to be attorney's fee contracts within the meaning of 737.306(l)(a) would open trustees to personal liability under every contract containing an attorney's fee clause.

The appellate court wisely rejected this. Section 737.306(1)(a) only applies when a trustee hires an attorney. Ultimately, the statute was repealed and expired on June 30, 2007.

In all cases, the deed, the trust, and any other instruments, such as mortgages and notes, should clearly state that the trustee has no personal liability in the matter. The trustee should have some rubber stamps made up to use on all documents signed as trustees. Such rubber stamps could read similar to the following:

For signing notes, mortgages, and similar documents:

It is expressly understood and agreed between the parties and all successors and assigns that this instrument is executed by the Trustee, not personally, but as Trustee in the exercise of the authority conferred upon such Trustee. No personal liability or responsibility is assumed by or shall be enforceable against said Trustee, either express or implied.

For signing other documents:

This statement is based solely upon information provided by beneficiaries of the trust to the undersigned. The undersigned has no personal knowledge of any of the facts contained herein.

For endorsing checks made out to the trust:

Pay to the order of: _____ without recourse. _____, as trustee of the _____ Land Trust dated _____ Signatory: _____

For providing copies of trust documents when requested by the beneficiary:

This is a true and correct copy of the original, containing _____ pages now held in our files. _____, as trustee of the _____ Land Trust dated _____ Signatory: _____

As long as such clauses are used on documents signed by the trustee, there should be no question of personal liability, even if the document being signed provides for some liability for the trustee. For example, in some loan documents, the mortgagor agrees to protect the lender against such liabilities as environmental problems. However, federal cases in Illinois have noted the unique nature of Illinois-type land trusts.

In other states, you must be sure no cases or statutes impose specific liabilities on trustees. If so, you may be able to form a corporation to serve as a land trust trustee. This corporation could have limited assets so that there would be no risk.

CERCLA

There was a serious concern for trustees for a while with the Comprehensive Environmental Response Compensation and Liability Act, known as "CERCLA." 42 U.S.C. §§ 9601-9675 (1988). This is the law regarding hazardous waste cleanup. Because this was the day's issue, the government had gotten excited and gone overboard. CERCLA provides for unlimited, strict, joint and several liability for owners, operators, and even past owners of properties contaminated by hazardous wastes. The result is that the courts have looked for the "deep pocket" to hold liable for cleanup, regardless of fault.

In one ridiculous case, a party that merely held a mortgage on a property was held liable because the mortgage gave it a "- capacity to influence" the borrower. *United States v. Fleet Factors Corp., 901 F2d 1550 (11th Cir 1990); cert. denied, No. 90- 504 (U.S., Jan. 14, 1991).* Other circuits declined to follow the reasoning of the court in Fleet Factors. Because Florida is in the circuit from which this case came, this case was a problem for a time for land trusts there, and trustees avoided any commercial properties or those near commercial properties.

Fortunately, Congress took action to protect trustees. The Asset Conservation, Lender Liability, and Deposit Insurance Protection Act was passed on September 28, 1996. It provides that the trustee's liability shall not exceed the trust's assets (unless the trustee is personally at fault). The Act is found in Subtitle E of Public Law 104-208, §§ 2501-2505.

This should settle the issue. However, if a trustee wants to avoid litigating the matter, he or she could avoid commercial property, require an environmental audit, or incorporate.

Corporate Trustees

Before 1992, a land trust trustee could not be a corporation unless it had $1 million in assets as required by Florida Statutes, Section 660.41, and also complied with Florida Statutes, Section 658.21. However, in 1992, Section 660.41 was repealed, and now corporations and LLCs can be trustees.

The 2006 revised land trust law clarified that other entities, such as limited liability companies (LLCs), can be used as trustees for a land trust. Some attorneys have used their law firm as trustee, but this appears to be impermissible under F.S. 621.08, which is the opinion of Attorneys Title Insurance Fund. See Title Note 11.09.02. So a completely separate trust company would be the best course.

Therefore, attorneys wishing to be land trustees should remember that their law firm cannot act as a trustee since Florida title insurers deem such an ultra vires activity that a law firm cannot do. The same rationale would likely apply to CPA firms, real estate brokerages, or any other professional association or limited liability company formed solely to practice its licensed profession and owned by licensed professionals.

Attorneys, CPAs, title insurance agents, title insurers, and real estate brokers should also remember their duties of disclosure (or non-disclosure) and ethical rules regarding conflicts of interest, client communications, and work product when preparing their land trust agreements. They should include provisions to ensure their professional obligations are adequately addressed, clarified, and maybe even waived inside the agreement with the beneficiary. It should be so clear that the beneficiary has no expectation that the trust company acting as trustee is also the beneficiary's CPA, real estate broker, title agent, or lawyer when trust services alone are provided.

Banks and licensed trust companies serving as land trustees will be subject to their usual federal and state banking and trust regulations when holding the title to the land as if they were holding funds in a bank account for a customer.

If an attorney, CPA, real estate broker, title agent, or any other person agrees to act as trustee as an individual for a client, they should understand that their name will likely appear as a defendant in lawsuits related to the property. While it may be clear that they are just the trustee of the trust, their personal name would still appear in all-caps, bold print on the summons and complaint (and news stories if the case is sensational enough), dragging their name, brand, and reputation into the mudslinging of a lawsuit. When those lawsuits are for foreclosure or unpaid taxes, they may appear in the "public records" section of the individual's credit report, damaging their credit rating. Further, if the lawsuit is alleging racial or other discrimination against a tenant, imagine the brand damage control that would need to be engaged to ensure that the media understands and accurately reports the story that you're not the one who discriminated; you just hold title to the property in trust. There's an old saying that if you have to explain why you're not really involved, it's already too late to save your reputation.

NOTE: A good manual for land trust trustees is Land Trust Administration, by Martin S. Edwards. Unfortunately, it is out of print, but some law libraries may still have a copy.

Bibliography

Florida Continuing Legal Education (CLE) Seminar Manuals

Trick or Treat: The Revised Land Trust Act - All Treats No Tricks (2013)

Land Trusts: Everything You Always Wanted to Know and More (2010)

Real Estate Transactions Involving Land Trusts (2005)

Land Trust Seminar (2002)

Land Trusts: Ownership and Conveyances Made Safe, Simple and Confidential (2000)

Land Trusts: Ownership and Conveyances Made Safe, Simple and Stealthy (1998)

Land Trust Seminar (1995)

1993 Land Trust Seminar (1993)

1989 Land Trust Seminar (1989)

1987 Land Trusts (1987)

Land Trusts (1985)

Land Trusts: An Important Vehicle for Ownership of Real Estate (1983)

Land Trusts: Their Formation and Uses in Florida (1981)

Books

Edwards, Martin S. Land Trust Administration. Springfield: Illinois Institute for Continuing Legal Education, 1999. (Out of Print) May be available from the Illinois Institute for Continuing Education, 2395 W. Jefferson, Springfield, IL 62702. www.iicle.com. An excellent book for corporate trust departments and others who serve as trustees.

Kenoe, Henry W. Kenoe on Land Trusts. Springfield: Illinois Institute for Continuing Legal Education, 1989. Published by Illinois Institute for Continuing Legal Education, 2395 W. Jefferson, Springfield, IL 62702. Out of print.

Lowell, David R. and John G. Grimsley. Florida Law of Trusts. 3rd ed. Norcross: The Harrison Company, 1984.

Warda, Mark. Land Trusts for Privacy and Profit. 3rd ed. Lake Wales: Galt Press, 2009. Available from Galt Press, galtpress@warda.net. A national version of this land trust book contains legal information about land trusts' status in all fifty states.

Articles

"Can a Beneficial Interest in an Illinois Land Trust Qualify for Tax Free Exchange Treatment?" Illinois Bar Journal. (1982): 178-181.

Dorsey, John C. and Walter H. Nunnallee. "A Shell Corporation May be a Good Devisee of Contaminated Realty." Estate Planning 20 (1993): 283- 288.

"The Florida Land Trust: An Overview." Nova Law Review. 6 (1982): 489.

"Florida Land Trust: Tax Planning and Problems." Florida Bar Journal 49 (1975): 308.

Garrau, Douglas M. "The Potentially Responsible Trustee: Probable Target for CERCLA Liability." Virginia Law Review 77 (1991): 113.

"Illinois Land Trust May Effect s. 1031 Exchange." Tax Management Memorandum 33 (1992): 387-388.

"Land Trust Act." University of Miami Law Review. 18 (1964): 669.

"Power of Direction in Illinois Land Trust Exercisable by Less Than All of the Beneficiaries is a S. 2038 Power." Tax Management Memorandum 36 (1995): 64-65.

"The Use of Revocable Trust to Defeat the Elective Share." Florida Bar Journal 57 (1983): 110.

Cases

Avila South Condo Assoc., Inc. v. Kappa Corp., 347 So2d 599 (1977)

Axtell v. Coons, 89 So.2d 419 (1921)

Breen v. Breen, 103 N.E. 2d 625 (1952)

Chicago Federal v. Caccitore, 185 N.E. 2d 670 (1962)

Chrysler Credit Corporation v. Louis Joliet Bank and Trust Co., 863 F.2d 534 (1988)

Comm. Nat'l. Bk.v. Hazel Manor Condo., Inc., 487 NE 2d 1145 (Ill. App. 2nd Dist. 1985)

Conkling v. McIntosh, 58 NE2d 304, 324 Ill.App. 292 (1944)

Conley v. Petersen, 25 Ill.2d 271, 184 NE2d 888 (1962)

Connor v. First Nat'l. Bk.and Tr. Co., 439 NE2d 122, 108 Ill.App.3d 534 (1982)

Coombs v. People, 64 N.E. 1056 (1902)

Cowen v. Knott, 252 So.2d 400 (1971)

Damen Savings v. Heritage Standard Bank, 431 N.E. 2d 34 (1982)

Datwani v. Netsch, 562 So.2d 721 (Fla. 3DCA 1990)

Devoigne v. Chicago Title & Trust Co., 136 N.E. 498 (1922)

Duncanson v. Lill, 322 Ill. 328 (1927)

Ellis Realty v. Chapelski, 329 N.E. 2d 370, 28 Ill. App.3d 1008 (1975)

Feinberg v. The Great Atlantic & Pacific Tea Co. 266 N.E. 2d 401 (Ill. 1970)

Ferraro v. Parker, 229 So.2d 621 (1969)

Field v. Mans, 516 US 59 (1995)

Fields v. Indiana Ave. Apts, Inc. 196 NE2d 485, 47 Ill.App.2d 55 (1964)

First D.M.V., Inc. v. Amster, 546 so.2d 936 (1989)

First Federal v. Pogue, 389 N.E. 2d 652 (1979)

First National Bank of Barrington v. Oldenberg, 427 N.E. 2d 1312 (1981)

First National Bank of Joliet v. Hampson, 88 Ill.App.3d 1057, 410 NE2d 1109 (1980)

Flagship Bank of Orlando v. Reinman, Harrell, et al, 503 So2d 913 (Fla 5DCA 1987)

Freeman as Trustee of Fiddlesticks Land Trust U/A/D September 25, 1984 v. Berrin, 352 So. 3d 452 (Fla. 2d DCA 2022)

Gallagher & Speck v. Chicago Title & Trust Co., 238 Ill. App 39 (1925)

Goldman v. Mandell, 403 So2d 511 (1981)

Grammer v. Roman, 174 So.2s 433 (1965)

Green v. First American Bk. and Trust, Tr. et al, 511 So2d 569 (Fla. 4DCA 1987)

Home Fed. S. & L. Assoc. of Chicago v. Zarkin, 89 Ill2d 232, 432 NE2d 841 (Ill. 1982)

Horney v. Hayes, 142 N.E. 2d 94 (1957)

Hubert Rutland, 36 CCH TCM 40 (1977)

IMM Acceptance v. First Nat'l. Bk.and Trust, 499 NE2d 1012 (Ill. App. 2d 1986)

In re Arehart, 52 B.R. 308, (Bankr. MD Fla 1985)

In re Argonne Construction Co. 10 B.R. 570 (N.D. Ill. 1981)

In re Dolton Lodge No. 35188, 22 B.R. 918 (Ill. Bkr. 1982)

In re Estate of Schaaf, 312 NE2d 348, 19 Ill. App. 3d 662 (1974)

In re Matter of Maidman, 2 B.R. 569 (Ill. Bkr. 1980)

In re Metro Palms I Trust, 153 B.R. 922, (Bankr. MD Fla 1993)

In re Saber, 233 B.R. 547 (S.D.Fla 1999)

In re Star Trust, 237 B.R. 827 (Bankr. MDFla. 1999)

In re St. Charles Land Trust, 206 So2d 128 (La.App 1967)

Jonathan D. Commander, P.A., v. McCann-Coyner-Clarke Real Estate, Inc., 830 So.2d 116 (Fla.DCA 2002)

Johnson v. First National Bank of Park Ridge, 463 NE2d 859, 123 Ill.App.3d 823 (1984)

Kirkland v. Miller, 702 So2d 620 (Fla 4DCA 1997)

Kuro, Inc. v. Department of Revenue, 713 So2d 1021 (Fla2DCA), appeal dismissed, 728 So2d 201 (Fla 1998)

Lake Shore S. & L. Assn. v. Amer. Nat'l Bk. & Tr. Co., 234 NE2d 418, 91 Ill.App.2d 143 (1968)

Landsdown Realty Trust v. Commissioner. 50 F2d 56 (1930)

Lawyer's Title Guaranty Fund v. Koch, 397 So2d 455 (Fla. 4th DCA, 1981)

Levi v. Adkay Heating & Cooling Corp., 274 NE2d 650, 1 Ill.App.3d 509 (1971)

Magnuson v. Jones, 491 So.2d 1315 (1986)

Mayo v. Barnett Bank of Pensacola, 448 F.Supp. 250 (N.D.Fla. 1978)

McClure v. United States, 608 F2d 478 (Ct Cl 1979)

Melrose Park Nat'l. Bk v. Melrose Park Nat'l. Bk, Tr., 462 NE2d 741 (Ill. App. 1st 1984)

Nelson v. Fogelstrom, 284 NE2d 339, 5 Ill.App3d 804 (1972)

Pieroni Building Trust v. Commissioner, 45 B.T.A. 157 (1941)

Pommier v. Commissioner, 52 CCH TCM 766 (1986)

Ridgewood Savings Bank v. Warda, Pinellas Co. Cir. Ct. Case No. 84-15780-7 (1985)

River Park Venture 315076 v. Dickenson, 303 So.2d 654 (1974)

Robinson v. Chicago National Bank, 176 NE2d 659, 321 Ill.App.2d 55 (1961)

Robinson v. Walker, 211 N.E. 2d 488 (1965)

Saeed v. Bank of Ravenswood, 427 NE2d 858, 101 Ill.App.3d 20 (1981)

Santo v. Santo, 497 NE2d 492, 146 Ill.App.3d 774 (1986)

Schneider v. Pioneer Trust and Savings Bank, 168 N.E. 2d 808 (1960)

Schwartz v. Hill, 562 So2d 779 (Fla. 2DCA 1990)

SEC v. W. J. Howey Co., 328 U.S. 293 (1946)

Southeast Village Associates v. Health Mgt Assn, 416 N.E. 2d 325 (1980)

State ex rel Stanley v. Cook, 146 Ohio St. 348, 66 NE2d 207 (1946)

State Street Houses, Inc. v. New York State Urban Development Corp., 356 F.3d 1345 (2004)

Taylor v. Richmond's New Approach Ass'n., Inc. 351 So.2d 1094 (1977)

Teeple v. Hunziker, 454 NE2d 1174, (Ill. App. 2d 1983)

Tick v. Cohen, 787 F2d 1490 (1986)

United Housing Foundation, Inc. v. Forman, 421 U.S. 837 (1975)

United States v. Aronson, 610 F.Supp 217 (1985)

United States v. Fleet Factors Corp., 901 F2d 1550 (11th Cir 1990)

Wachta v. First Federal, 430 N.E. 2d 708 (1981)

Williamson v. Tucker, 645 F2d 404 (1981)

Yandle Oil Co. v. Crystal River Seafood, Inc., 563 So2d 839 (Fla. 5DCA 1990)

Appendix - A

Statutes and Regulations

This appendix includes the following Florida Statutes (F.S.) and Florida Administrative Code (F.A.C.) regulations:

Statutes

Section 689.071 (Land Trust Act)

Section 689.073 (Deed Powers Act)

Section 689.07 (Deeds Designating Trustees)

Section 736.0102 (Non-applicability to land trusts)

Section 736.08125 (Non-liability of Successor Trustees)

Section 736.1013 (Non-liability of Trustees)

Administrative Code

Section 12B-4.013 (Documentary Stamp Taxes)

Section 12D-7.011 (Homestead for Trusts)

Statutes

689.071 Florida Land Trust Act.

(1) SHORT TITLE.—This section may be cited as the "Florida Land Trust Act."

(2) DEFINITIONS.—As used in this section, the term:

(a) "Beneficial interest" means any interest, vested or contingent and regardless of how small or minimal such interest may be, in a land trust which is held by a beneficiary.

(b) "Beneficiary" means any person or entity having a beneficial interest in a land trust. A trustee may be a beneficiary of the land trust for which such trustee serves as trustee.

(c) "Land trust" means any express written agreement or arrangement by which a use, confidence, or trust is declared of any land, or of any charge upon land, under which the title to real property, including, but not limited to, a leasehold or mortgagee interest, is vested in a trustee by a recorded instrument that confers on the trustee the power and authority prescribed in s. 689.073(1) and under which the trustee has no duties other than the following:

1. The duty to convey, sell, lease, mortgage, or deal with the trust property, or to exercise such other powers concerning the trust property as may be provided in the recorded instrument, in each case as directed by the beneficiaries or by the holder of the power of direction;

2. The duty to sell or dispose of the trust property at the termination of the trust;

3. The duty to perform ministerial and administrative functions delegated to the trustee in the trust agreement or by the beneficiaries or the holder of the power of direction; or

4. The duties required of a trustee under chapter 721, if the trust is a timeshare estate trust complying with s. 721.08(2)(c)4. or a vacation club trust complying with s. 721.53(1)(e).

However, the duties of the trustee of a land trust created before June 28, 2013, may exceed the limited duties listed in this paragraph to the extent authorized in subsection (12).

(d) "Power of direction" means the authority of a person, as provided in the trust agreement, to direct the trustee of a land trust to convey property or interests, execute a lease or mortgage, distribute proceeds of a sale or financing, and execute documents incidental to the administration of a land trust.

(e) "Recorded instrument" has the same meaning as provided in s. 689.073(1).

(f) "Trust agreement" means the written agreement governing a land trust or other trust, including any amendments.

(g) "Trust property" means any interest in real property, including, but not limited to, a leasehold or mortgagee interest, conveyed by a recorded instrument to a trustee of a land trust or other trust.

(h) "Trustee" means the person designated in a recorded instrument or trust agreement to hold title to the trust property of a land trust or other trust.

(3)   OWNERSHIP VESTS IN TRUSTEE.—Every recorded instrument transferring any interest in real property to the trustee of a land trust and conferring upon the trustee the power and authority prescribed in s. 689.073(1), whether or not reference is made in the recorded instrument to the beneficiaries of such land trust or to the trust agreement or any separate collateral unrecorded declarations or agreements, is effective to vest, and is hereby declared to have vested, in such trustee both legal and equitable title, and full rights of ownership, over the trust property or interest therein, with full power and authority as granted and provided in the recorded instrument to deal in and with the trust property or interest therein or any part thereof. The recorded instrument does not itself create an entity, regardless of whether the relationship among the beneficiaries and the trustee is deemed to be an entity under other applicable law.

(4)   STATUTE OF USES INAPPLICABLE.—Section 689.09 and the statute of uses do not execute a land trust or vest the trust property in the beneficiary or beneficiaries of the land trust, notwithstanding any lack of duties on the part of the trustee or the otherwise passive nature of the land trust.

(5)   DOCTRINE OF MERGER INAPPLICABLE.—The doctrine of merger does not extinguish a land trust or vest the trust property in the beneficiary or beneficiaries of the land trust, regardless of whether the trustee is the sole beneficiary of the land trust.

(6)   PERSONAL PROPERTY.—In all cases in which the recorded instrument or the trust agreement, as hereinabove provided, contains a provision defining and declaring the interests of beneficiaries of a land trust to be personal property only, such provision is controlling for all purposes when such determination becomes an issue under the laws or in the courts of this state. If no such personal property designation appears in the recorded instrument or in the trust agreement, the interests of the land trust beneficiaries are real property.

(7)   TRUSTEE LIABILITY.—In addition to any other limitation on personal liability existing pursuant to statute or otherwise, the provisions of ss. 736.08125 and 736.1013 apply to the trustee of a land trust created pursuant to this section.

(8)   LAND TRUST BENEFICIARIES.—

(a)   Except as provided in this section, the beneficiaries of a land trust are not liable, solely by being beneficiaries, under a judgment, decree, or order of court or in any other manner for a debt, obligation, or liability of the land trust. Any beneficiary acting under the trust agreement of a land trust is not liable to the land trust's trustee or to any other beneficiary for the beneficiary's good faith reliance on the provisions of the trust agreement. A beneficiary's duties and liabilities under a land trust may be expanded or restricted in a trust agreement or beneficiary agreement.

(b)1.   If provided in the recorded instrument, in the trust agreement, or in a beneficiary agreement:

a.   A particular beneficiary may own the beneficial interest in a particular portion or parcel of the trust property of a land trust;

b.   A particular person may be the holder of the power of direction with respect to the trustee's actions concerning a particular portion or parcel of the trust property of a land trust; and

c.   The beneficiaries may own specified proportions or percentages of the beneficial interest in the trust property or in particular portions or parcels of the trust property of a land trust.

2.   Multiple beneficiaries may own a beneficial interest in a land trust as tenants in common, joint tenants with right of survivorship, or tenants by the entireties.

(c)   If a beneficial interest in a land trust is determined to be personal property as provided in subsection (6), chapter 679 applies to the perfection of any security interest in that beneficial interest. If a beneficial interest in a land trust is determined to be real property as provided in subsection (6), then to perfect a lien or security interest against that beneficial interest, the mortgage, deed of trust, security agreement, or other similar security document must be recorded in the public records of the county that is specified for such security documents in the recorded instrument or in a declaration of trust or memorandum of such declaration of trust recorded in the public records of the same county as the recorded instrument. If no county is so specified for recording such security documents, the proper county for recording such a security document against a beneficiary's interest in any trust property is the county where the trust property is located. The perfection of a lien or security interest in a beneficial interest in a land trust does not affect, attach to, or encumber the legal or equitable title of the trustee in the trust property and does not impair or diminish the authority of the trustee under the recorded instrument, and parties dealing with the trustee are not required to inquire into the terms of the unrecorded trust agreement or any lien or security interest against a beneficial interest in the land trust.

(d)   The trustee's legal and equitable title to the trust property of a land trust is separate and distinct from the beneficial interest of a beneficiary in the land trust and in the trust property. A lien, judgment, mortgage, security interest, or other encumbrance attaching to the trustee's legal and equitable title to the trust property of a land trust does not attach to the beneficial interest of any beneficiary; and any lien, judgment, mortgage, security interest, or other encumbrance against a beneficiary or beneficial interest does not attach to the legal or equitable title of the trustee to the trust property held under a land trust, unless the lien, judgment, mortgage, security interest, or other encumbrance by its terms or by operation of other law attaches to both the interest of the trustee and the interest of such beneficiary.

(e)   Any subsequent document appearing of record in which a beneficiary of a land trust transfers or encumbers any beneficial interest in the land trust does not transfer or encumber the legal or equitable title of the trustee to the trust property and does not diminish or impair the authority of the trustee under the terms of the recorded instrument. Parties dealing with the trustee of a land trust are not required to inquire into the terms of the unrecorded trust agreement.

(f)   The trust agreement for a land trust may provide that one or more persons have the power to direct the trustee to convey property or interests, execute a mortgage, distribute proceeds of a sale or financing, and execute documents incidental to administration of the land trust. The power of direction, unless provided otherwise in the trust agreement of the land trust, is conferred upon the holders of the power for the use and benefit of all holders of any beneficial interest in the land trust. In the absence of a provision in the trust agreement of a land trust to the contrary, the power of direction shall be in accordance with the percentage of individual ownership. In exercising the power of direction, the holders of the power of direction are presumed to act in a fiduciary capacity for the benefit of all holders of any beneficial interest in the land trust, unless otherwise provided in the trust agreement.

A beneficial interest in a land trust is indefeasible, and the power of direction may not be exercised so as to alter, amend, revoke, terminate, defeat, or otherwise affect or change the enjoyment of any beneficial interest in a land trust.

(g)   A land trust does not fail, and any use relating to the trust property may not be defeated, because beneficiaries are not specified by name in the recorded instrument to the trustee or because duties are not imposed upon the trustee. The power conferred by any recorded instrument on a trustee of a land trust to sell, lease, encumber, or otherwise dispose of property described in the recorded instrument is effective, and a person dealing with the trustee of a land trust is not required to inquire any further into the right of the trustee to act or the disposition of any proceeds.

(h)   The principal residence of a beneficiary shall be entitled to the homestead tax exemption even if the homestead is held by a trustee in a land trust, provided the beneficiary qualifies for the homestead exemption under chapter 196.

(i)   In a foreclosure against trust property or other litigation affecting the title to trust property of a land trust, the appointment of a guardian ad litem is not necessary to represent the interest of any beneficiary.

(9)   SUCCESSOR TRUSTEE.—

(a)   If the recorded instrument and the unrecorded trust agreement are silent as to the appointment of a successor trustee of a land trust in the event of the death, incapacity, resignation, or termination due to dissolution of a trustee or if a trustee is unable to serve as trustee of a land trust, one or more persons having the power of direction may appoint a successor trustee or trustees of the land trust by filing a declaration of appointment of a successor trustee or trustees in the public records of the county in which the trust property is located. The declaration must be signed by a beneficiary or beneficiaries of the land trust and by the successor trustee or trustees, must be acknowledged in the manner provided for acknowledgment of deeds, and must contain:

1.   The legal description of the trust property.

2.   The name and address of the former trustee.

3.   The name and address of the successor trustee or trustees.

4.   A statement that one or more persons having the power of direction of the land trust appointed the successor trustee or trustees, together with an acceptance of appointment by the successor trustee or trustees.

(b)   If the recorded instrument is silent as to the appointment of a successor trustee or trustees of a land trust but an unrecorded trust agreement provides for the appointment of a successor trustee or trustees in the event of the death, incapacity, resignation, or termination due to dissolution of the trustee of a land trust, then upon the appointment of any successor trustee pursuant to the terms of the unrecorded trust agreement, the successor trustee or trustees shall file a declaration of appointment of a successor trustee in the public records of the county in which the trust property is located. The declaration must be signed by both the former trustee and the successor trustee or trustees, must be acknowledged in the manner provided for acknowledgment of deeds, and must contain:

1.   The legal description of the trust property.

2.   The name and address of the former trustee.

3.   The name and address of the successor trustee or trustees.

4.   A statement of resignation by the former trustee and a statement of acceptance of appointment by the successor trustee or trustees.

5.   A statement that the successor trustee or trustees were duly appointed under the terms of the unrecorded trust agreement.

If the appointment of any successor trustee of a land trust is due to the death or incapacity of the former trustee, the declaration need not be signed by the former trustee and a copy of the death certificate or a statement that the former trustee is incapacitated or unable to serve must be attached to or included in the declaration, as applicable.

(c)   If the recorded instrument provides for the appointment of any successor trustee of a land trust and any successor trustee is appointed in accordance with the recorded instrument, no additional declarations of appointment of any successor trustee are required under this section.

(d)   Each successor trustee appointed with respect to a land trust is fully vested with all the estate, properties, rights, powers, trusts, duties, and obligations of the predecessor trustee, except that any successor trustee of a land trust is not under any duty to inquire into the acts or omissions of a predecessor trustee and is not liable for any act or failure to act of a predecessor trustee. A person dealing with any successor trustee of a land trust pursuant to a declaration filed under this section is not obligated to inquire into or ascertain the authority of the successor trustee to act within or exercise the powers granted under the recorded instruments or any unrecorded trust agreement.

(e)   A trust agreement may provide that the trustee of a land trust, when directed to do so by the holder of the power of direction or by the beneficiaries of the land trust or legal representatives of the beneficiaries, may convey the trust property directly to another trustee on behalf of the beneficiaries or to another representative named in such directive.

(10)   TRUSTEE AS CREDITOR.—

(a)   If a debt is secured by a security interest or mortgage against a beneficial interest in a land trust or by a mortgage on trust property of a land trust, the validity or enforceability of the debt, security interest, or mortgage and the rights, remedies, powers, and duties of the creditor with respect to the debt or the security are not affected by the fact that the creditor and the trustee are the same person, and the creditor may extend credit, obtain any necessary security interest or mortgage, and acquire and deal with the property comprising the security as though the creditor were not the trustee.

(b)   A trustee of a land trust does not breach a fiduciary duty to the beneficiaries, and it is not evidence of a breach of any fiduciary duty owed by the trustee to the beneficiaries for a trustee to be or become a secured or unsecured creditor of the land trust, the beneficiary of the land trust, or a third party whose debt to such creditor is guaranteed by a beneficiary of the land trust.

(11)   NOTICES TO TRUSTEE.—Any notice required to be given to a trustee of a land trust regarding trust property by a person who is not a party to the trust agreement must identify the trust property to which the notice pertains or include the name and date of the land trust to which the notice pertains, if such information is shown on the recorded instrument for such trust property.

(12)   DETERMINATION OF APPLICABLE LAW.—Except as otherwise provided in this section, chapter 736 does not apply to a land trust governed by this section.

(a)   A trust is not a land trust governed by this section if there is no recorded instrument that confers on the trustee the power and authority prescribed in s. 689.073(1).

(b)   For a trust created before June 28, 2013:

1.   The trust is a land trust governed by this section if a recorded instrument confers on the trustee the power and authority described in s. 689.073(1) and if:

a.   The recorded instrument or the trust agreement expressly provides that the trust is a land trust; or

b.   The intent of the parties that the trust be a land trust is discerned from the trust agreement or the recorded instrument,

without regard to whether the trustee's duties under the trust agreement are greater than those limited duties described in paragraph (2)(c).

2.   The trust is not a land trust governed by this section if:

a.   The recorded instrument or the trust agreement expressly provides that the trust is to be governed by chapter 736, or by any predecessor trust code or other trust law other than this section; or

b.   The intent of the parties that the trust be governed by chapter 736, or by any predecessor trust code or other trust law other than this section, is discerned from the trust agreement or the recorded instrument,

without regard to whether the trustee's duties under the trust agreement are greater than those limited duties listed in paragraph (2)(c), and without consideration of any references in the trust agreement to provisions of chapter 736 made applicable to the trust by chapter 721, if the trust is a timeshare estate trust complying with s. 721.08(2)(c)4. or a vacation club trust complying with s. 721.53(1)(e).

3.   Solely for the purpose of determining the law governing a trust under subparagraph 1. or subparagraph 2., the determination shall be made without consideration of any amendment to the trust agreement made on or after June 28, 2013, except as provided in paragraph (d).

4.   If the determination of whether a trust is a land trust governed by this section cannot be made under either subparagraph 1. or subparagraph 2., the determination shall be made under paragraph (c) as if the trust was created on or after June 28, 2013.

(c)   If a recorded instrument confers on the trustee the power and authority described in s. 689.073(1) and the trust was created on or after June 28, 2013, the trust shall be determined to be a land trust governed by this section only if the trustee's duties under the trust agreement, including any amendment made on or after such date, are no greater than those limited duties described in paragraph (2)(c).

(d)   If the trust agreement for a land trust created before June 28, 2013, is amended on or after such date to add to or increase the duties of the trustee beyond the duties provided in the trust agreement as of June 28, 2013, the trust shall remain a land trust governed by this section only if the additional or increased duties of the trustee implemented by the amendment are no greater than those limited duties described in paragraph (2)(c).

(13)   UNIFORM COMMERCIAL CODE TRANSITION RULE.—This section does not render ineffective any effective Uniform Commercial Code financing statement filed before July 1, 2014, to perfect a security interest in a beneficial interest in a land trust that is determined to be real property as provided in subsection (6), but such a financing statement ceases to be effective at the earlier of July 1, 2019, or the time the financing statement would have ceased to be effective under the law of the jurisdiction in which it is filed, and the filing of a Uniform Commercial Code continuation statement after July 1, 2014, does not continue the effectiveness of such a financing statement. The recording of a mortgage, deed of trust, security agreement, or other similar security document against such a beneficial interest that is real property in the public records specified in paragraph (8)(c) continues the effectiveness and priority of a financing statement filed against such a beneficial interest before July 1, 2014, if:

(a)   The recording of the security document in that county is effective to perfect a lien on such beneficial interest under paragraph (8)(c);

(b)   The recorded security document identifies a financing statement filed before July 1, 2014, by indicating the office in which the financing statement was filed and providing the dates of filing and the file numbers, if any, of the financing statement and of the most recent continuation statement filed with respect to the financing statement; and

(c)   The recorded security document indicates that such financing statement filed before July 1, 2014, remains effective.

If no original security document bearing the debtor's signature is readily available for recording in the public records, a secured party may proceed under this subsection with such financing statement filed before July 1, 2014, by recording a copy of a security document verified by the secured party as being a true and correct copy of an original authenticated by the debtor. This subsection does not apply to the perfection of a security interest in any beneficial interest in a land trust that is determined to be personal property under subsection (6).

(14)   REMEDIAL ACT.—This act is remedial in nature and shall be given a liberal interpretation to effectuate the intent and purposes hereinabove expressed.

(15)   EXCLUSION.—This act does not apply to any deed, mortgage, or other instrument to which s. 689.07 applies.

History.—ss. 1, 2, 3, 4, 5, 6, ch. 63-468; s. 1, ch. 84-31; s. 2, ch. 2002-233; s. 21, ch. 2006-217; s. 1, ch. 2006-274; s. 7, ch. 2007-153; ss. 1, 2, 4, ch. 2013-240.

689.073 Powers conferred on trustee in recorded instrument.

(1) OWNERSHIP VESTS IN TRUSTEE.—Every conveyance, deed, mortgage, lease assignment, or other instrument heretofore or hereafter made, hereinafter referred to as the "recorded instrument," transferring any interest in real property, including, but not limited to, a leasehold or mortgagee interest, to any person or any corporation, bank, trust company, or other entity duly formed under the laws of its state of qualification, which recorded instrument designates the person, corporation, bank, trust company, or other entity "trustee" or "as trustee" and confers on the trustee the power and authority to protect, to conserve, to sell, to lease, to encumber, or otherwise to manage and dispose of the real property described in the recorded instrument, is effective to vest, and is declared to have vested, in such trustee full power and authority as granted and provided in the recorded instrument to deal in and with such property, or interest therein or any part thereof, held in trust under the recorded instrument.

(2) NO DUTY TO INQUIRE.—Any grantee, mortgagee, lessee, transferee, assignee, or person obtaining satisfactions or releases or otherwise in any way dealing with the trustee with respect to the real property or any interest in such property held in trust under the recorded instrument, as hereinabove provided for, is not obligated to inquire into the identification or status of any named or unnamed beneficiaries, or their heirs or assigns to whom a trustee may be accountable under the terms of the recorded instrument, or under any unrecorded separate declarations or agreements collateral to the recorded instrument, whether or not such declarations or agreements are referred to therein; or to inquire into or ascertain the authority of such trustee to act within and exercise the powers granted under the recorded instrument; or to inquire into the adequacy or disposition of any consideration, if any is paid or delivered to such trustee in connection with any interest so acquired from such trustee; or to inquire into any of the provisions of any such unrecorded declarations or agreements.

(3) BENEFICIARY CLAIMS.—All persons dealing with the trustee under the recorded instrument as hereinabove provided take any interest transferred by the trustee thereunder, within the power and authority as granted and provided therein, free and clear of the claims of all the named or unnamed beneficiaries of such trust, and of any unrecorded declarations or agreements collateral thereto whether referred to in the recorded instrument or not, and of anyone claiming by, through, or under such beneficiaries. However, this section does not prevent a beneficiary of any such unrecorded collateral declarations or agreements from enforcing the terms thereof against the trustee.

(4) EXCLUSION.—This section does not apply to any deed, mortgage, or other instrument to which s. 689.07 applies.

(5) APPLICABILITY.—The section applies without regard to whether any reference is made in the recorded instrument to the beneficiaries of such trust or to any separate collateral unrecorded declarations or agreements, without regard to the provisions of any unrecorded trust agreement or declaration of trust, and without regard to whether the trust is governed by s. 689.071 or chapter 736. This section applies both to recorded instruments

that are recorded after June 28, 2013, and to recorded instruments that were previously recorded and governed by similar provisions contained in s. 689.071(3), Florida Statutes 2012, and any such recorded instrument purporting to confer power and authority on a trustee under such provisions of s. 689.071(3), Florida Statutes 2012, is valid and has the effect of vesting full power and authority in such trustee as provided in this section.

History.—ss. 2, 3, ch. 63-468; s. 21, ch. 2006-217; ss. 1, 4, ch. 2013-240.

689.07 "Trustee" or "as trustee" added to name of grantee, transferee, assignee, or mortgagee transfers interest or creates lien as if additional word or words not used.

(1) Every deed or conveyance of real estate heretofore or hereafter made or executed in which the words "trustee" or "as trustee" are added to the name of the grantee, and in which no beneficiaries are named, the nature and purposes of the trust, if any, are not set forth, and the trust is not identified by title or date, shall grant and is hereby declared to have granted a fee simple estate with full power and authority in and to the grantee in such deed to sell, convey, and grant and encumber both the legal and beneficial interest in the real estate conveyed, unless a contrary intention shall appear in the deed or conveyance; provided, that there shall not appear of record among the public records of the county in which the real property is situate at the time of recording of such deed or conveyance, a declaration of trust by the grantee so described declaring the purposes of such trust, if any, declaring that the real estate is held other than for the benefit of the grantee.

(2) Every instrument heretofore or hereafter made or executed transferring or assigning an interest in real property in which the words "trustee" or "as trustee" are added to the name of the transferee or assignee, and in which no beneficiaries are named, the nature and purposes of the trust, if any, are not set forth, and the trust is not identified by title or date, shall transfer and assign, and is hereby declared to have transferred and assigned, the interest of the transferor or assign or to the transferee or assignee with full power and authority to transfer, assign, and encumber such interest, unless a contrary intention shall appear in the instrument; provided that there shall not appear of record among the public records of the county in which the real property is situate at the time of the recording of such instrument, a declaration of trust by the assignee or transferee so described declaring the purposes of such trust, if any, or declaring that the interest in real property is held other than for the benefit of the transferee or assignee.

(3) Every mortgage of any interest in real estate or assignment thereof heretofore or hereafter made or executed in which the words "trustee" or "as trustee" are added to the name of the mortgagee or assignee, and in which no beneficiaries are named, the nature and purposes of the trust, if any, are not set forth, and the trust is not identified by title or date, shall vest and is hereby declared to have vested full rights of ownership to such mortgage or assignment and the lien created thereby with full power in such mortgagee or assignee to assign, hypothecate, release, satisfy, or foreclose such mortgage unless a contrary intention shall appear in the mortgage or assignment; provided that there shall not appear of record among the public records of the county in which the property constituting security is situate at the time of recording of such mortgage or assignment, a declaration of trust by such mortgagee or assignee declaring the purposes of such trust, if any, or declaring that such mortgage is held other than for the benefit of the mortgagee or assignee.

(4) Nothing herein contained shall prevent any person from causing any declaration of trust to be recorded before or after the recordation of the instrument evidencing title or ownership of property in a trustee; nor shall this section be construed as preventing any beneficiary under an unrecorded declaration of trust from enforcing

the terms thereof against the trustee; provided, however, that any grantee, transferee, assignee, or mortgagee, or person obtaining a release or satisfaction of mortgage from such trustee for value prior to the placing of record of such declaration of trust among the public records of the county in which such real property is situate, shall take such interest or hold such previously mortgaged property free and clear of the claims of the beneficiaries of such declaration of trust and of anyone claiming by, through or under such beneficiaries, and such person need not see to the application of funds furnished to obtain such transfer of interest in property or assignment or release or satisfaction of mortgage thereon.

(5)   In all cases in which tangible personal property is or has been sold, transferred, or mortgaged in a transaction in conjunction with and subordinate to the transfer or mortgage of real property, and the personal property so transferred or mortgaged is physically located on and used in conjunction with such real property, the prior provisions of this section are applicable to the transfer or mortgage of such personal property, and, where the prior provisions of this section in fact apply to a transfer or mortgage of personal property, then any transferee or mortgagee of such tangible personal property shall take such personal property free and clear of the claims of the beneficiaries under such declaration of trust (if any), and of the claims of anyone claiming by, through, or under such beneficiaries, and the release or satisfaction of a mortgage on such personal property by such trustee shall release or satisfy such personal property from the claims of the beneficiaries under such declaration of trust, if any, and from the claims of anyone claiming by, through, or under such beneficiaries.

History.—s. 1, ch. 6925, 1915; s. 10, ch. 7838, 1919; RGS 3793; CGL 5666; s. 1, ch. 59-251; s. 1, ch. 2004-19.

736.0102 Scope.

(1) Except as otherwise provided in this section, this code applies to express trusts, charitable or noncharitable, and trusts created pursuant to a law, judgment, or decree that requires the trust to be administered in the manner of an express trust.

(2) This code does not apply to constructive or resulting trusts; conservatorships; custodial arrangements pursuant to the Florida Uniform Transfers to Minors Act; business trusts providing for certificates to be issued to beneficiaries; common trust funds; trusts created by the form of the account or by the deposit agreement at a financial institution; voting trusts; security arrangements; liquidation trusts; trusts for the primary purpose of paying debts, dividends, interest, salaries, wages, profits, pensions, or employee benefits of any kind; and any arrangement under which a person is nominee or escrowee for another.

(3) This code does not apply to any land trust under s. 689.071, except to the extent provided in s. 689.071(7), s. 721.08(2)(c)4., or s. 721.53(1)(e). A trust governed at its creation by this chapter, former chapter 737, or any prior trust statute superseded or replaced by any provision of former chapter 737, is not a land trust regardless of any amendment or modification of the trust, any change in the assets held in the trust, or any continuing trust resulting from the distribution or retention in further trust of assets from the trust.

History.—s. 1, ch. 2006-217; s. 10, ch. 2007-153; s. 3, ch. 2013-240.

736.08125 Protection of successor trustees.

(1)   A successor trustee is not personally liable for actions taken by any prior trustee, nor does any successor trustee have a duty to institute any proceeding against any prior trustee, or file any claim against any prior trustee's estate, for any of the prior trustee's actions as trustee under any of the following circumstances:

(a)   As to a successor trustee who succeeds a trustee who was also the settlor of a trust that was revocable during the time that the settlor served as trustee;

(b)   As to any beneficiary who has waived any accounting required by s. 736.0813, but only as to the periods included in the waiver;

(c)   As to any beneficiary who has released the successor trustee from the duty to institute any proceeding or file any claim;

(d)   As to any person who is not an eligible beneficiary; or

(e)   As to any eligible beneficiary:

1.   If a super majority of the eligible beneficiaries have released the successor trustee;

2.   If the eligible beneficiary has not delivered a written request to the successor trustee to institute an action or file a claim against the prior trustee within 6 months after the date of the successor trustee's acceptance of the trust, if the successor trustee has notified the eligible beneficiary in writing of acceptance by the successor trustee in accordance with s. 736.0813(1)(a) and that writing advises the beneficiary that, unless the beneficiary delivers the written request within 6 months after the date of acceptance, the right to proceed against the successor trustee will be barred pursuant to this section; or

3.   For any action or claim that the eligible beneficiary is barred from bringing against the prior trustee.

(2)   For the purposes of this section, the term:

(a)   "Eligible beneficiaries" means:

1.   At the time the determination is made, if there are one or more beneficiaries as described in s. 736.0103(19)(c), the beneficiaries described in s. 736.0103(19)(a) and (c); or

2.   If there is no beneficiary as described in s. 736.0103(19)(c), the beneficiaries described in s. 736.0103(19)(a) and (b).

(b)   "Super majority of eligible beneficiaries" means at least two-thirds in interest of the eligible beneficiaries if the interests of the eligible beneficiaries are reasonably ascertainable, otherwise, at least two-thirds in number of the eligible beneficiaries.

(3)   Nothing in this section affects any liability of the prior trustee or the right of the successor trustee or any beneficiary to pursue an action or claim against the prior trustee.

History.—s. 8, ch. 2006-217; s. 19, ch. 2013-172; s. 42, ch. 2021-183.

736.1013 Limitation on personal liability of trustee.

(1)   Except as otherwise provided in the contract, a trustee is not personally liable on a contract properly entered into in the trustee's fiduciary capacity in the course of administering the trust if the trustee in the contract disclosed the fiduciary capacity.

(2)   A trustee is personally liable for torts committed in the course of administering a trust or for obligations arising from ownership or control of trust property only if the trustee is personally at fault.

(3)   A claim based on a contract entered into by a trustee in the trustee's fiduciary capacity, on an obligation arising from ownership or control of trust property, or on a tort committed in the course of administering a trust may be asserted in a judicial proceeding against the trustee in the trustee's fiduciary capacity, whether or not the trustee is personally liable for the claim.

(4)   Issues of liability between the trust estate and the trustee individually may be determined in a proceeding for accounting, surcharge, or indemnification or in any other appropriate proceeding.

History.—s. 10, ch. 2006-217.

Administrative Code

12B-4.013 Conveyances Subject to Tax.

(1) Exchange of Property: In an exchange of real property by the respective owners of the property exchanged, lands are given as consideration for the transfer of other lands between the parties. The consideration has a reasonably determinable value, (DeVore v. Gay, 39 So. 2d 796 (Fla. 1949)) and is property other than money. The consideration for each deed is the fair market value of the property transferred up by the transferor plus any other consideration given.

(2) Defaulting Mortgagor: Where a mortgagor, in full or partial satisfaction of the mortgage indebtedness or in lieu of foreclosure of a mortgage, conveys the mortgaged premises to the mortgagee, documentary stamp taxes are due on the transaction. The tax will be due on the unpaid portion of any mortgages or other encumbrances the property is subject to, plus any other consideration as defined in Section 201.02(1), F.S., including accrued interest.

(3)(a) Clerk of the Court, Master, Sheriff. A conveyance by a master in chancery, a sheriff, or a clerk of the court for realty sold under foreclosure or execution is subject to tax. The tax is computed on the amount of the highest and best bid received for the property at the foreclosure sale. The Clerk of the Court is required to collect the tax from the highest bidder when the Certificate of Title is recorded.

(b) The documentary stamp taxes cannot reduce the claim of the mortgagee when the mortgagee is an agent of the federal government. The mortgagor is liable for the payment of the tax from any funds paid to the mortgagor after the payment of prior claims of, or in connection with the foreclosure. (1960 Op. Att'y. Gen. Fla. 060-125 (July 29, 1960))

Cross Reference – subsection 12B-4.013(6), F.A.C.

(4) Eminent Domain Proceedings, Threat of: Conveyances of realty made to a governmental entity under threat of condemnation or as part of an out-of-court settlement of condemnation proceedings are not subject to documentary stamp tax. Threat of condemnation exists when a property owner is informed in writing by a representative of a governmental body or public official authorized to acquire property for public use, that such body or official has decided to acquire the property and the property owner has reasonable grounds to believe that the necessary steps to condemn the property will be instituted if a voluntary sale is not arranged. Conveyances to nongovernmental entities are subject to tax.

Cross-Reference – subsection 12B-4.014(13), F.A.C.

(5) State, County, Municipality: Conveyance to or by the state, a county, a municipality or other public agency to or by a non-exempt party is subject to tax. The state, county, municipality or other public agency is exempt from payment of tax but the non-exempt party is not exempt. (1936 Op. Att'y. Gen. Fla. 1935-36 Biennial Report, Page 29 (April 10, 1936); 1962 Op. Att'y. Gen. Fla. 062-150 (Nov. 8, 1962); 1968 Op. Att'y. Gen. Fla. 068-10 (Jan. 19, 1968); 1971 Op. Att'y. Gen. Fla. 071-100 (May 12, 1971))

Cross Reference – subsection 12B-4.002(3), F.A.C.

(6) United States, Its Agencies or Instrumentalities: Conveyance to the United States, its agencies or instrumentalities from non-exempt party, except as provided in subsection 12A-4.014(11), F.A.C., is subject to tax. (1960 Op. Att'y. Gen. Fla. 060-125 (July 29, 1960); 1961 Op. Att'y. Gen. Fla. 061-84 (May 19, 1961); 1961 Op. Att'y. Gen. Fla. 061-122 (Aug. 1, 1961); 1965 Op. Att'y. Gen. Fla. 065-59 (July 15, 1965); 1971 Op. Att'y. Gen. Fla. 071-100 (May 12, 1971))

(7) Timber, Oil, Gas, and Mineral – Contracts or Assignments: Contracts, agreements, leases, and other documents conveying any interest in standing timber, pine stumps, oil or gas leases and assignments or conveyances of oil, gas, mineral rights or royalty interests affecting lands in this state are subject to tax. (1945 Op. Att'y. Gen. Fla. 045-328 (Oct. 19, 1945); 1950 Op. Att'y. Gen. Fla. 050-140 (Mar. 22, 1950); 1962 Op. Att'y. Gen. Fla. 062-114 (Aug. 29, 1962); 1971 Op. Att'y. Gen. Fla. 071-30 (Feb. 19, 1971))

(8) Cooperative Units: Instruments by which the right is granted to a tenant-stockholder to occupy a unit owned by a cooperative corporation are subject to tax.

Cross Reference – subsection 12B-4.011(2), F.A.C.

(9) Condominium Units: Instruments conveying interest or ownership in a condominium unit are subject to tax.

(10) Cemetery Lots, Interment Rights, Sepulcher Rights: Documents conveying cemetery lots, interment rights, sepulcher rights or any other interest in realty are subject to tax. (1932 Op. Att'y. Gen. Fla. 1931-32 Biennial Report, Page 1000 (June 11, 1932); 1970 Op. Att'y. Gen. Fla. 070-169 (Dec. 4, 1970))

(11) Easements: Easements constitute transfers of interest in realty are subject to tax. (Letter from Att'y. Gen. Fla. to State Comptroller (April 15, 1932))

(12) Banks: Conveyances executed to or by State or National banks are subject to tax.

(13) Savings and Loan Associations: Conveyances executed to or by savings and loan associations are subject to tax.

(14) Agreement or Contract for Deed: Consideration for the conveyance of an equitable interest in real property pursuant to an agreement or contract for deed includes the amount of any payments made and the unpaid balance of the agreement or contract. Tax is therefore calculated on the full contract price and tax shall be paid on the contract when made. No stamp tax is due on the recorded deed made when the proper amount of taxes have been paid on the contract. The deed shall indicate, by notation on the contract, that the proper amount of stamp tax has been paid. The agreement may also be subject to tax under Section 201.08, F.S. (1959 Op. Att'y. Gen. Fla. 059-244 rev. (Feb. 25, 1960); 1970 Op. Att'y. Gen. Fla. 070-171 (Dec. 8, 1970))

(15) Cancellation of Contract or Agreement for Deed: A conveyance of the purchaser's interest to the seller in satisfaction of the purchaser's obligation under a contract or agreement for deed where the indebtedness of the purchaser is canceled or otherwise rendered unenforceable is subject to tax. The measure of the tax payable is determined by the amount of the indebtedness canceled or otherwise rendered unenforceable and any other consideration given by the seller. (1960 Op. Att'y. Gen. Fla. 060-165 (Oct. 11, 1960))

Cross Reference – subsection 12B-4.014(12), F.A.C.

(16) Assignment of Contract for Deed: The assignment of a prior purchaser's interest under a contract or agreement for deed to a new purchaser is a conveyance of an equitable interest which the prior purchaser had in the real property. Consideration for the transfer includes the amount paid by the new purchaser and the unpaid balance of the contract for deed. Tax is due based on the total consideration. No stamp tax is due on the recorded deed when the proper amount of tax has been paid on the assignment. The deed shall indicate by notation that proper stamp tax has been paid. Tax is also due under Section 201.08, F.S., if the remaining balance of the contract is assumed by the new purchaser. (1959 Op. Att'y. Gen. Fla. 059-244 Rev. (Feb. 25, 1960); Department of Revenue v. Mesmer, 345 So. 2d 384 (Fla. 1st DCA 1977))

(17) Industrial Development Authority and Florida Housing Finance Corporation: Conveyances of realty by industrial development authorities and the Florida Housing Finance Corporation to private corporations are taxable.

Cross Reference – subsection 12B-4.054(26), F.A.C.

(18) Gift Transactions; Mortgage on Property: A gift of mortgaged realty is taxable based upon the unpaid balance of the mortgage at the time of transfer.

(19) Combined Sale of Land and Improvements: Where conveyance of realty is made by a corporation or person engaged in the business of land sales and construction of buildings and other improvements, stamp tax is imposed on the conveyance based on the amount of consideration paid or to be paid upon delivery of the deed to the purchaser. If the deed is not delivered to the purchaser until construction is completed, stamp tax is required on the total consideration paid for the land and improvements, regardless of the date of recordation. However, proper stamp tax shall be paid when the deed is recorded.

(20) "Wrap-Around" Mortgages: Where a "wrap-around" mortgage is given to secure the unpaid balance of the purchase price for the transfer of realty, documentary stamp tax is to be paid on the total consideration which shall include the amount of any "wrap-around" mortgage. (Department of Revenue v. Brookwood Associates, Limited, 324 So. 2d 184 (Fla. 1st DCA 1975))

(21) Mortgage on Property: When computing the tax under Section 201.02, F.S., on a deed of conveyance, the total consideration includes any mortgages encumbering the property being transferred.

Cross Reference – subsections 12B-4.013(7), (8), (10) and (31), F.A.C.

(22) Mobile Homes: A mobile home which has been permanently affixed to land and taxed as real property is issued an "RP" series license plate by the appropriate county tax collector. Tax applies to the sale of mobile homes in the following manner:

(a) When a mobile home is affixed to realty, bears an "RP" license tag and is sold in conjunction with the sale of realty as a package deal, the transaction constitutes the transfer of an interest in real property and is taxable under Chapter 201, F.S., and the instrument by which the interest in real property is transferred must evidence payment of documentary stamp tax and surtax levied under Chapter 201, F.S., based upon the consideration paid.

(b) When a mobile home is affixed to realty and bears an "MH" tag or is untagged, the sale of the mobile home does not constitute the transfer of an interest in real property even though the land is sold in conjunction with the mobile home. However, the land which is sold in conjunction with the sale of the mobile home is taxable under Chapter 201, F.S., based upon the fair market value of the land conveyed and the instrument by which the interest in the real property is conveyed must evidence payment of documentary stamp tax and surtax levied under Chapter 201, F.S., based upon the consideration paid.

(c) Where members of a mobile home park have practical dominion over designated sites on which a mobile home is located which is essentially equivalent to ownership, each member's interest in the site on which his home is affixed constitutes "ownership" rendering mobile homes taxable as real property. Therefore, any instruments transferring interest, ownership or membership in a site owned by a cooperative mobile home corporation are subject to tax. Mikos v. King's Gate Club, Inc., 426 So. 2d 74 (Fla. 2nd DCA, 1983); Nordbeck v. Williamson, 529 So. 2d 360 (Fla. 2nd DCA 1988).

(23) Assignment of Lease or Other Conveyance of Leasehold Interest in Realty: All assignments of leases or other conveyances of leasehold interests in real property are taxable under Section 201.02, F.S., based upon the consideration paid, including leasehold mortgages encumbering the interest conveyed. However, mortgages encumbering the fee title are not consideration, except when assumed by the assignee.

(24) Assignment of Successful Bid – An interest in realty transferred or conveyed by assignment of successful bid at a foreclosure sale is taxable under Section 201.02, F.S.

(25) Assignment of Beneficial Interest in Trust created under Chapter 689, F.S.: Effective July 3, 1979, any document which conveys any beneficial interest in a trust agreement is subject to tax, and the tax is to be paid upon execution of the document. The provision in Section 689.071(4), F.S., which defines the interest of a beneficiary under a trust agreement to be personal property only, does not exempt a transfer of the beneficial interest in the trust from documentary stamp tax. Tax is due on any assignment of a beneficial interest in a trust created under Chapter 689, F.S., based on the consideration paid for such assignment.

(26) Construction Mortgage: When realty is conveyed subject to a construction mortgage, the deed is subject to tax based upon the unpaid balance of the mortgage debt at the time of conveyance, in addition to any other consideration given.

(27) Deeds Between Spouses.

(a) A deed that transfers any interest in Florida real property between spouses is taxable based on the consideration for the property interest transferred. When the property is encumbered, the consideration includes the mortgage balance in proportion to the interest transferred.

(b) No tax is due on a deed that transfers the marital home, or an interest therein, between spouses or former spouses pursuant to an action for dissolution of marriage when the transfer is made at the time of or following divorce. The marital home means the primary residence of the married couple. Tax is due on a deed that transfers the marital home, or an interest therein, between spouses when the transfer is made prior to the final dissolution of the marriage. Tax paid on such deed within one year prior to the final dissolution of the marriage may be refunded.

To request a refund, a completed Form DR-26, Application for Refund, must be submitted with proof of payment of the tax, including a copy of the final divorce decree. Proof that the real property was the marital home is also required.

(c) No tax is due on a deed that transfers any interest in homestead property between spouses, when the only consideration for the transfer is the amount of a mortgage or other lien encumbering the homestead property at the time of the transfer. When there is consideration other than a mortgage or other lien encumbering the homestead property, tax is due on the total consideration including any mortgages or liens encumbering the property at the time of the transfer. For the purpose of this paragraph, the term "homestead property" has the same meaning as the term "homestead" as defined in Section 192.001, F.S., and s. 6(a), Art. VII of the State Constitution.

(28) Trusts Pursuant to Chapter 689, F.S.: A deed to or from a trustee conveying real property is taxable to the extent that the deed transfers the beneficial ownership of the real property and to the extent that there is consideration for the transfer. The following are examples of taxable and exempt conveyances to or from a trustee.

(a) No change in Beneficial Ownership: A deed from X to a trustee is exempt from the stamp tax to the extent of X's beneficial ownership interest as a trust beneficiary, whether or not the real property is encumbered by a mortgage. For example, if X owns encumbered or unencumbered real property and conveys it to the trustee of a trust of which X is the sole beneficiary, the conveyance is exempt from the stamp tax.

(b) Change in Beneficial Ownership: If persons other than X are trust beneficiaries, then a deed from X to a trustee is taxable to the extent of the consideration, if any, for the beneficial interest in the real property transferred to such other persons. The stamp tax is based on any cash, note, release or other consideration from the trust beneficiaries other than X, including their proportionate share of any mortgage encumbering the real property. For example, if X owns unencumbered real property valued at $100 and X conveys the property to the trustee of a trust of which X and Y are each 50% beneficiaries, and Y pays $50 cash for the conveyance to the trustee, then stamp tax would be due based on a consideration of $50.

(c) Gift in Trust: A deed from X to a trustee is exempt from the stamp tax if persons other than X are trust beneficiaries, the transfer is a gift from X to those beneficiaries, and the real property is not encumbered by any mortgage. If the real property is encumbered by any mortgage, then the stamp tax is based on the other beneficiaries' proportionate share of the mortgage indebtedness allocated according to their respective percentage beneficial interest. For example, if X owns real property valued at $100 which is encumbered by a mortgage of $50 and X conveys the property to the trustee of a trust of which X and X's daughter are each 50% beneficiaries, and there is no consideration other than the mortgage, then stamp tax would be due based on a consideration of $25 (one-half of the mortgage indebtedness).

(d) Successor or Substitute Trustee: A deed from a trustee to a successor or substitute trustee of the same trust is not subject to the stamp tax.

(e) Trustee's Deed to Beneficiary: A deed of real property from a trustee to X is not subject to the stamp tax to the extent of X's beneficial ownership interest as a trust beneficiary immediately before the conveyance, whether or not the real property is encumbered by a mortgage. Except as provided in paragraph (f) of this rule below, however, the stamp tax applies to the extent that the trustee transfers to X an ownership interest in the real property greater than X's percentage beneficial ownership interest as a trust beneficiary immediately before the transfer, based on the consideration, if any, for the transfer of the additional interest, including the proportionate share of any mortgage indebtedness encumbering the additional percentage interest in the real property transferred to X by the trustee. For example, if X and X's spouse are each beneficiaries of a trust of which X owns 60% interest and X's spouse owns 40% interest and the trustee conveys to X real property valued at $100 which is encumbered by a mortgage of $50, and there is no consideration other than the mortgage, then stamp tax would be due based on a consideration of $20 (40% of the mortgage indebtedness).

(f) Trustee's Power to Apportion: When trust beneficiaries hold undivided percentage interests in the corpus of the trust rather than specific interests in each parcel of real property held in the trust, and a trust instrument grants the trustee the power to apportion and distribute the various assets of the trust among the beneficiaries, then stamp tax is due on the conveyance of real property from the trustee to a beneficiary only to the extent that the value of that real property exceeds the value of the beneficiary's undivided percentage interest in the trust. For example, a grantor conveys Blackacre and Whiteacre to a trustee for the benefit of the grantor's two children, X and Y, who each have an undivided 50% interest in the trust. The terms of the trust provide that when both X and Y reach 21 years of age, the trustee will liquidate the trust and distribute the assets of the trust between X and Y as the trustee shall determine provided that each beneficiary shall receive property of approximately equal value. Blackacre and Whiteacre are equal in value when X and Y reach 21, and the trustee conveys Blackacre to X and Whiteacre to Y. Stamp tax is due on the initial conveyance from the grantor to the trustee to the extent of any taxable consideration, such as a mortgage on the property (see foregoing paragraph (c) of this rule), but no stamp tax is due on the subsequent conveyances from the trustee to X and Y, regardless of whether any mortgage then encumbers the property.

(g) Trustee's Deed to Non-Beneficiary: The stamp tax applies to a trustee's deed of real property to grantees that are not beneficial owners as trust beneficiaries immediately before the conveyance, to the extent of the consideration given, if any, for the interest in the real property transferred to the non-beneficiary grantees. The stamp tax is based on any cash, note, release or other consideration from the non-beneficiary grantees, including their proportionate share of any mortgage encumbering the real property. For example, if X is the sole beneficiary of a trust and the trustee conveys to X and Y, as 50% tenants-in-common, real property valued at $100 which is encumbered by a mortgage of $60, and Y pays $20 cash for Y's 50% interest in the property, then stamp tax would be due based on the consideration of $50 ($20 cash plus 50% of the mortgage indebtedness).

(h) Identity of Parties; Nature of Trust: All conveyances to or from a trustee are equally taxable or exempt as provided in this rule, regardless of:

1. Whether the trustee is the same person as grantor, grantee, or beneficiary,

2. Whether the trustee or grantor or grantee or beneficiary is a natural person or an entity, and,

3. Whether a recorded instrument confers on the trustee the powers and authority specified in Section 689.07 1(1), F.S., or declares the interest of the beneficiaries is personal property as specified in Section 689.071(4), F.S.

(i) Revocable Trust: A deed to a trustee from a grantor who has the power to revoke the trust instrument, and a deed back to the grantor from the trustee upon revocation of the trust, are not transfers of ownership subject to the stamp tax.

Rulemaking Authority 201.11, 213.06(1) FS. Law Implemented 201.01, 201.02 FS. History–New 8-18-73, Formerly 12A-4.13, Amended 12-11-74, 2-21-77, 5-23-77, 12-26-77, 7-3-79, 9-16-79, 11-29-79, 3-27-80, 12-23-80, 12-30-82, Formerly 12B-4.13, Amended 12-5-89, 6-4-90, 2-13-91, 2-16-93, 10-18-94, 12-30-97, 7-28-98, 1-4-01, 5-4-03, 4-5-07, 7-30-13, 12-12-19.

12D-7.011 Homestead Exemptions – Trusts.

The beneficiary of a passive or active trust has equitable title to real property if he is entitled to the use and occupancy of such property under the terms of the trust; therefore, he has sufficient title to claim homestead exemption. AGO 90-70. Homestead tax exemption may not be based upon residence of a beneficiary under a trust instrument which vests no present possessory right in such beneficiary.

Rulemaking Authority 195.027(1), 213.06(1) FS. Law Implemented 196.001, 196.031, 196.041 FS. History–New 10-12-76, Formerly 12D-7.11, Amended 2-25-96.

Appendix - B
Checklists

The following checklists should make the steps in each procedure easier to follow:

1. Land Trust Formation Checklist

2. Mortgage of Land Trust Property Checklist

3. Pledge of Land Trust Beneficial Interest Checklist

4. Sale of Land Trust Beneficial Interest Checklist

5. Sale of Land Trust Property and Closing Trust Checklist

Land Trust Formation Checklist

1. Complete Land Trust Data Sheet ☐

2. Check beneficiary for RICO liens ☐

3. Check mortgage for due-on-sale clause ☐

3a. Obtain approval for transfer if necessary ☐

4. Check with Property Appraiser if homestead exemption desired ☐

5. Check with insurance agent for proper beneficiary designation ☐

6. Deed to Trustee

prepared ☐

executed ☐

recorded ☐

7. Trust Agreement

prepared ☐

executed ☐

8. Beneficiary Agreement

prepared ☐

executed ☐

9. Trust certificates (if needed/desired)

prepared ☐

executed ☐

10. If foreign beneficiary, comply with all laws ☐

11. IRS Form 56 or equivalent

prepared ☐

executed ☐

filed ☐

12. Copies distributed to all parties ☐

Mortgage of Land Trust Property Checklist

1. Direction to Trustee

   prepared ☐

   executed by beneficiary ☐

   2. Promissory Note

   prepared ☐

   executed by beneficiary ☐

   3. Mortgage

   prepared ☐

   executed by trustee ☐

   recorded ☐

Pledge of Land Trust Beneficial Interest Checklist

1. Promissory Note

   prepared ☐

   executed by beneficiary ☐

2. Security Agreement

   prepared ☐

   executed by beneficiary ☐

3. Collateral Assmt of B.I.

   prepared ☐

   executed by beneficiary ☐

4. UCC-1

   prepared ☐

   filed ☐

Sale of Land Trust Beneficial Interest Checklist

1. Assignment of B. I.

   prepared ☐

   executed by beneficiary, assignee, and trustee ☐

2. Form DR-228

   prepared ☐

   executed ☐

   filed ☐

3. Form DR-430

   prepared ☐

   executed ☐

   filed ☐

4. IRS Form 56 (terminate old)

   prepared ☐

   executed by trustee ☐

   filed ☐

5. IRS Form 56 (new beneficiary)

   prepared ☐

   executed by trustee ☐

   filed ☐

Sale of Land Trust Property and Closing Trust Checklist

1. Direction to trustee

   prepared ☐

   executed ☐

   2. Send instructions to closing agent ☐

   3. Check that trustee fees are current ☐

   4. Obtain RICO lien search on beneficiary ☐

   5. Deed

   prepared ☐

   executed ☐

   recorded ☐

   6. Closing documents

   prepared ☐

   rubber stamp exculpatory clause ☐

   executed ☐

   7. If foreign beneficiary comply with all laws ☐

   8. IRS Form 56

   prepared ☐

   executed ☐

   filed ☐

   9. Copies distributed to all parties ☐

Appendix - C

Forms

This appendix contains forms that can be used to set up and maintain land trusts.

You should not use them unless you have read this book and the forms and understand them completely. If you do not understand them, you should consult an attorney knowledgeable about land trusts.

These forms are basic in nature and are not intended to be relied upon as legal advice. They are not identical to the forms that the authors use in their own trustee business or law practice. Forms and provisions change from time to time, and the authors do not undertake to provide any notice of revisions, amendments, updates, or deletions of any forms — or any portion thereof — provided here.

The formatting of the forms may be incorrectly rendered in electronic versions or even print versions of this book. For this reason, these forms are also available in Word format from the publisher. To order access to the forms or additional copies of this book, visit www.landtrustbook.com

Form 1 – Land Trust Data Sheet

Trust # or Name   Date

   Trustee   Address & Phone   Trustee's compensation   Successor trustee

Address & Phone   Alternate successor

   Address & Phone

   Beneficiaries:

   Name 1: _____

     %   SS#   Address   Phone   Email _____

   Name 2: _____

     %   SS#   Address   Phone   Email _____

   ☐ Husband & wife in estate by the entireties

   Successor Beneficiaries:

   Name 1: _____

     %   SS#   Address   Phone

   Email   _____

   Name 2: _____

     %   SS#   Address   Phone

   Email   _____

   Property going into trust:

   Street Address_____   Legal Description   _____

   Tax Parcel #   County

   Mortgagee   Loan Number _____ Balance   _____

   Second Mortgagee   Loan Number _____ Balance _____

    I/we certify that the above information is true, that the land trust is not being set up for any illegal or criminal purpose, that I am / we are U.S. residents for tax purposes, and that I/we agree to indemnify the trustee for any liability regarding this trust.

_____

   Signatures of Acknowledgment

Form 2 – Warranty Deed to Trustee

Prepared by/When recorded, return to:

No title search, examination, or assurance requested nor provided in preparation of this instrument

WARRANTY DEED TO TRUSTEE UNDER LAND TRUST NO. _____

THIS WARRANTY DEED made this {$Day} day of {$Month}, {$Year} by {$Grantor1} and {$Grantor2}, a {$GrantorMaritalStatus} hereinafter called "Grantor," to {$TrusteeName}, {$TrusteeStatus}, as Trustee under Land Trust No. _____ dated _____ (hereinafter referred to as "Trustee") with full power and authority to protect, conserve and to sell, or to lease or to encumber, or to otherwise manage and dispose of the property hereinafter described and whose Post Office address is: {$TrusteeStreetAddress}, {$TrusteeCityStateZip}.

WITNESSETH:

That the Grantor, for and in consideration of love and affection, and other good and valuable consideration, receipt of which is hereby acknowledged, hereby grants, bargains, sells, aliens, remises, releases, conveys and confirms unto Trustee, all that certain land situate in {$PropCounty} County, Florida, to-wit:

See Exhibit A attached hereto and by Reference incorporated herein.

Note to Examiner: This deed is exempt from documentary stamp taxes pursuant to 12 FL ADC 12B-4.013(2 8)(a).

This conveyance is subject to:

1. Taxes and Assessments for the year {$Year} and subsequent years.

2. Zoning and other governmental regulations.

TO HAVE AND TO HOLD the above-described real estate in fee simple with the appurtenances upon the trust and for the purposes set forth in this Deed and in Land Trust Number _____ dated _____ (Trust Agreement).

Full power and authority is hereby granted to said Trustee to improve, subdivide, protect, conserve, sell, lease, encumber and otherwise manage and dispose of said property or any part thereof, to hold mortgages and notes, to foreclose, to dedicate parks, streets, highways or alleys and to vacate any subdivision or part thereof, and to re-subdivide said property as often as desired, to contract to sell, to grant options to purchase, to sell on any terms, to convey either with or without consideration, to convey said property or any part thereof to a successor or successors in trust and to grant to such successor or successors in trust all of the title, estate, powers and authorities vested in said trustee, to donate, to dedicate, to mortgage, pledge or otherwise encumber said property, or any part thereof, to lease said property, or any part thereof, from time to time, in possession or reversion, by leases to commence in present or future, and upon any terms and for any period or periods of time, not exceeding in the case of any single demise the term of 99 years, and to renew or extend leases upon any terms and for any period or periods of time and to amend, change or modify leases and the terms and provisions thereof at any time or times hereafter, to contract to make leases and to grant options to lease and options to renew leases and options to purchase the whole or in any part of the reversion and to contract respecting the manner of fixing the amount of present or future rentals, to partition or to exchange said property, or any part thereof, for other real or personal property, to submit said property or any part thereof to condominium, to place restrictions on the property or any part thereof, to grant easements or charges of any kind, to release, convey or assign any right, title or interest in or about or easement appurtenant to said premises or any part thereof and to deal with said property and every part thereof in all other ways, and for such other considerations as it would be lawful for any person owning the same to deal with the same, whether similar to or different from the ways above specified, at any time or times hereafter.

In no case shall any party dealing with the Trustee in relation to the real estate or to whom the real estate or any part of it shall be conveyed, contracted to be sold, leased or mortgaged by Trustee, be obliged to see to the application of any purchase money, rent or money borrowed or advanced on the premises, or be obliged to see that the terms of this trust have been complied with, or be obliged to inquire into the necessity or expediency of any act of the Trustee, or be obliged or privileged to inquire into any of the terms of the Trust Agreement or Declaration of Trust or the identification or status of any named or unnamed beneficiaries, or their heirs or assigns to whom the Trustee may be accountable; and every deed, trust deed, mortgage, lease or other instrument executed by Trustee in relation to the real estate shall be conclusive evidence in favor of every person relying upon or claiming under any such conveyance, lease or other instrument (a) that at the time of its delivery the trust created by this Indenture and by the Trust Agreement and Declaration of Trust was in full force and effect, (b) that the conveyance or other instrument was executed in accordance with the trusts, conditions and limitations contained in this Indenture and in the Trust Agreement and Declaration of Trust and is binding upon all beneficiaries under those instruments, (c) that Trustee was duly authorized and empowered to execute and deliver every such deed, trust deed, lease, mortgage or other instrument and (d) if the conveyance is made to a successor or successors in trust, that the successor or successors in trust have been appointed properly and vested fully with all the title, estate, rights, powers, duties and obligations of the predecessor in trust. If there are co-trustees, it is specifically understood that the signature of only one of the Co-Trustees shall be required to accomplish the foregoing.

Any contract, obligation or indebtedness incurred or entered into by Trustee in connection with said property shall be as Trustee of an express trust and not individually and the Trustees shall have no obligations whatsoever with respect to any such contract, obligation or indebtedness except only as far as the trust property and funds in the actual possession of Trustee shall be applicable for the payment and discharge thereof; and it shall be expressly understood that any representations, warranties, covenants, undertakings and agreements hereinafter made on the part of the Trustee, while in form purporting to be the representations, warranties, covenants, undertakings and agreements of said Trustee, are nevertheless made and intended not as persona representations, warranties, covenants, undertakings and agreements by the Trustee or for the purpose or with the intention of binding said Trustee personally, but are made and intended for the purpose of binding only the trust property specifically described herein; and that no personal liability or personal responsibility is assumed by nor shall at any time be asserted or enforceable against the trustee individually on account of any instrument executed by or on account of any representation warranty, covenant, undertaking or agreement of the said Trustee, either expressed or implied, all such personal liability, if any, being expressly waived and released and all persons and corporations whomsoever and whatsoever shall be charged with notice of this condition from the date of the filing for record of this Deed.

In the event of the death or dissolution of the Trustee, the successor trustee under the trust agreement referred to above shall be Land Trust Service Corporation, and upon a recording in the public records of {$PropCounty} County, Florida, of a death certificate or certificate of dissolution of the Trustee or of any successor trustee, title to the land described herein shall be deemed to be held by the successor trustee and to pass to the successor trustee without the requirement of recording any further or additional documents.

This deed is given and accepted in accordance with Sections 689.071 and 689.073, Florida Statutes. The Trustee shall have no personal liability whatsoever for action as trustee under the trust agreement referred to above or by virtue of taking title to the land described above and the sole liability of Trustee hereunder shall be limited to the property which the Trustee holds under the trust agreement referred to above.

{DELETE THIS PARAGRAPH IF THE PROPERTY WILL NOT BE THE BENEFICIARY'S HOME-STEAD} NOTE TO EXAMINER: The Beneficiaries reserve the right to reside upon any real property placed in this Trust as the Beneficiaries' permanent residence during the Beneficiaries' life, it being the intent of this provision to retain for the Beneficiaries' the requisite beneficial interest and possessory right in and to such real property to comply with Sections 193.1554(b)(5) and 194.041 of the Florida Statutes such that said beneficiary interest and possessory right constitute in all respects "equitable title to the real estate" as that term is used in Section 6, Article VII of the Constitution of the State of Florida. Notwithstanding anything contained in this Trust inconsistent with this provision, the Beneficiaries' interest in any real property in which the Beneficiaries' reside pursuant to the provisions of this Trust shall be deemed to be an interest in real property and not personalty, and shall be deemed to be the homestead of the Beneficiary.

And the Grantor by this Deed fully warrants the title to the above-described real estate and will defend the title against the lawful claims of all persons whomsoever. "Grantor", "Grantee", "Trustee", and "Beneficiary" are used for singular or plural, as context requires.

IN WITNESS WHEREOF, the Grantor aforesaid has set its hand and seal this Day and Year set forth above.

Signed, sealed, and delivered in the presence of:

_____ Witness #1

Printed Name: _____

Address:_____

_____ Witness #2

Printed Name: _____

Address:_____

_____

{$Grantor1}

{$Grantor1Mailing}

_____

{$Grantor2}

{$Grantor2Mailing}

STATE OF _____

COUNTY OF _____

The foregoing instrument was acknowledged before me by means of [ ] physical presence or [ ] online notarization, this _____ day of _____, _____ by {$Grantor1} and {$Grantor2} whom I know personally or who produced _____ as identification.

_____ [Notary Seal]

Notary Public – State of _____

My Commission Expires:

EXHIBIT"A"

{$LegalDesc}

Tax Parcel ID: {$PropAppraiserNo}

Form 3 – Quitclaim Deed to Trustee

QUITCLAIM DEED TO TRUSTEE

THIS QUIT CLAIM DEED Made this   day of , 20 , by

and   Grantors, to

as Trustee under Trust No.   dated

, 20 with full power and authority, to protect, conserve, sell, lease, encumber or otherwise manage and dispose of said property pursuant to Florida Statutes sections 689.071 and 689.073, Grantee, whose post office address is

.

WITNESSETH, that the said first party, for and in consideration of the sum of

$10.00 in hand paid by the said second party, the receipt whereof, is hereby acknowledged does hereby remise, release and quitclaim unto the said second party forever, all the right, title, interest, claim and demand which the said first party has in and to the following described lot, piece, or parcel of land, to wit:

Tax Parcel I.D. No.

TO HAVE AND TO HOLD the same together with all and singular the appurtenances thereunto belonging or in anywise appertaining and all the estate, right, title, interest, lien, equity and claim whatsoever of said first party, either in law or equity, to the only proper use, benefit and behoof of the said second party forever.

THE INTEREST of the beneficiaries under said trust is personal property. Persons dealing with the Trustee are not obligated to look to the application of purchase monies. The interest of the beneficiaries is solely in the rights proceeds and avails of trust property, not in the title, legal or, equitable, of said real estate. The liability of the Trustee under this deed and the trust agreement, is limited to the assets of the trust and the Trustee hereunder has no personal liability whatsoever.

Signed, sealed, and delivered in the presence of:

_____ Witness #1

Printed Name: _____

Address:_____

_____ Witness #2

Printed Name: _____

Address:_____

_____

{$Grantor1}

{$Grantor1Mailing}

_____

{$Grantor2}

{$Grantor2Mailing}

STATE OF _____

COUNTY OF _____

The foregoing instrument was acknowledged before me by means of [ ] physical presence or [ ] online notarization, this _____ day of _____, _____ by {$Grantor1} and {$Grantor2} whom I know personally or who produced _____ as identification.

_____ [Notary Seal]

Notary Public – State of _____

My Commission Expires:

Form 4 – Land Trust Agreement

LAND TRUST AGREEMENT

THIS TRUST AGREEMENT known as Trust No.   dated   , 20 by and between

_____ as Trustee, and the following beneficiaries in the percentages

set opposite their names:

_____ , 100% of the entire beneficial interest hereunder, with full pow-

er to assign and deal with all of the rights and interests of the beneficial interest. In the event of the

death of the said beneficiary during the existence of this trust, provided that said interest shall not have

been previously assigned or otherwise disposed, then the interest herein shall vest in and be vested in

_____.

1. TRUST. The Trustee is about to take title to real estate under the provisions of Florida Statutes sections 689.071 and 689.073, with full power and authority, to protect, conserve, sell, lease, encumber or otherwise manage and dispose of said property, and agrees to hold title and the proceeds, profits, and avails thereof, if any, which may come into its possession, in Trust for the uses and purposes and under the terms herein set forth.

2. PROPERTY. The Trustee will take title to the following property:

[Insert legal description or say See Exhibit A]

Property Appraiser's Parcel Identification Number:

  Street Address:

3. BENEFICIARIES' INTEREST. The interests of the beneficiaries hereunder and of any person who becomes entitled to any interest under this Trust shall consist solely of a power of direction to deal with the title to said property and to manage and control said property and the right to receive the proceeds from rentals, mortgages, sales or other dispositions shall be deemed to be personal property and may be treated, assigned and transferred as such. No beneficiary now has, or shall hereafter at any time have, any right, title or interest in or to any portion of said real estate as such, either legal or equitable, but only an interest in the earnings, avails and proceeds as aforesaid; it being the intention of this instrument to vest the full legal and equitable title to said premises in the Trustee under Florida statutes sections 689.071 and 689.073. The beneficiaries shall have the power to sign offers to purchase property, listing agreements to offer the trust property for sale, and to sign real estate sales contracts to sell the property out of the trust. The landlord and signer on leases of the real property owned by the trust may be the beneficiary, or the beneficiary's property manager, or the trustee.

4. POWER OF DIRECTION. {$Ben1} or {$Ben2}, acting jointly or alone is/are hereby appointed as the Holder(s) of the Power of Direction under this Trust Agreement. The Holder of the Power of Direction has full authority and power to perform all acts and make all decisions that the Beneficiary would have the power to perform or make, specifically including all powers set forth in Florida Statutes, the power to collect rents and profits, or to confirm how they will be made payable, the power to authorize purchase of insurance, and the power to direct or

instruct the Trustee as to the handling of any claim or litigation affecting the Property. A Trustee may be removed from power by the Holder of the Power of Direction, which specifically includes the power to remove Trustees and successor Trustees without cause, and to name successor Trustees. In the event that no successor Trustee is named in this Trust Agreement or the deed of conveyance into the Land Trust created by this instrument, or that no named successor is available to serve, or that a Trustee or successor Trustee is removed, a successor Trustee shall be designated and appointed by the Holder of the Power of Direction. The appointment shall be proven by a Declaration executed by the Holder of the Power of Direction and recorded in the public records of the county in which the Property is located.

5. DEATH OF BENEFICIARY. Except as herein otherwise specifically provided, the right and interest of any beneficiary hereunder who is a natural person shall pass at death to his Personal Representative and not to his heirs at law. The death of any beneficiary hereunder shall not terminate the Trust or in any manner affect the powers of the Trustee hereunder.

6. OWNERSHIP. Upon request each beneficiary hereunder shall be issued a Trust Participation Certificate in a form approved by the Trustee, which shall indicate the beneficiary's percentage interest in the Trust and the land held by the Trustee.

7. ASSIGNMENT. If Trust Participation Certificates have been issued, no assignment of any beneficial interest hereunder shall be binding on the Trustee until the Trust Participation Certificate representing the assigned share is surrendered to the Trustee with the assignment noted thereon and a new Certificate or Certificates are issued by the Trustee. If no Trust Participation Certificates have been issued, assignment shall be by an assignment form approved by the Trustee and shall not be binding until signed by the Trustee.

8. LOST CERTIFICATES. In the event a beneficiary's Trust Participation Certificate is lost, stolen or destroyed, the Trustee shall cancel it on the records of the Trust and issue a new Certificate after receiving an Affidavit as to the circumstances of the loss attested to by the beneficiary.

9. PURCHASERS. It shall not be the duty of the purchaser of the trust property or any part thereof to see to the application of the purchase money paid therefor; nor shall anyone who may deal with the Trustee be privileged or required to inquire into the necessity or expediency of any act of the Trustee, or as to the provisions of this instrument.

10. DUTY OF TRUSTEE. While the Trustee is sole owner of the real estate held by it hereunder so far as the publicis concerned and has full power to deal with it, it is understood and agreed by the persons in interest hereunder, and by any persons who may hereafter become interested, that the Trustee will deal with it only when authorized to do so in writing and that it will execute contracts, deeds or other instruments dealing with the said real estate or any part thereof only on the written direction of all of the beneficiaries hereunder at the time.

10. TERMINATION BY TRUSTEE. If the trust property or any part thereof remains in the trust twenty (20) years from this date, the Trustee shall, unless otherwise agreed by all parties in writing, convey and deliver the same to the beneficiaries in accordance with their respective interests.

11. LIMITATION ON BENEFICIARIES. No beneficiary hereunder shall have any authority to contract for or in the name of the Trustee, or use the name of the Trustee in any advertising or other publicity or to bind the Trustee individually. Beneficiary shall not open any financial or utility accounts or obtain any licenses in the name of the Trustee.

12. LIMITATION OF TRUSTEE'S LIABILITY. The liability of the Trustee hereunder shall be limited to the assets of this Trust. All obligations incurred by the Trustee hereunder shall be the obligations of this Trust only and not the Trustee in an individual capacity. The Trustee shall not be required to enter into any obligation or liability in dealing with the Trust property nor to expend any personal sums to defend or protect the Trust property.

13. NONINVOLVEMENT IN TRANSACTIONS. It is understood and agreed by the beneficiaries, directors and any parties becoming beneficiaries or directors in the future, that the trustee hereto is only following the directions of the parties to this trust and is not involved in any way in the agreements, negotiations or deals between them or with third parties. Any party with any interest in this trust or any other agreements related to this trust should seek the advice of a competent attorney. The parties hereto shall indemnify and hold harmless the trustee for any claims related to involvement with this trust.

14. NOTIFICATION OF CLAIMS. In the event the Trustee shall receive notice of claims or actions against the Trust, it shall notify the beneficiaries at their last known addresses.

15. TRUSTEE'S COMPENSATION. The Trustee shall receive for its services the sum of $ for preparing the trust documents, executing the closing documents if necessary, and the first year trustee fee and the sum of $ for each future year or fraction thereof as long as any property remains in this Trust. Also, it shall receive reasonable compensation for making deeds or other instruments, performing additional services, or retaining attorneys or agents. Such fees shall be provided to beneficiaries upon request. Such fees and the annual fee hereunder may be modified upon giving sixty (60) days' notice to the beneficiary. The beneficiaries hereunder jointly and severally agree to pay the fees hereunder, and the Trustee shall have a lien on the property of the Trust for any trustee fees owed by beneficiary. Trustee shall have the right to convey the title to the property of this trust subject to any outstanding trustee fees.

16. INDEMNIFICATION. The beneficiaries hereunder, jointly and severally, agree to hold the Trustee harmless and indemnify the trustee for any costs, obligations, liabilities or other amounts including reasonable attorney fees, expended on behalf of the property of the trust, or in defense of any claims related to the property of the trust. Trustee shall notify beneficiaries upon receipt of any such claims and give beneficiaries an opportunity to defend or cure such claims.

17. WARRANTY. The beneficiaries hereunder and any parties accepting an interest hereunder warrant that this trust is not set up or maintained for any illegal or criminal purpose. In the event any beneficiary becomes aware of any possible illegality regarding this trust he or she shall immediately inform the Trustee. The Trustee may, at any time it becomes convinced that the trust is or has become illegal or in violation of any law of the State of Florida or the United States, immediately resign as provided in paragraph 20.

18. LIMITATIONS ON AGREEMENTS. This Agreement shall not be deemed to be, create, or evidence the existence of a corporation de facto or de jure, or a Massachusetts Trust, or any other type of business trust, or an association in the nature of a corporation or a general or limited partnership, or a joint venture by or between the Trustee and the beneficiaries.

19. TAXES. Nothing herein contained shall be construed as imposing any obligation on the Trustee to file any income, profit or other tax reports or schedules, it being expressly understood that the beneficiaries hereunder from time to time will individually make all such reports and pay any and all taxes growing out of their interest under this Trust Agreement.

20. REPLACEMENT OF TRUSTEE. The Trustee may be replaced in any of the following manners:

a. Resignation. The Trustee may resign at any time by mailing a notice of its intention to do so to each of the beneficiaries at each's last known address. In the event of such resignation the beneficiaries may appoint a successor trustee, by lodging an instrument with the Trustee signed by all the beneficiaries and accepted by the Successor Trustee. If no Successor Trustee is appointed within thirty (30) days, the Trustee may convey the Trust property to the beneficiaries according to their interests and this Trust shall terminate. If, in the opinion of the Trustee, the Trustee may be subjected to embarrassment, litigation, insecurity, liability or hazard, the Trustee may at any time and without notice resign as to all or part of the trust property and convey such trust property to the beneficiaries.

b. Replacement. The beneficiaries may at any time replace the Trustee by lodging with it an instrument naming a Successor Trustee, signed by all beneficiaries and accepted by the Successor Trustee. Upon receipt of said instrument and if there shall be no fees due and owing to him, the Trustee shall quit claim the property to the Successor Trustee.

c. Death or Incapacity. In the event of the death or incapacity of the trustee, the following, in order of their listing, is appointed Successor Trustee:

Successor Trustee 1: _____

Successor Trustee 2: _____

Any successor Trustee under this Trust shall have all of the powers, properties and duties of the original Trustee. Any replacement of the Trustee shall not affect his first lien on the Trust property, for his costs, expenses, attorney's fees and reasonable compensation.

21. RECORDING. This Trust shall not be recorded except as herein provided or required by law.

22. DISCLOSURE. The Trustee shall not release information regarding this Trust except as required by law. In making a disclosure required by law, the Trustee shall supply beneficiaries with copies of any reports filed and shall be subject to no liability for the filing of such reports.

23. FLORIDA RICO ACT. Notwithstanding any provision of this Trust to the contrary, the Trustee shall have no obligation to convey title to real property held by the Trustee pursuant to this Agreement until it has performed or caused to be performed, at the expense of the beneficiaries of this Trust Agreement, a search of the official records of all counties in which such real property is located. If such search discloses that no Rico lien notices have been filed against any person for whom the Trustee holds legal or record title to real property pursuant to this Trust Agreement, then the Trustee may convey its legal or record title to such real property in accordance with the written

instructions of the beneficiary. If such search discloses that one or more Rico lien notices have been filed against any person for whom the Trustee holds legal or record title to real property pursuant to this Trust Agreement then the Trustee shall not convey its legal or record title to such real property unless:

a) All such Rico lien notices have been released or terminated or such real property has been released from all such Rico lien notices, or b. Such persons named in the Rico lien notice agree in writing that the total amount of all proceeds that would otherwise be received directly by such person as a result of the conveyance, will be paid directly to the Trustee, and that the Trustee shall have the right to hold such proceeds, together with the total amount of all such proceeds that would otherwise be paid or distributed to such person or at the direction of such person or his designee, until such time as the provisions of subsection a. above have been satisfied, and also agrees, in writing, that at the request of the Department of Legal Affairs of the State of Florida, or the office of any state attorney of the State of Florida, the Trustee, without any liability to the person named in the Rico lien notice, may pay the total amount of such proceeds held by the Trustee pursuant to the provisions of this subsection b. to the Department of Legal Affairs of the State of Florida or the office of any state attorney of the State of Florida.

24. STATE OR LOCAL TAXES. In the event that any documentary stamp tax, or other state or local taxes or fees are due regarding this trust, these shall be the sole responsibility of the beneficiaries who shall hold the trustee harmless from any claims or liens for such amounts.

25. LIMITATION ON BENEFICIARIES' LIABILITY. With regard to claims by third parties, the Beneficiarries' liability shall be limited to the assets of the trust as provided by F.S. 689.071(8)(a).

26. DISCLOSURE OF ASSIGNMENTS. Trustee shall have no duty to file any reports of the assignment of any beneficial interests under this trust. Any such duty shall be the obligation of the beneficiaries.

27. PROCEEDS. In the event of sale or rental of the trust property, any proceeds and rents shall be payable to the beneficiaries of the trust, or as they direct, and not the Trustee. Upon request the Trustee shall provide written instructions to the closing agent or lessee as to how to make payment.

28. PARTITION. The remedy of partition shall not be available to the beneficiaries of this Land Trust.

29. PARTIES BOUND. This Agreement shall extend to and be obligatory upon the heirs, successors, administration and assigns of the respective parties.

30. GENDER. Any references to he or him in this Agreement shall apply to parties of either gender.

31. PARAGRAPH TITLES. The titles of paragraphs are for convenience only and shall in no way be used for the purpose of construing the meaning of this Agreement.

32. GOVERNING LAW. This Agreement shall be construed under the laws of the State of Florida.

33. COUNTERPARTS. This agreement, and any documents related to it, may be signed in one or more counterparts, each of which shall be deemed an original, and all of which together shall be considered one instrument.

34. ADDRESSES. The addresses of the parties as of the date of this Agreement for the purpose of notices are:

Trustee:

Beneficiary:

32. NO FOREIGN INTEREST. Beneficiary does not hold any interest under this trust for the benefit of any foreign national or contrary to any regulation or law of the United States of America or of the state wherein the Property is located pertaining to the control of foreign funds, assets or property. No foreign national has any interest of any nature, direct or indirect, in the Property. Further, Beneficiary is not a Foreign Principal as defined in §692.201, F.S. and as such is in compliance with the requirements set out in §692.202-205, F.S.

33. USA PATRIOT ACT. The Beneficiary warrants and represents to Trustee that no Beneficiary herein, is identified in any list of known or suspected terrorists published by any United States government agency (individually, as each such list may be amended or supplemented from time to time, referred to as a "Blocked Persons List") including, without limitation, (a) the annex to Executive Order 13224 issued on September 23, 2001 by the President of the United States and (b) the Specially Designated Nationals List published by the United States Office of Foreign Assets Control. Beneficiary covenants with the Trustee that if Beneficiary becomes aware that it, any other Beneficiary or any respective affiliate is identified on any Blocked Persons List, the Beneficiary shall immediately notify the Trustee in writing of such information. The Beneficiary further agrees that in the event it or any respective affiliate is at any time identified on any Blocked Persons List, such event shall entitle Trustee to terminate this Trust by conveying the Trust Property to such Beneficiary. In addition, the Trustee may immediately contact the Office of Foreign Assets Control and any other government agency the Trustee deems appropriate in order to comply with its legal obligations. Upon the occurrence of such event, Trustee will forbear terminating the Trust so long as (1) the person identified in a Blocked Persons List is contesting in good faith by appropriate legal proceedings such person's inclusion in a Blocked Persons List, and (2) the Trustee determines, in its sole and absolute discretion, that such forbearance will not adversely affect Trustee.

34. BENEFICIARY IDENTIFICATION. The Beneficiary will provide any personal information and documentation as may be requested by Trustee to comply with Federal and State law, and Trustee is permitted to provide this information as required by the appropriate agency.

35. MISCELLANEOUS.

Recitals

The recitals set forth herein above are true and accurate in all material respects and are adopted and incorporated herein.

Governing Law.

This Agreement shall be construed by and governed under the laws of the State of Florida, including its principles of conflicts of laws and the parties hereby irrevocably agree to submit to the jurisdiction and venue of the Circuit Courts of the State of Florida, County of _____, to resolve any dispute arising hereunder or relating hereto. Particularly, but in no way of limitation, the parties agree that they are subject to the personal jurisdiction of the state and federal courts of the Middle District of Florida, and the parties waive the right to challenge the personal jurisdiction of those courts over the party.

Mediation / Arbitration of Disputes.

In the event that there is a dispute among the Parties hereto, the parties agree to first attempt to negotiate their differences among themselves in good faith. If such negotiation is unsuccessful, the parties agree to submit the deadlocked decision to a local center for mediation ("local" shall mean a center within the locality of the primary office of the company) or an equivalent mediation center for a non-binding mediation session in an attempt to resolve the dispute. If such non-binding mediation is unsuccessful, the parties agree to submit the decision to legally binding arbitration which shall be governed by the Rules of Procedure of the American Arbitration Association or an equivalent set of Rules of Procedure agreed upon by the parties. This section shall not apply to any dispute wherein the relief sought is injunctive in nature.

Attorney's Fees and Costs.

The parties will split equally any mediation or arbitration fee incurred in any mediation or arbitration permitted by this Agreement, and each party will pay their own costs, expenses and fees, including attorney's fees, incurred in conducting the mediation or arbitration. In any litigation permitted by this Agreement, the prevailing party shall be entitled to recover from the non-prevailing party costs and fees, including reasonable attorney's fees, incurred in conducting the litigation.

The costs that the prevailing party shall be entitled to recover shall include all costs taxable pursuant to any applicable statute, rule, or guideline, including, but not limited to the Statewide Uniform Guidelines for Taxation of Costs, as well as costs deemed not taxable pursuant to those Statewide Uniform Guidelines. Such recoverable costs specifically include, but are not limited to 1) costs of investigation, 2) costs of copying documents and other materials whether for discovery, litigation, internal review, or other purpose, 3) costs of electronic discovery, including but not limited to upload and storage costs, 4) electronic research service charges, 5) telephone charges, 6) mailing, commercial delivery services, and courier charges, 7) travel expenses, whether for investigation, deposition, hearings, trial, or any other purpose, 8) information technology support charges, 9) any and all consultant and expert witness fees, whether or not incurred in connection with reports, depositions, hearings, or trial, 10) court reporter and transcript fees whether for deposition, trial, evidentiary, or non-evidentiary hearings or other purposes, 11) mediation charges and mediator fees, and 12) any other reasonable cost incurred by the prevailing party in connection with the dispute.

Partial Enforceability – Waiver.

All rights, powers and remedies provided herein may be exercised only to the extent that the exercise thereof does not violate any applicable law, and they are intended to be limited to the extent necessary so that they will not render this Agreement invalid, illegal or unenforceable under any applicable law. If any provision of this Agreement, or the application of the provision to any person or circumstance shall be held invalid by law, the remainder of this Agreement, or the application of that provision to persons or circumstances other than those with respect to which it is held invalid by law, shall not be affected thereby. Failure by either party at any time to require performance by the other party or to claim a breach of any provision of this Agreement will not be construed as a waiver of any right accruing under this Agreement, nor affect any subsequent breach, nor affect the effectiveness of this Agreement or any part hereof, nor prejudice either party as regards any subsequent action.

Effect.

Except as herein otherwise specifically provided, this Agreement shall be binding upon and inure to the benefit of the parties and their legal representatives, heirs, administrators, executors, successors, and assigns.

Pronouns and Number.

Wherever from the context it appears appropriate, each term stated in either the singular or the plural shall include the singular and the plural, and pronouns stated in either the masculine, the feminine, or the neuter gender shall include the masculine, feminine, and neuter.

Captions.

Captions or section headings contained in this Agreement are inserted only as a matter of convenience and in no way define, limit, or extend the scope or intent of this Agreement or any provision hereof. The "Recitals" contained in this Agreement are for convenience of purpose only and shall have no effect upon the interpretation of this Agreement.

Counterparts and E-Signing.

This Agreement may be executed in several counterparts, each of which shall be deemed an original but all of which shall constitute one and the same instrument. This Agreement may contain more than one counterpart of the signature page and may be executed by the affixing of the signatures of each of the parties to one of these counterpart signature pages. All the counterpart signature pages shall be read as though one, and they shall have the same force and effect as though all of the signers had signed a single signature page. Any exhibits or schedules attached to this Agreement are incorporated herein by reference. The parties signing below agree that this Agreement shall be governed by the Electronic Signatures in Global and National Commerce Act and may be executed in electronic form, including but not limited to an electronic signature made through an electronic signature platform.

Entire Agreement – Modification - Survival

This written document, along with any recitals, schedules, exhibits or attachments herewith, embodies the entire agreement between the parties here, and there are no other understandings, agreements or representations, express or implied. All modifications to the Agreement must be in writing and signed by the party against whom enforcement of such modification is sought. All covenants and obligations of this Agreement shall survive the termination or expiration of this Agreement.

Construction

The Parties acknowledge that this is a negotiated agreement and that in no event shall the terms hereof be construed against either party on the basis that such party, or its counsel, drafted this Agreement. The Parties further acknowledge that they have had a full and complete opportunity to review the Agreement and seek attorneys' advice before executing the Agreement.

Time

Time is of the essence in this Agreement. The end of a day shall be at 5:00 p.m. in Orange County, Florida on the date in question. In computing time periods of less than six (6) days, Saturdays, Sundays and Florida state or national legal holidays shall be excluded. Any time periods provided for herein which shall end on a Saturday, Sunday or a legal holiday shall extend to 5:00 p.m. of the next business day in Orange County, Florida.

Confidentiality

The parties agree that the terms of this Agreement are confidential and that they shall not disclose to or discuss the terms of this Agreement with any other person except their attorneys, accountants, and immediate family members. They shall inform any of those people to whom they disclose the terms of this Agreement the existence of this confidentiality provision and the fact that a breach of this provision by those people to whom they disclose the terms is equal to a breach by the disclosing party for which that party will be liable.

IN WITNESS WHEREOF, the Beneficiary and Trustee have executed this agreement to be effective as of the date and year above written.

Beneficiary 1: _____

Beneficiary 2: _____

Signed, sealed, and delivered in the presence of:

Witness #1: _____

Witness #2: _____

ACCEPTED BY TRUSTEE:

_____

NOTICE: FLORIDA RESTRICTS THE SALE OF PROPERTY TO FOREIGN PRINCIPALS (Secs. 692.202-205, F.S.)

Effective July 1, 2023, foreign principals of these foreign countries of concern are prohibited from purchasing or acquiring any interest in certain types of Florida real property, subject to limited exceptions:

1. The People's Republic of China

2. The Russian Federation

3. The Islamic Republic of Iran

4. The Democratic People's Republic of Korea

5. The Republic of Cuba

6. The Venezuelan regime of Nicolás Maduro

7. The Syrian Arab Republic

8. Any agency of or any other entity of significant control of such foreign country of concern

BUYERS ARE A FOREIGN PRINCIPAL IF ANY OF THESE APPLY TO THEM:

1. The government or any official of the government of a foreign country of concern;

2. A political party or member of a political party or any subdivision of a political party in a foreign country of concern;

3. A partnership, association, corporation, organization, or other combination of persons organized under the laws of or having its principal place of business in a foreign country of concern, or a subsidiary of such entity;

4. Any person who is domiciled in a foreign country of concern and is not a citizen or lawful permanent resident of the United States, or

5. Any person, entity, or collection of persons or entities, described in paragraphs (a) through (d) having a controlling interest in a partnership, association, corporation, organization, trust, or any other legal entity or subsidiary formed for the purpose of owning real property in Florida.

IF A BUYER IS A FOREIGN PRINCIPAL, FLORIDA LAW PROHIBITS THEM:

1. From purchasing or acquiring any interest in real property in Florida classified as agricultural land or within 5 miles of a military installation.

2. With limited exceptions, from purchasing or acquiring any interest in real property in Florida within 10 miles of a critical infrastructure facility or military installation

NOTE: Foreign principals of the People's Republic China are prohibited from purchasing or acquiring any interest in any real property in Florida regardless of its classification, subject to the Limited Residential Exception and Diplomatic Purposes Exception described below

CERTAIN EXCEPTIONS MAY APPLY:

Limited Residential Exception - If the Buyer is a 'natural person' subject to the law, they may still purchase one residential real property, up to 2 acres in size, if all of the following apply:

1. The parcel is not on or within 5 miles of any military installation;

2. Buyer has a current verified United States visa that is not limited to authorizing tourist-based travel or official documentation confirming that the person has been granted asylum in the United States and such visa or documentation authorizes the person to be legally present in Florida;

3. The purchase is in the Buyer's name, i.e., the name of the person who holds the visa or official documentation described in paragraph (b), and

4. The Buyer is only entitled to one residential property as described above.

Diplomatic Purposes Exception - The real property is for diplomatic purposes as recognized, acknowledged, or allowed by the Federal Government

CAUTION: PERSONS WHO ARE OR MAY BE DEFINED AS "FOREIGN PRINCIPALS OF FOREIGN COUNTRIES OF CONCERN" SHOULD CONSULT WITH AN ATTORNEY BEFORE PURCHASING OR ACQUIRING ANY INTEREST IN REAL PROPERTY IN FLORIDA ON OR AFTER JULY 1, 2023. LAND ACQUIRED IN VIOLATION OF THIS LAW MAY BE FORFEITED TO THE STATE.

BY SIGNING BELOW, I ACKNOWLEDGE HAVING REVIEWED THE ABOVE NOTICE.

_____ BENEFICIARY:

SSN/EIN:

Form 5 – Direction to Trustee

DIRECTION TO TRUSTEE

The undersigned, being all the beneficiaries of Land Trust No. _____ dated _____ hereby authorize and direct the Trustee thereunder to execute and deliver the following selected documents affecting the property held in the trust (initial as appropriate):

Lease Agreement with _____ as tenant

Listing Agreement/other documents needed by agent/broker to list for: _____ sale or _____ lease.

Seller disclosure statements regarding property condition.

Settlement statements.

Mortgage encumbering the Trust Property in favor of _____.

Promissory note made to _____ for $_____ for a term of _____ years with an annual rate of interest of _____%.

Any/all affidavits regarding the status of the title.

As-Is Statements.

All other documents needed by lender, closing agent, seller or purchaser to:

purchase,

finance, or

sell/convey.

Warranty Deed to _____ as grantee.

Please direct the closing agent on sale/refinance to disburse the proceeds as follows:

$/%_____ to _____ whose Social Security # is _____.

$/%_____ to _____ whose Social Security # is _____.

$/%_____ to _____ whose Social Security # is _____.

$/%_____ to _____ whose Social Security # is _____.

I understand that the 1099-S on any sale will be reported on my Social Security/FEIN #, and not on the Trustee's Tax ID #.

I/We hereby certify that we have examined the above documents and have found them to be satisfactory. It is understood that the Trustee executes these documents not personally, but only as Trustee aforesaid, in the exercise of the power and authority conferred upon and vested in the Trustee as such and pursuant to this Direction. The undersigned agrees to indemnify and save harmless said Trustee as to any claim or litigation arising from compliance with this Direction.

Date:

_____

Beneficiary: (sign and print name)

Date:

_____

Beneficiary: (sign and print name)

Trustee: _____

Form 6 – Assignment of Beneficial Interest

Assignment of Beneficial Interest

City, State: _____

Dated: _____, 20

FOR VALUE RECEIVED the undersigned hereby sells, assigns and transfers unto _____ whose tax identification number(s) is/are _____, _____% of all rights, powers, privileges and beneficial interests in and to that certain Trust Agreement known as Trust No. _____ dated _____, 20_____, including all interest to the property subject to said Trust Agreement.

Acceptance by Assignee

The undersigned hereby accept the foregoing Assignment subject to all of the provisions of said Trust Agreement, acknowledge receipt of a copy thereof and of this Assignment, verify the above taxpayer identification numbers to be true and correct, and name

as successor beneficiaries in the event of our death. We understand that any documentary stamp tax due on this assignment is our responsibility if not previously paid and that we may be required to file Form DR-430. Notices, inquiries and other matters regarding the trust property should be mailed to us at

_____.

Acceptance by Trustee

The Trustee hereby accepts the foregoing Assignment subject to all of the provisions of the Trust Agreement.

_____

Trustee

Form 7 – Acceptance of Beneficial Interest by Successor Beneficiary after death of prior beneficiary

ACCEPTANCE OF BENEFICIAL INTEREST AND RATIFICATION OF TRUST AGREEMENT UPON DEATH OF BENEFICIARY

_____, Florida

Date: _____, 20_____

Decedent:

Date of death:

Trust No. dated , 20 provided that the beneficiary was , and that in the event of beneficiary's death beneficiary's interest would pass to . The beneficiary died on

, 20 , and a copy of the death certificate has been provided to the trustee.

The undersigned does hereby accept 100% ownership in said beneficial interest in Trust No. dated , 20 , subject to all of the provisions of said trust agreement. Mail received by the trustee should be forwarded to .

Beneficiary:

, as Trustee aforesaid, does hereby acknowledge receipt of a copy of the foregoing and acknowledges that the current beneficiary of Trust No.

dated , 20 is .

Trustee:_____

Form 8 – Trustee's Deed Out of Trust

Prepared by/Return to:

_____

_____

_____

TRUSTEE'S DEED

THIS DEED executed this   day of , 20 , between   as Trustee under Trust No. _____ dated _____, 20_____ with full power and authority to protect, conserve, sell, lease, encumber or otherwise manage and dispose of said property under Florida Statutes sections 689.071 and 689.073, as GRANTOR whose mailing address is   , and   as GRANTEE, whose mailing address is:

WITNESSETH, that the said Grantor, for and in consideration of the sum of $10.00 and other good and valuable considerations to said Grantor in hand paid by the said Grantee, the receipt whereof is hereby acknowledged, does hereby remise, release and quit-claim unto the said Grantee forever, all the right, title, interest, claim and demand which the said Grantor has in and to the following described lot, piece, or parcel of land, to wit:

PARCEL IDENTIFICATION NUMBER: _____

TO HAVE AND TO HOLD the same together with all and singular the appurtenances thereunto belonging or in anywise appertaining, and all the estate, right, title, interest, lien, equity and claim whatsoever of said Grantor, either in law or equity, to the only proper use, benefit and behoof of the said Grantee forever.

THIS DEED is executed pursuant to and in the exercise of the power and authority granted to and vested in said Trustee by the terms of said deed or deeds in trust delivered to said Trustee in pursuance of the Trust agreement above mentioned. This deed is made subject to the lien of every trust deed or mortgage (if there be any) of record in said county given to secure the payment of money, remaining unreleased at the date of the delivery hereof, and covenants, conditions, restrictions, and easements of record.

IN WITNESS WHEREOF, the said Grantor has hereunto signed and sealed this deed this day and year first above written.

Signed, sealed, and delivered in the presence of:

_____ Witness #1

Printed Name: _____

Address:_____

_____ Witness #2

Printed Name: _____

Address:_____

_____

{$Grantor1}

{$Grantor1Mailing}

_____

{$Grantor2}

{$Grantor2Mailing}

STATE OF _____

COUNTY OF _____

The foregoing instrument was acknowledged before me by means of [ ] physical presence or [ ] online notarization, this _____ day of _____, _____ by {$Grantor1} and {$Grantor2} whom I know personally or who produced _____ as identification.

_____ [Notary Seal]

Notary Public – State of _____

My Commission Expires:

Form 9 – IRS Form 56

This form changes from time to time. Therefore, it is best to download it directly from the IRS Website at www.irs.gov. Search for "Form 56," and you will receive a response with links to the form in fillable PDF format and the instructions if needed.

Form 10 – IRS Form 56-A

This form is no longer available for download, therefore we are no longer providing it as a form with this book to avoid confusion at the Internal Revenue Service.

Form 11 – Beneficiaries' Co-Venture Agreement, Simple

Co-Venture Agreement

THIS AGREEMENT made this   day of , 20 , by and between

Beneficiary 1:

And

Beneficiary 2:

IN CONSIDERATION of the mutual covenants herein contained the parties hereto agree as follows:

1. That they will form and enter into a Land Trust Agreement.

2. That their interests in said Trust shall be as follows:

3. That they agree to contribute funds as necessary to the maintenance of said trust in proportion to their interests. In the event one beneficiary has paid more toward necessary maintenance expense than other beneficiaries, he or she shall be reimbursed at the time subject property is sold.

4. That they agree to share in the management of the property in said Trust.

5. That they will share in the proceeds of said Trust in proportion to their interests.

6. That no beneficiary shall sell his beneficial interest without first offering it, at an equal price to the other beneficiaries of this trust.

7. That in the event of death or incapacity of one of the beneficiaries, the remaining beneficiaries shall have the right to acquire said beneficiary's interest at fair market value.

8. That no party shall have the authority to obligate the other parties and no party shall incur any obligation on behalf of the trust without the consent of all other parties.

9. That no party shall be personally liable for any act or debt of the trustee unless that party shall agree in writing to assume such liability.

IN WITNESS WHEREOF, the parties hereto have signed this agreement the day and year first above written.

_____

Beneficiary 1

_____

Beneficiary 2

Form 12 – Beneficiaries' Partnership Agreement – Extended

Partnership Agreement of

_____

A Florida General Partnership

THIS PARTNERSHIP AGREEMENT is made this _____ day of _____ ,_____, by and between the parties listed on Schedule "A" who have signed this agreement.

IN CONSIDERATION of the mutual covenants herein contained, the undersigned partners hereby form a general partnership under the partnership laws of the State of on the terms and conditions as follows:

1. PURPOSE. The purpose of the partnership is to invest in real estate for profit.

2. NAME. The name of the partnership shall be _____.

3. PLACE OF BUSINESS. The principal place of business of the partnership shall be and each other place as may be agreed on by the partners.

4. DURATION. The partnership shall commerce on , , and continue until dissolved pursuant to paragraph 18 of this Agreement.

5. INITIAL CAPITAL. The initial capital of the partnership shall be $ and consist of the payments from each partner as indicated on Schedule "A".

6. SUBSEQUENT CAPITAL. Upon a vote of % of the Partnership, each partner shall contribute additional capital as needed, in proportion to the present ownership of the Partnership. In the event any partner fails to make such subsequent capital contribution, the partners who have contributed may consider the sums so advanced as loans to the Partnership at % interest, or as purchases of additional Partnership interests.

7. PARTNERSHIP PROPERTY. All property originally paid or brought into the Partnership as contributions to capital by the partners, or subsequently acquired by purchases or otherwise on account of the Partnership shall be Partnership property and held in the name of the Partnership.

8. PARTNERSHIP REAL ESTATE. All interests in real property owned or held by the Partnership shall be held by a Trustee for the Partnership in a land trust.

9. PARTNERSHIP FUNDS. All funds of the Partnership shall be deposited in an account in a bank designated by a majority in interest of the partners. All withdrawals shall be made by checks to be signed as authorized by such majority in interest.

10. PARTNERSHIP RECORDS. Books of account and partnership records shall be maintained at the principal office of the Partnership and shall be open to inspection by any of the partners or their agents at any time, including determination of value for purposes of this Agreement, which shall be made by the regular accountants selected by the partners.

11. PARTNERSHIP INTERESTS. Each initial partner shall have an interest in the partnership in proportion to his or her capital contribution as listed on Schedule "A." New partners shall have an interest in proportion to their contribution as determined from the previous contributions and the intervening appreciation of the assets of the Partnership. All contributions shall be made in units of $100.

12. MANAGEMENT. The affairs of the Partnership shall be managed by all of the partners. Decisions shall be made by a majority vote of the partners. Each partner shall at all times inform the others of all work for and transactions on behalf of the Partnership. The Partnership may, upon prior approval, make payments to any partners for work done on behalf of the Partnership.

13. PROHIBITIONS. During the continuance of the Partnership, no partner shall, without the written consent of all the partners, do any of the following:

a. Assign the Partnership property in trust for creditors or on the assignee's promise to pay the debts of the Partnership;

b. Dispose of the good will of the business;

c. Submit a Partnership claim or liability to arbitration or reference;

d. Confess judgment against the Partnership;

e. Do any act which would make it impossible to carry on the ordinary business of the Partnership;

f. Make, execute or deliver in the name of the Partnership any bond, trust deed, mortgage, indemnity bond, guaranty, surety bond or accommodation paper or accommodation endorsement;

g. Borrow money in the name of the accommodation or use as collateral any accommodation property;

h. Assign, pledge, transfer, release or compromise any debt owing to, or claim of, the accommodation except for full payment.

If any partner violates any of the provisions hereof and, after written notice thereof to him by any partner, fails to remedy the violation within ten (10) days after receipt of such notice, the other partners shall have the right within ninety (90) days after acquiring notice of such violation to terminate this Agreement and purchase such partner's interests, at its then value as determined by Paragraph 15, making payment therefore as provided in Paragraph 15.

Any partner who shall violate any of the provisions of this Agreement, in addition to being subject to other remedies, liabilities and obligations herein or by law imposed therefore, shall keep and save harmless the Partnership property and shall also indemnify the other partners from any and all claims, demands and actions of every kind whatever which may arise from such violation.

14. ASSIGNMENT. No partner shall have the right to transfer all or any interest in the Partnership unless all other partners agree to accept the assignee as a partner and such assignee shall accept this Agreement in writing.

15. WITHDRAWAL OR DEATH. In the event any partner dies, is declared incompetent, files for bankruptcy or desires to withdraw from the Partnership, the Partnership shall purchase such partner's interest. Such interest shall be purchased at a price based upon the following schedule:

16. PROPERTIES. The properties purchased by the Partnership shall be determined by a majority vote, but shall conform to the parameters outlined in Schedule "B." If a vote determines a property will not be acquired by

the Partnership, those voting in favor of the acquisition are free to acquire the property on their own outside of this Partnership.

17. PROFITS. The profits of the Partnership shall be distributed upon a majority vote of the partners according to the proportional interest of the Partners.

18. DISSOLUTION. This Partnership shall be dissolved upon a vote of a majority of the partners, or in any event, by , 20 . Upon any voluntary dissolution, the Partnership shall immediately commence to wind up its affairs. The proceeds from liquidation of Partnership assets shall be applied as follows:

a. Debts of the Partnership, other than to partners;

b. Amounts owed to partners for loans, unpaid salaries, and for the credit balances in their respective drawing accounts;

c. The equity of the partners as reflected in the books of accounts.

Any gain or loss on depreciation of Partnership properties in the process of liquidation shall be credited or charged to the partners in the proportion of their interests in profit and loss. Any property distributed in kind in the liquidation shall be valued and treated as though the property were sold and the cash proceeds were distributed.

19. LIABILITY. No partner shall be personally liable for any act or debt of the trustee unless that partner shall agree in writing to assume such liability.

20. AMENDMENTS. This Agreement except with respect to vested rights of the partners may be amended at any time by a majority vote of the partners.

21. NOTICES. All notices given under this Agreement shall be sent by Certified Mail.

22. SUCCESSORS. This Agreement shall be binding upon the successors, heirs and assigns of any partner.

23. DIRECTION TO TRUSTEE. All direction to Trustees for the Partnership shall be effective upon signing by a majority of interest of the partners.

IN WITNESS WHEREOF, the parties have executed the foregoing Partnership Agreement.

_____, Partner

_____, Partner

_____, Partner

_____, Partner

Note: Attach Schedule A listing partners, contributions and interests, and Schedule B listing types of properties to be acquired by partnership.

Form 13 – Designation of Florida registered agent for alien business organization

This form is promulgated by the Florida Department of State and is updated or amended from time to time. The best way to ensure you have the latest form is to visit Sunbiz online, go to the Forms Section, and navigate to "miscellaneous forms." This is where this form is typically maintained.

As of August, 2024, this is the website to download the latest forms: https://dos.fl.gov/sunbiz/forms/miscellaneous-forms/

The form itself, as of this date is at https://form.sunbiz.org/pdf/inhs80.pdf

Form 14 – Promissory Note for Beneficiary

PROMISSORY NOTE

$_____

City, State: _____

Date: _____

FOR VALUE RECEIVED, the undersigned, jointly and severably promise to pay to the order of:

the principal sum of   Dollars ($) together with interest from date at the rate of   per cent (%) per annum on the balance from time to time remaining unpaid. Said principal and interest shall be payable in lawful money of the United States of America at

or at such place as may be designated by written notice from the holder to the maker of this note. Payment shall be made as follows:

This note with interest is secured by a security agreement pledging the beneficial interest in a land trust and a UCC financing statement, of even date herewith, made by the maker hereof in favor of the above payee. The terms of the security agreement are by this reference made a part hereof.

If default be made in the payment of any sums or interest herein payable, or in the terms of said security agreement, then the entire balance due hereunder shall, at the option of the holder, be immediately due and payable, without notice, time being of the essence. From default, all sums due shall bear interest at the highest rate allowed by law. Failure to exercise this option shall not constitute a waiver of the right to exercise the same in the event of a subsequent default.

Each person liable hereunder, whether maker or endorser, hereby waives presentment, protest, notice, notice of protest and notice of dishonor and agrees to pay all costs of collection, including a reasonable attorney's fee whether suit be brought or not.

_____

Beneficiary - Borrower

Form 15 – Guaranty of Promissory Note By Beneficiary

GUARANTY AGREEMENT

GUARANTY given by and

_____, the undersigned, to induce the acceptance of the

Promissory Note payable to _____ dated

in the amount of _____

Dollars ($_____).

1. Obligation. In consideration of the loan made upon such note, the undersigned hereby unconditionally guarantee to _____, its successors and assigns and to every subsequent holder of such note that all sums stated therein to be payable on such note shall be promptly paid in full, in accordance with the terms thereof, at maturity, by acceleration or otherwise, and in the case of any extension of time of payment or renewal in whole or in part, all sums shall be promptly paid when due according to such extensions or renewals, at maturity or otherwise.

2. Consent. The undersigned hereby consent that at any time, without notice to the undersigned, payment of any sums payable on such note, or of any of the collateral therefore, may be extended, or such note or collateral may be exchanged, surrendered, or otherwise dealt with as the holder of such note may determine, and that any of the acts mentioned in such note may be done, without affecting the liability of the undersigned.

3. Endorsement. The signature of the undersigned hereto shall constitute an endorsement of such note.

4. Waiver. The undersigned hereby waives presentment, demand for payment by the maker or anyone else, protest, and notice of nonpayment, dishonor, or protest of such note and all other notices and demands.

Date: _____, 20

_____

Guarantor

_____

Guarantor

Form 16 – Collateral Assignment of Beneficial Interest

COLLATERAL ASSIGNMENT OF BENEFICIAL INTEREST

City, State: _____

FOR VALUE RECEIVED the undersigned hereby sells, assigns and transfers unto

whose tax identification number(s) is/are _____, _____% of all rights, powers, privileges and beneficial interests in and to that certain Trust Agreement known as _____ dated _____ including all interest to the property subject to said Trust Agreement.

SAID ASSIGNMENT, however, is for collateral security only, for a promissory note executed today in the amount of $_____ and the assignee by acceptance of this assignment does not assume or become liable for any obligations or liabilities of the assignor.

_____
Beneficiary/Debtor

_____
Beneficiary/Debtor

Acceptance by Assignee

The undersigned hereby accept the foregoing Assignment subject to all of the provisions of said Trust Agreement and agrees to re-assign this interest in the trust upon payment in full of the promissoory note and all interest due thereunder. Notices, inquiries and other matters regarding the trust property should be directed to me at _____.

_____
Secured Party

_____
Secured Party

Acceptance by Trustee

The trustee hereby accepts the foregoing Assignment subject to all of the provisions of the Trust Agreement and agrees not to accept further assignments, or to sign documents affecting the title to the trust property, without the consent of both parties.

_____
Trustee

Form 17 – Security Agreement (Chattel Mortgage)

Security Agreement (Chattel Mortgage)

City, State: _____ Date:_____, 20_____

FOR VALUE RECEIVED, receipt of which is hereby acknowledged, the undersigned debtor hereby grants a security interest in the beneficial interest of the land trust known as

_____

to _____ as secured party.

This security agreement is to secure indebtedness in the amount of   Dollars ($) evidenced by a promissory note of even date.

The undersigned warrants that he/she is the owner of _____ percent (_____ %) interest in said land trust and that such interest is subject to no other liens, charges encumbrances or claims.

This agreement shall be secured with a UCC financing statement. A copy of this security agreement and the UCC financing statement shall be lodged with the trustee of said land trust and the undersigned consents that no further pledge of the beneficial interest shall be made, or conveyance or encumbrance of the real property of the trust without the consent of the secured party.

Upon default the secured party shall have all the rights and remedies provided a secured party under the Uniform Commercial Code of this state, including the right to sell the beneficial interest at a public or private sale, with or without advertising. The undersigned agrees that the requirements of the UCC shall be met if notice is mailed to the undersigned address at the address below not less than five days prior to the sale or other disposition.

Default shall be any failure to pay principal or interest under the promissory note as it comes due, breach of any warranty made by the debtor, attachment, seizure, foreclosure, forfeiture or levy on the beneficial interest of the trust or the real property held by the trust, institution of any action in bank- ruptcy by or against debtor, or any reasonable insecurity of the secured party.

The undersigned acknowledges receipt of a completed copy of this security agreement. Secured party:

_____

Debtor

_____

Debtor

Address:

_____

Secured Party

Form 18 – UCC-1 Financing Statement

This form is now filed online at https://floridaucc.com/

For this reason, this form is no longer provided as part of this book.

Form 19 – UCC-3 Amended Financing Statement / Termination of Financing Statement

This form is now filed online at https://floridaucc.com/

For this reason, this form is no longer provided as part of this book.

Form 20 – DR-228 (Documentary Tax Remittance)

This form is available to download in fillable PDF at https://floridarevenue.com/Forms_library/current/dr228.pdf

Form 21 – DR-430 (Disclosure to Property Appraiser)

This form is available to download as a fillable Word document at https://floridarevenue.com/property/Documents/dr430.doc

Form 22 – Trust Participation Certificate

TRUST PARTICIPATION CERTIFICATE

    THIS IS TO CERTIFY that

is/are entitled to participate to the extent of % of the profits and avails of the land trust known as

_____ and the interest represented by this Certificate is an undivided interest

in said trust.

    THE REAL PROPERTY of the trust consists of the property described on the reverse side of this Certificate.

    THIS CERTIFICATE is transferable only upon the books of the Trustee by the holder hereof in person or by duly authorized attorney, upon surrender hereof properly endorsed, and by paying to the Trustee his transfer fee. No assignment shall be recognized until notification in writing is received by the Trustee and acknowledged.

_____

Trustee

Form 23 – Memorandum of Option

Prepared by/return to:

MEMORANDUM OF OPTION

This Memorandum of Option is made this   day of , 20 . Notice is hereby given that   as trustee of Trust No.   dated   , 20 , with full power and authority to protect, conserve, sell, lease, encumber or otherwise manage and dispose of said property, pursuant to Florida Statutes sections 689.071 amd 689.073 has granted an option, for good and valuable consideration, to   whose address is .

The option is on the following described real property:

Property Identification Number:

IN WITNESS WHEREOF, the said trustee has hereunto signed and sealed this memorandum the day and year first above written.

_____

Trustee

_____

Witness #1

Printed Name: _____

Address:_____

_____

Witness #2

Printed Name: _____

Address:_____

STATE OF _____

COUNTY OF _____

The foregoing instrument was acknowledged before me by means of [ ] physical presence or [ ] online notarization, this _____ day of _____, _____ by {$Grantor1} and {$Grantor2} whom I know personally or who produced _____ as identification.

_____ [Notary Seal]

Notary Public – State of _____

My Commission Expires:

Form 24 – FIRPTA Affidavit

Non-Foreign Certification by Individual Transferor

(Seller's FIRPTA Affidavit)

Transferor:

Transferee:

Property:

Closing Date:

Before me, the undersigned authority, personally appeared the person(s) named in paragraph 2(b) below who, after being duly sworn, stated as follows:

1. This certificate is to inform the transferee that withholding Federal Income Tax is not required, upon the sale of the following described real property:

[insert legal description of real property]

2. The undersigned Transferor certifies and declares as follows:

a. I am not a foreign person for purposes of United States income taxation and am not subject to the tax withholding requirements of Section 1445 of the Internal Revenue Code of 1954, as amended.

b. My United States taxpayer identification or Social Security Number is: _____

c. My home address is: _____

3. There are no other persons who have an ownership interest in the above described property other than those persons listed in paragraph 2(b) above.

a. The undersigned hereby further certifies and declares:

b. I understand the purchaser of the described property intends to rely on the foregoing representations in connection with the United States Foreign Investment in Real Property Tax Act (FIRPTA).

4. I understand this certification may be disclosed to the Internal Revenue Service by the transferee and that any false statements contained in this certification may be punished by fine, imprisonment or both.

Under penalties of perjury, I state that this declaration was carefully read and is true and correct.

_____

Affiant

Print Name:

State of:

County of:

The foregoing instrument was sworn to and acknowledged before me by means of [ ] physical presence or [ ] online notarization this _____ day of _____, _____, by _____ who is [ ] personally known to me or [ ] who produced _____ as identification.

_____

Notary Public

Form 25 – Assignment of Mortgage to Trustee

Prepared by/ When recorded return to:

ASSIGNMENT OF MORTGAGE

The undersigned owner and holder of a mortgage (and of the indebtedness secured by it) made by {$BorrowerName}, to {$LenderName} securing ${$LoanAmount} on {$MortgageDate}, which was recorded in Official Records at Book {$BookRecordingRef}, at Page {$PageRecordingRef} or Instrument {$InstrumentNumber}, of the public records of {$RecordingCounty} County, Florida, for valuable consideration, the receipt and sufficiency of which is hereby acknowledged, does assign and transfer without recourse to {$MortgageAssignee}, whose address is {$MortgageAssigneeAddress} the above-described mortgage and indebtedness secured by it together with all financing statements, assignments of rent and leases, and other instruments related to the mortgage, including but not limited to modifications, with full power and authority, to protect, conserve, sell, lease, encumber or otherwise manage and dispose of, pursuant to Florida Statutes §689.071 and §689.073, as well as to satisfy and assign said mortgage, and to hold title to any property acquired through foreclosure of said mortgage or deed-in-lieu of foreclosure.

Dated Effective {$EffectiveDate}, nunc pro tunc.

{$LENDERNAME}

By: _____

{$LenderSigner}, {$LenderSignerTitle}

{$LenderAddress}

State of Flordia

County of _____

The foregoing instrument was acknowledged before me by means of [ ] physical presence or [ ] online notarization, this _____ day of _____, 20__, by {$LenderSigner}, as {$LenderSignerTitle}of {$LenderName}, who is personally known to me or has produced _____ as identification.

_____

Notary Public - State of Florida

Form 26 – Assignment of Purchase Contract to Trustee

Assignment of Purchase Contract to Trustee

   Date:

   The undersigned, as Buyer of that certain real property known as _____

in a purchase and sale contract with _____ as Seller, hereby assigns said contract to

_____ as Trustee of Trust No. _____.

   Buyer/Assignor: _____

   Assignee: _____

   as Trustee of Trust No. _____, and not individually

   Consent by Seller: (if necessary): _____

Form 27 – Assignment of Sale Contract to Trustee

Assignment of Sale Contract to Trustee

Date:

The undersigned, as Seller of that certain real property known as _____

in a purchase and sale contract with _____ as Buyer, hereby assigns said contract to

_____ as Trustee of Trust No. _____ who presently holds title to said property.

Seller/Assignor: _____

Assignee: _____

as Trustee of Trust No. _____, and not individually

Form 28 – Authorization to Sign Closing Documents

Authorization to Sign Closing Documents

    Date:

    To:

    Fax/E-mail:

    Re: Trust No._____, dated _____

    Property being sold/purchased: _____

    We hereby authorize _____ to sign any closing documents for the ☐ purchase ☐ sale of the above-referenced property on behalf of the named trust.

    This authorization is to act on behalf of the trust only and not on behalf of the trustee individually or in any capacity other than as trustee of this designated trust and the above property.

    By: _____

    Trustee of Trust No. _____ dated _____

    Note: This document cannot be used for the deed since since the trustee holds record title, but it can be used for other closing docs, for example, if the closing statement (ALTA settlement statement) changes at the last minute.

Form 29 – Authorization to Disburse Closing Proceeds

Authorization to Disburse Closing Proceeds

Date:

To:

Fax/E-mail:

Re: Trust No._____, dated _____

Property being sold/refinanced: _____

You are hereby authorized and directed to disburse any and all net proceeds from the sale/refinance of property referenced above to: _____

The undersigned trustee will hold you harmless from any claims made as a result of compliance with this authorization.

By: _____

Trustee of Trust No. _____ dated _____

Form 30 – Authorization to Represent Owner

Authorization to Represent Owner

Date:

To:

Fax/E-mail:

Re: Trust No._____, dated _____

Property: _____

This is to certify that _____ is hereby authorized to represent the above-referenced trust as owner of the above-referenced property regarding

_____

This authority only relates to the above property and trust. No authority is given to represent the trustee individually or regarding any other properties trustee may hold in other trusts.

By: _____

Trustee of Trust No. _____ dated _____

Form 31 – Closing Instructions for Purchase

Purchase Closing Instructions

Date:

To:

Fax/E-mail:

Re: Trust No._____, dated _____

Property: _____

IMPORTANT CLOSING INSTRUCTIONS!

We understand that you will be preparing the closing documents for the above-referenced property. The deed should name the grantee as follows:

{Grantor}   to   Trust   No.   _____,   dated   _____,   with _____ as Trustee with full power and authority, to protect, conserve, sell, lease, encumber or otherwise manage and dispose of said property pursuant to Florida Statutes §689.071 and §689.073, Grantee, whose post office address is _____.

In addition, the following statement should be placed somewhere on the deed:

Persons dealing with the Trustee are not obligated to look to the application of purchase monies. The interest of the beneficiaries is solely in the rights, proceeds and avails of trust property, not in the title, legal or, equitable, of said real estate. The liability of the Trustee under this deed and the trust agreement is limited to the assets of the trust and the Trustee hereunder has no personal liability whatsoever.

We must see a copy of the deed before the closing so that we can be sure that it conforms to the trust.

We will not attend the closing so any papers that need to be signed by us as buyer can be emailed, or delivered to our office prior to closing, with enough time for us to return them by closing. We have not collected a courier fee from our client, so if you need them returned by courier please provide a FedEx or UPS label or account number and charge the buyer's side of the closing statement.

Please provide us with the closing documents as early as possible. If they arrive after noon the day before the closing we might not be able to get them notarized and back in time for the closing.

If you have any questions, feel free to call or email us.

By: _____

Trustee of Trust No. _____ dated _____

Form 32 – Closing Instructions for Sale

Sale Closing Instructions

Date:

To:

Fax/E-mail:

Re: Trust No._____, dated _____

Property: _____

IMPORTANT CLOSING INSTRUCTIONS!

We understand that the sale of the above-referenced property will be closed through your office. In order to complete the transaction we will need the following:

• All documents to be executed by seller should be made out to be signed as follows:

_____, as Trustee of Trust No. _____, dated _____, 20_____. In no case can any document be signed "individually" by the trustee.

• Under Florida criminal law, §895.07(7) we are required to obtain a name search, in the county records where the property is located, on the following beneficiary of the trust _____

• Under the terms of the land trust agreement we can accept no money. Therefore the proceeds check should be made out to _____. You can accept this letter as authorization, or you can provide us with your own form, or you can put it somewhere on the closing statement. But in any case, no proceeds should be payable to the trustee except our trustee fee.

• Our trustee fee of $_____ should be collected at closing on the seller's side of the closing statement and forwarded to us after closing.

• We will not attend the closing so the documents should be sent to us by courier, email. If you wish to have the documents returned by FedEx or UPS, please provide a label or your account number as we have not collected this fee from our client.

• Please provide us with the closing documents as early as possible so that we can get them notarized and back to you on time.

If you have any questions, feel free to call or email us.

By: _____

Trustee of Trust No. _____ dated _____

Form 33 – Property Management Agreement

PROPERTY MANAGEMENT AGREEMENT

THIS AGREEMENT is made on _____, 20____ between

_____ as Owner and _____ as Manager, of

the Property, known as _____

WHEREAS Owner wishes to hire Manager to take over the day to day management of the Property and Manager wishes to take over such duties,

THEREFORE, in consideration of the mutual agreements contained herein, the parties agree as follows:

1. Authority. Manager is hereby appointed exclusive agent with power and authority to lease and manage the Property.

2. Term. This agreement shall be for a term of _____ months, beginning _____, 20____ and ending _____, 20____.

3. Duties. Manager shall rent, manage and control the property using its best efforts to find and keep tenants. Manager shall negotiate all leases on terms agreed by Owner. Manager shall contract for all necessary repairs to the property. Manager shall collect all rents and remit to Owner after payment of _____. Payments shall be made to Owner of net amounts, less $_____ kept on deposit for expenses, at least once every _____ days.

4. Leases. Manager shall execute all leases and rental agreements in Owner's name. Manager is hereby appointed as Owner's attorney-in-fact to execute such agreements on behalf of owner.

5. Manager shall have authority to serve any legal notices on tenants and to take any legal action as is permitted by law to enforce leases, evict tenants or collect money owed.

6. Compensation. The manager shall be paid as follows:

.

7. Sale of Property. In the event of a bona fide sale of the property, the Owner may terminate this contract upon giving thirty days' notice.

Owner: _____

Manager: _____

Form 34 – Amendment to Trust Agreement

Amendment to Trust Agreement

    The undersigned, being all of the beneficiaries of Land Trust No. _____ dated _____ hereby amend the terms of said trust as follows:

    All other terms of said trust not amended hereby remain in effect.

    IN WITNESS WHEREOF, the parties have hereunder set their hands and seals the date set forth.

_____

Beneficiaries

Date:

_____

Trustee

Date:

Form 35 – Warranty Deed to Trustee – Homestead Property

This form has been replaced by Form 2 which includes a homestead paragraph which may be deleted if not applicable.

Form 36 – Trustee's Deed to Successor Trustee

Prepared by/Return to:

QUIT CLAIM DEED TO SUCCESSOR TRUSTEE

THIS QUIT CLAIM DEED Made this _____ day of _____, 20___, by _____, as Trustee under Trust No. _____ dated _____, Grantors, to_____, as Successor Trustee under Trust No. _____ dated _____, _____ with full power and authority, to protect, conserve, sell, lease, encumber or otherwise manage and dispose of said property pursuant to Florida Statutes sections 689.071 and 689.073, Grantee, whose post office address is _____.

WITNESSETH, that the said first party, for and in consideration of the sum of $10.00 in hand paid by the said second party, the receipt whereof, is hereby acknowledged does hereby remise, release and quitclaim unto the said second party forever, all the right, title, interest, claim and demand which the said first party has in and to the following described lot, piece, or parcel of land, to wit:

Tax Parcel I.D. No.

TO HAVE AND TO HOLD the same together with all and singular the appurtenances thereunto belonging or in anywise appertaining, and all the estate, right, title, interest, lien, equity and claim whatsoever of said first party, either in law or equity, to the only proper use, benefit and behoof of the said second party forever.

THIS DEED is executed pursuant to and in the exercise of the power and authority granted to and vested in said Trustee by the terms of said deed or deeds in trust delivered to said Trustee in pursuance of the Trust agreement mentioned above. This deed is made subject to the lien of every trust deed or mortgage (if there be any) of record in said county given to secure the payment of money, remaining unreleased at the date of the delivery hereof, and covenants, conditions, restrictions, and easements of record.

IN WITNESS WHEREOF, the said first party has signed and sealed these presents the day and year first above written.

_____

Trustee of Trust No. _____ dated _____

_____

Witness #1

Printed Name: _____

Address:_____

_____

Witness #2

Printed Name: _____

Address:_____

STATE OF _____

COUNTY OF _____

The foregoing instrument was acknowledged before me by means of [ ] physical presence or [ ] online notarization, this _____ day of _____, _____ by _____ as trustee of Trust No. _____ dated _____ whom I know personally or who produced _____ as identification.

_____ [Notary Seal]

Notary Public – State of _____

My Commission Expires:

Form 37 – Declaration of Appointment of Successor Trustee (B)

Prepared by/Return to:

DECLARATION OF APPOINTMENT OF A SUCCESSOR TRUSTEE

(F.S. 689.071(9)(b))

This declaration made this _____ day of _____, _____, by and between {$HolderofthePowerofDirection} (hereinafter collectively referred to as "Holder of the Power of Direction"), whose address is {$Holder Address} and {$SuccessorTrusteeName} (hereinafter "Successor Trustee"), whose address is {$SuccessorTrusteeAddress}.

Whereas {$FormerTrusteeName} (hereinafter "Former Trustee") is currently the trustee of that certain land trust created pursuant to Section 689.071, Florida Statutes, commonly known as {$LandTrustName} Dated {$LandTrustDate}, (hereinafter, the "Land Trust"), and Former Trustee's current mailing address is {$FormerTrusteeAddress}.

Whereas the real property held pursuant to the terms and conditions of the Land Trust is more particularly described as:

{$LegalDescription}

Whereas the Land Trust provides for the appointment by the beneficiaries or the holder of the power of direction of a successor trustee or trustees in the event of the death, incapacity, resignation, inability, or termination due to dissolution of the Former Trustee;

Now therefore, pursuant to Section 689.071(9)(b), the Holder of the Power of Direction and Successor Trustee hereby declare that:

1. The Holder of the Power of Direction hereby appoints {$SuccessorTrusteeName} as Successor Trustee of the aforesaid land trust.

2. Successor Trustee hereby accepts appointment as Successor Trustee of the Land Trust.

3. The Successor Trustee was duly appointed as such under the terms of the unrecorded Land Trust agreement.

4. The Successor land Trustee appointed herein is fully vested with all the estate, properties, rights, powers, trusts, duties, and obligations of the predecessor land trustee, except that any successor land trustee is not under any duty to inquire into the acts or omissions of a predecessor trustee and is not liable for any act or failure to act of a predecessor trustee. A person dealing with any successor trustee pursuant to this declaration is not obligated to inquire into or ascertain the authority of the successor trustee to act within or exercise the powers granted under the recorded instruments or any unrecorded declarations or agreements.

This agreement is made as of the date and year set forth above.

HOLDER OF THE POWER OF DIRECTION

{$HolderofthePowerofDirection}

_____ _____(L.S.)

Witness 1:

Witness 1 Address:

    By:_____

_____ Its:_____

Witness 2:

Witness 2 Address:

STATE OF _____, COUNTY OF _____

The foregoing instrument was acknowledged before me by [ ] physical presence or [ ] online notarization this ____ day of _____, by _____, on behalf of {$HolderofthePowerofDirection}, who is personally known to me or has provided _____ as identification

_____

Notary Public - State of Florida

Printed Name:

My Commission Expires:

My Commission Number:

    SUCCESSOR TRUSTEE

_____ _____(L.S.)

Witness 1:   {$SuccessorTrusteeName}

Witness 1 Address:

    By:_____

_____ Its:_____

Witness 2:

Witness 2 Address:

STATE OF _____, COUNTY OF _____

The foregoing instrument was acknowledged before me by [ ] physical presence or [ ] online notarization this ____ day of _____, by {$SuccessorTrusteeName}, who is personally known to me or has provided _____ as identification

_____

Notary Public - State of Florida

Printed Name:

My Commission Expires:

My Commission Number:

Form 38 – Declaration of Appointment of Successor Trustee (C)

Prepared by/Return to:

DECLARATION OF APPOINTMENT OF A SUCCESSOR TRUSTEE

(F.S. 689.071(9)(c))

This declaration made this _____ day of {$SigningMonth}, {$SigningYear}, by and between {$FormerTrusteeName} (hereinafter "Former Trustee"), whose address is {$FormerTrusteeAddress}, and {$SuccessorTrusteeName} (hereinafter "Successor Trustee"), whose address is {$SuccessorTrusteeAddress}.

Whereas Former Trustee is currently the trustee of that certain land trust created pursuant to Section 689.071, Florida Statutes, commonly known as the {$LandTrustName} Land Trust Dated {$LandTrustDate} (hereinafter, the "Land Trust");

Whereas the real property held pursuant to the terms and conditions of the Land Trust is more particularly described as

{$PropertyLegalDescription}

Whereas the Land Trust provides for the appointment of a successor trustee or trustees in the event of the death, incapacity, resignation, or termination due to dissolution of the Former Trustee;

Now therefore, pursuant to Section 689.071(9)(c), the Former Land Trustee and Successor Land Trustee hereby declare that:

1. Former Trustee hereby resigns as trustee of the Land Trust.

2. Successor Trustee hereby accepts appointment as Successor Trustee of the Land Trust.

3. The Successor Trustee was duly appointed as such under the terms of the unrecorded Land Trust agreement.

4. The Successor land Trustee appointed herein is fully vested with all the estate, properties, rights, powers, trusts, duties, and obligations of the predecessor land trustee, except that any successor land trustee is not under any duty to inquire into the acts or omissions of a predecessor trustee and is not liable for any act or failure to act of a predecessor trustee. A person dealing with any successor trustee pursuant to this declaration is not obligated to inquire into or ascertain the authority of the successor trustee to act within or exercise the powers granted under the recorded instruments or any unrecorded declarations or agreements.

This agreement is made effective as of the date and year set forth above.

_____

Witness:

Printed Name:_____

Address: _____

_____

Witness:

Printed Name:_____

Address: _____

 FORMER TRUSTEE

{$FormerTrusteeName}

By:_____(L.S.)

{$FormerTrusteeSigner}, {$FormerTrusteeSignerTitle}

STATE OF FLORIDA

COUNTY OF _____

The foregoing instrument was acknowledged before me by [__] physical presence or [__] remote online notarization this _____ day of {$SigningMonth}, {$SigningYear}, by {$FormerTrusteeSigner}, as {$FormerTrusteeSignerTitle}on behalf of {$FormerTrusteeName}.

_____

Notary Public - State of _____

Printed Name:

My Commission Expires:

My Commission Number:

[____] Personally known or

[____] Produced identification; Identification Produced: _____

_____

Witness:

Printed Name:_____

Address: _____

_____

Witness:

Printed Name:_____

Address: _____

 SUCCESSOR TRUSTEE

{$SuccessorTrusteeName}

By:_____(L.S.)

{$SuccessorTrusteeSigner}, {$SuccessorTrusteeSignerTitle}

STATE OF FLORIDA

COUNTY OF _____

The foregoing instrument was acknowledged before me by [__] physical presence or [__] remote online notarization this _____ day of {$SigningMonth}, {$SigningYear}, by {$SuccessorTrusteeSigner}as {$SuccessorTrusteeSignerTitle} on behalf of {$SuccessorTrusteeName}.

_____

Notary Public - State of _____

Printed Name:

My Commission Expires:

My Commission Number:

[____] Personally known or

[____] Produced identification; Identification Produced: _____

Form 39 – Contract to Sell Beneficial Interest in Land Trust

AGREEMENT TO SELL BENEFICIAL INTEREST

ARTICLES OF AGREEMENT, made this _____ day of _____ 20_____, between {$BuyerName} as buyer whose mailing address is {$Buyer Address} and {$SellerName} as seller, whose mailing address is {$Seller-Address}.

WHEREAS, _____ as Trustee under Trust known as Trust No. _____, dated _____, is the owner of real property known as:

Property address: {$PropertyAddress}

County: {$PropertyCounty}

Short form legal description: {$PropertyShortLegal}

Parcel ID No.: {$PropertyTaxPIN}

WHEREAS, Seller owns, or conditionally owns, the Beneficial Interest in the Land Trust;

WHEREAS, Buyer wishes to purchase said Beneficial Interest and

WHEREAS, Seller is willing to contract for the sale of the beneficial interest in said trust to Buyer, which interest entitles Buyer to all the rights and privileges of said trust including the right to obtain a deed from the trustee to said property,

NOW THEREFORE, in consideration of the mutual promises herein contained, it is agreed that if the Buyer shall make the payments and perform the covenants hereinafter mentioned on his part to be made and performed, the said Seller hereby covenants to convey, assign and assure to the Buyer, his heirs, executors, administrators, or assigns, 100% of the beneficial interests in said Trust,

Buyer covenants and agrees to pay of the Seller the Purchase Price in the manner following:

Purchase Price: $_____

Loan Amount: $_____ *

Term: _____ years

Interest Rate: _____% per year

Payment Amount: $_____ per month

Balloon Amount at End of Term $_____

*The loan amount does not include the closing costs related to this transaction. Those costs include, but are not limited to, document preparation fees of approximately $950.00; escrow fees of $1,000.00, documentary stamp taxes based on the purchase price; and a Title Search (if requested) for $150.00. As a part of this transaction, the County Real Property Taxes, and any Homeowners Association dues will be pro-rated based upon the date of the transfer.

All sums remaining unpaid shall become due and payable no later than _____ (the "Maturity Date" the note). There shall be no prepayment penalty. Buyer shall pay all taxes, assessments or impositions that may be legally levied or imposed upon the property subsequent to the date of the closing. Buyer agrees to maintain hazard insurance at his expense with the seller/lender and any other lien-holder or prior owner, as applicable, named as loss payee.

In the case of buyer failing to make any of the payments or any part thereof or to perform any of the covenants on their part hereby made and entered into, for the space of thirty (30) days, this contract shall, at the option of the Seller be forfeited and terminated and the Buyer shall forfeit all payments made by him on this contract; and such payments shall be retained by the Seller in full satisfaction and liquidation of all damages by them sustained and the Seller shall have the right to re-enter and take possession of the property owned by the trust without being liable to any action therefore. A late fee of 5% is due on any payment received after 5 days after each due date.

This is a contract solely for 100% of the Beneficial Interest in, and power of direction over a Land Trust. Said power of direction and assignment shall revert to the Seller upon Buyer's default of any term of this agreement or subsequent note or conditional assignment of beneficial interest.

IT IS MUTUALLY AGREED, by and between the parties hereto, that the time of payment shall be an essential part of this contract, and that all covenants and agreements herein contained shall extend to and be obligatory upon the heirs, executors, administrators and assigns of the respective parties.

For the Closing of the transaction contemplated by this Contract, the parties agree to execute such conditional or absolute assignments of beneficial interest, promissory note, settlement statement, and other documents reasonably deemed necessary by Joseph E. Seagle, P.A., the closing agent for this transaction.

IN WITNESS WHEREOF, the parties to these presents have hereunder set their hands and seals the day and year first written above.

_____

{$BuyerName}

_____

{$SellerNamc}

Index

A

B

C

D

www.ingramcontent.com/pod-product-compliance
Lightning Source LLC
Chambersburg PA
CBHW051117200326
41518CB00016B/2532